MEDIA PLANNING

MEDIA PLANNING

SECOND EDITION

JAMES R. ADAMS, MCAM

Published in association with
Communication Advertising and Marketing Education Foundation

BUSINESS BOOKS
COMMUNICA - EUROPA

First published 1971
Second Edition 1977

ISBN 0 220 66335 1 (Hardback)
      0 220 66337 8 (Paperback)

This book has been set 10 on 11 point Press Roman.
Printed in Great Britain at the Alden Press, Oxford
for the publishers, Business Books Limited,
24 Highbury Crescent, London N5

Contents

Foreword

The first edition of this book has been for six years a valuable contribution to the subject of media planning. This is why a second edition which brings the discussion up-to-date and expands it in several significant ways is so much to be welcomed.

Media planning is one of the parts of the advertising planning process which is subject to a reasonable degree of systematic thought and analysis. There is a respectable amount of information and ideas available which enable one to study the subject and, thereby, to acquire a recognisable degree of expertise.

However, media planning is inextricably a part of the total advertising plan: in my opinion, it does damage to that plan if one treats media planning as an activity in its own right. This does not mean that one cannot or should not study its methods and concepts separately — which is exactly what has been done quite admirably by James Adams in this book.

JOHN TREASURE
J. Walter Thompson Company Limited

Preface to the Second Edition

The chief impetus for the second edition of *Media Planning* has been the degree of change in the advertising and media scene since the first, in particular, the establishment of local commercial radio. This meant that the first edition left students with an awkward gap in this area, and with a considerable patina of age on some of the press media comments. In updating these, and other references, note has also been taken of the change in the basis of the book's function for the student, now to prepare for the Media Diploma examination of CAM.

Other changes have attempted to make the book more useful to practitioners, as well as students. Although it is usually assumed that these practitioners will work in advertising agencies, more are finding their way into client organisations. Over the last six years I have been asked for advice on many practical media planning questions which should have been addressed in a book of this title, but which were not. In particular, subjects like budget setting and the timing of campaigns, are dealt with seriously this time, even though the media planner may not have much influence on the eventual decisions.

Probably the major change in this area in the last six years has been the steady drift apart between what can be attained and what is. The sixties saw the art of media planning in the UK develop as far as it could, without dramatic developments in the understanding of marketing generally, with the best principles normally being applied in practice. Since then, real gains have been made on the marketing side, allowing media planning to take further steps forward. In practice, regression has been the order of the day. Life has become too short for the consideration of abstractions; brand managers have become too concerned with the next dealer-loader to bother with response functions; and the language of the special offer has spilled over into media to the extent that buying is, once more, seen as more important than planning. Enough of the basic technology is remembered for the media models still to be given a whirl on the way to the schedule, but invariably by the media owners, who, for the modest cost of a run, can exercise a high degree of influence on their own chances of success.

The squeezing of agency margins has brought about this state of affairs, and advertisers do not seem to mind. However, they might if they better understood the options, and this new edition of *Media Planning* is written with the hope of *xiv* aiding this understanding. It still deals with the practicalities of media life in the UK today, but will refer readers to the work of Little and Lodish, Rao, and others, who have established means of controlling the advertising and marketing process to degrees only dreamt of when the first edition was written.

Another feature that it is hoped will prove useful is the inclusion of more case histories. These now deal not only with the media planning process, but also the successful use of media in selling goods and services. My grateful thanks are due to those supplying these cases, and particularly those who allowed their data to be published, namely: L'Oreal, Playtex Limited and Spillers French (Baking) Limited.

My gratitude is also due to Norman Hart, and the CAM Foundation, for encouraging the production of this edition, and to Shirley, my wife, for once again shouldering the task of typing the manuscript.

Camberley   JAMES R. ADAMS
June 1977

1 What this book is about

It is intended that reading this book should give the student and non-specialist a sound basic idea of how media planning is best done. At the same time, it is hoped that it will provide a useful reference point for the practitioner.

These are large aims, because advertising in general, and media in particular, are subjects normally learned by practice, and the practice is often a long way from the theory. However, most readers will be undertaking, or have undertaken, some course of instruction, and will often find it rewarding when they find a divergence between what they have learnt and what they observe to wonder why this should be.

Two main forces tend to act against the implementation of the best media planning practice. The first is time: no plan can be evolved through the stages recommended in this book in less than a fortnight, give or take a few days, especially if, as is usually the case, those concerned will be simultaneously involved in a host of other problems. Therefore, when the client says to the account man, 'I must have the plan by 11.0 tomorrow, because ....' and the account man does not demur, the client will not get as good a plan as he should have.

The second is ignorance: the client only asks for the impossible because he does not realise that it *is* impossible, or because he feels that a plan produced after all the due processes will not be significantly different, in terms of profit for his brand, than the one which he will get tomorrow.

Of course, he may be right. If the area of choice is concentrated on the alternatives of the *Daily Mirror* or the *Sun*, he probably will. But the critical areas today are budget setting, area allocation and allocation over time. Unless the agency has an on-line model of the client's business that can provide immediate answers to these problems, it will be worth his while to wait the two weeks.

But is it not quite impracticable to tell the client who wants a plan tomorrow that he will have to wait two weeks? Yes, it is. The solution must be so to organise one's activities (client and agency alike) that needs are reasonably anticipated, and the planning cycle so timed that the account man actually has the documents in his brief case, when the client asks for them. This is a counsel of perfection, but I see nothing wrong in that.

1

Indeed, if the media planner's sole contribution is to cause the marketing team to structure their approach along rational lines, making the best possible use of the available data, then it will have been a considerable one. It is a sad fact of life that people are broadly divided into thinkers and doers. Given this crude choice, marketers have to be doers; but an injection of thought will do both them and their brands a power of good. (As long as it is clarifying rather than confusing thought.)

The media detail in the book may become dated rapidly, and the reader will have to make allowance for this. However, it is hoped that the basic principles laid down will be applicable at least until a further up-date becomes essential. Viable marketing models are probably now in the same stage as were media models a decade ago. It would be very sad to see them equally ignored, because the should-be users are 'too busy'.

2 Media planning and the advertiser

2.1 Resource allocation and profit

Media planning to the advertiser is simply a facet of the general problem of allocating financial resources in such a way as to optimise long-term profits. In this respect the area of influence that the media planner, or the agency, can exert, is fairly narrow. It is often difficult, for instance, to persuade a client to allocate more money to media as a whole. It is, in the present state of financial skills, very difficult to suggest that money allocated for advertising would better be allocated to, say, research and development.

Although the question 'should we buy a colour page in the *Daily Express*, or build another room on the laboratory?' may never be asked, there are two fairly direct competitors for the advertising budget. The first of these is promotional expenditure, i.e. the allocation of money 'below the line'. The balance between media and advertising expenditure and expenditure on deals, either to the consumer or to the trade, is one that exercises the minds of leading advertisers to a considerable extent.

The next most directly competitive cost is probably that of the sales force. There are times when the best advice an agency can give to its client is that, unless they invest more money in salesmen, their advertising expenditure will largely be wasted. To generate consumer demand by advertising, which cannot be satisfied because of lack of distribution, not only involves short-term loss of profits, but may well generate long-term hostility towards a company.

We have already mentioned research and development as an indirect competitor to the advertising budget, and clearly any form of expenditure will influence the company's profitability either more or less than expenditure on advertising. It may be, for instance, that to create extra demand that can only be met by overtime production, will be less profitable to the company than would be meeting a lower level of demand through standard production facilities, spending less on advertising. Unfortunately, few advertisers are in possession of financial analyses of this nature which really should be made available when advertising campaigns are planned.

At the beginning of this chapter we qualified the word profit by the word long-term. The reason for this is simple. It may be true that the way to increase this year's profits most easily is to cancel all advertising. (In Figure 4.2, where X, the most profitable level of advertising expenditure in one year, is zero). The two classic cases of companies which have actually done this are Guinness in the late twenties and Batchelor's Soups during the fifties. In both cases, although a profit peak was produced, so much was lost by way of sales that a great deal of money had to be spent in successive years in order to re-coup the positions. In both cases long-term profit objectives would have been better met by continuation of advertising.

Two special cases of this are the launches of new products and the running down of products considered to have reached the downward trend in their life cycle. It is common practice for manufacturers to forego any profits during the first three years of a brand's life in the attempt to secure by the end of the third year a successful sales situation producing good profits in the fourth year and beyond. It is also common for manufacturers who have decided that a product has no long-term future, to suspend advertising and to 'cream' as much profit from it as is possible during its remaining economic life.

The importance of advertising to the life of a manufacturing company varies enormously from industry to industry and to some extent from firm to firm within the same industry. At one extreme are the companies to whom advertising is an extremely important product ingredient — for instance the toiletry and cosmetic industries. In such companies, advertising expenditure can run to as high as a third of total costs and clearly the way in which the advertising budget is deployed can have a critical effect on the total company's fortunes. At the other end of the scale come a number of Britain's largest companies which, principally because they are basically engaged in selling products to other industries, make very little use of advertising.

Agency people tend to think of industry as a group of 'advertisers'. Company people tend to think of a group of manufacturing and commercial enterprises, some of which use consumer advertising, as a marketing tool. Table 2.1 shows how very important 'advertisers' — in the sense that their accounts are highly prized — spend very small proportions of their sales revenue on advertising. The discerning reader may note that the companies are ranked in order of profitability, as well as advertising/sales ratio. A more scientific sample would show that the general relationship is similar. Note that this does not mean (necessarily) that a high A/S ratio brings high profitability. An American study some years back showed that businessmen with a median income of $20,000 p.a. consumed four times as much alcohol as those with a median income of 10,000. Anyone concluding that to double his salary he had only to quadruple his drinking would probably have been disappointed.

2.2 Division of the advertising budget

Most of the advertising money is spent on media space and time, but some has to be spent on production of the advertisements or commercials to fill space and time. What the relative proportions are will vary considerably from medium to medium and from campaign to campaign. There is no scientific way of calculating what the ratio should be, but it is common to find an average produc-

TABLE 2.1

Company	UK turnover (1974)*	Net profit before depreciation and interest	Press and TV advertising+ expenditure	Avertising/ sales
	£m	£m	£m	%
H.J.Heinz Co Ltd	129.6	12.8	3.1	2.38
Gallaher Ltd	530.0	39.7	4.6	0.87
Ford Motor Co Ltd	628.3	27.8	0.5	0.08

*Times 1000   +MEAL

tion bill running at 10 per cent of the total advertising budget, with most falling between 5 and 15 per cent. Since it is now generally believed that the effectiveness of the advertising message is very much more important than the amount of money spent on conveying it to the consumer, it may be argued that considerably more than 15 per cent could be profitable.

Most managers would have two worries about this. Firstly, many people suspect that there is not necessarily a positive correlation between the amount of money spent on the preparation of an advertisement and the effectiveness of that advertisement — indeed sometimes there may even be an inverse correlation. Secondly, the advertising pre-testing facilities that we have produce measurements so imprecise that we would have great difficulty in saying whether a particular piece of production was worth the money or not.

The general way in which advertisers allocate their money between media is that low-cost, high frequency-of-purchase products tend to be advertised mostly on TV, and high-cost, low frequency-of-purchase products in the Press. This is illustrated in Table 2.2, although it should be noted that this excludes Retail and Mail Order advertisers (who currently top all MEAL categories) and also those restricted to one medium, e.g. cigarette manufacturers. There is also a tendency for the bigger appropriations to favour TV; the average of the appropriations listed in Table 2.2 is £978,000 for TV, against £594,000 for Press.

2.3   The relevance of media planning

We have so far suggested that advertising is not of great importance to many manufacturing companies and that media planning usually has a much less dramatic effect on the effectiveness of the advertising campaign than does the creative content of the advertisements. At this point the reader may wonder why there is so much to follow in this book.

It is simple to show that one media plan is X or Y per cent more efficient than another. This means that the total impact which the better schedule achieves is that much more than the total impact which the other achieves, however this may be defined. We shall not seriously wrestle with these definitions until Chapters 25 and 26, but it is most unusual for the measurement to relate to the sales or profits for the advertiser. Clearly, it would be possible for the agency and the advertiser to agree on a target figure for the impact of a media plan and for the appropriation to be reduced by the extent which the planner beat this target. This would almost certainly result in a genuine profit increase to the advertiser, but with the present method of agency remuneration it does not provide a great deal of incentive for the media planning department of the agency.

However, some comfort can be derived from actual case histories. The first relates to a direct response advertiser for whom a number of experiments were carried out with the aim of increasing the total response for a given appropriation. These experiments resulted in improvements both in copy and in media scheduling. It was possible in this case to estimate that the improvement due to improved media planning was of the order of 30 per cent. Note that this does not mean 30 per cent more opportunities to see, or 30 per cent more impact, but 30 per cent more sales for the advertising pound. (Further examples are

TABLE 2.2

Leading TV advertisers	TV percentage
Kelloggs Cornflakes	93
Guinness	84
Omo	86
Drive detergent	98
Martini	63
Coca Cola	100
Kodak cameras	77
Heinz soups	90
Stork SB	97
Milk	76

Leading Press advertisers	Press percentage
Austin Morris	82
British Airways	55
Halifax Building Society	89
Nationwide Building Society	99
Chrysler	54
Martini	37
Leeds Perm. Building Society	87
Barclays Bank	55
Tate & Lyle Industries	100
National Westminster Bank	41

Source: MEAL 1975

given in the chapter on direct response, Chapter 19.) The second example is less direct, though perhaps more dramatic. It concerns a well-known consumer good which had been selling at the rate of about £1 million per annum at MSP for five years. A change of agency brought a change in thinking and a decision to concentrate the whole of the budget, which had previously been spread over a number of media, into television. Within 4 years sales had trebled. The point of this example is that, although the creative content of the advertising was almost certainly the reason for the upsurge in sales, unless the media planner has recommended the change in medium, the creative opportunity would not have occurred, as the creative treatment was hardly translatable into any other medium.

Although it is difficult to find examples of this type, the search for them is one of the things that gives media planning so much interest.

2.4   Related reading

O.J. Firestone, *The economic implications of advertising*, Methuen (1967).
Simon Broadbent, *Spending advertising money*, Business Books (Second
    edition, 1975).

3 Media planning in the advertising agency

3.1 The work flow

The various stages through which a media plan evolves within an agency are quite complex. They will vary from agency to agency, and within agencies, from account to account. The variations will depend on the size of the problem to be tackled, the agency's organisation and its relations with its clients. Figure 3.1 illustrates the sequence which will be followed, more or less, in the planning of most large campaigns conducted by sophisticated advertising agencies on behalf of sophisticated clients. The development of almost all media plans must follow a similar pattern, although the stages may be telescoped and considerations made implicitly rather than being discussed at meetings.

The initial planning meeting is usually a large one and will comprise senior people working on the account, and possibly the agency management: the account director and his team, and creative and media personnel will take part. In some cases the client may be represented. The purpose of this meeting is formally to evaluate the current progress of the brand, and its market, and the intentions for the period under review (usually the following financial year). The end-product of the meeting should be a draft marketing strategy which outlines the way in which the agency feels the brand's targets should best be achieved.

This draft will then be thrashed out with the client, the agency being represented possibly by the management, certainly by the account team. When approved, the marketing objectives form the basis for both creative and media work.

At the next stage the creative and media departments work separately, although it is necessary for them to confer together as frequently as possible. The media plan for the current year will be critically examined for its strengths and weaknesses and the evidence of any available media tests considered. (This point is elaborated in Chapter 27.) Changes that have taken place in the media scene since the current plan was developed, together with necessary changes in strategy flowing from changed marketing objectives, will be discussed. Most importantly, the likely effect on the media choice of the basic creative appeals which

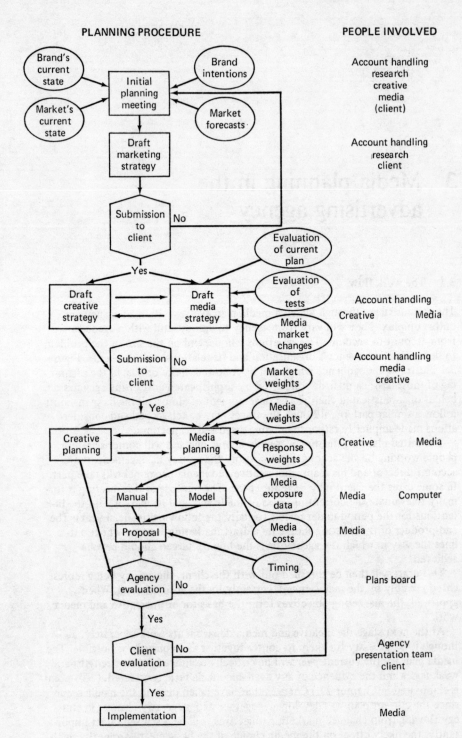

PLANNING PROCEDURE

PEOPLE INVOLVED

Brand's current state

Market's current state

Initial planning meeting

Brand intentions

Market forecasts

Account handling
research
creative
media
(client)

Draft marketing strategy

Account handling
research
client

Submission to client — No

Yes

Evaluation of current plan

Draft creative strategy

Draft media strategy

Evaluation of tests

Media market changes

Account handling

Creative   Media

Submission to client — No

Yes

Market weights

Media weights

Account handling
media
creative

Creative planning

Media planning

Response weights

Media exposure data

Creative   Media

Manual

Model

Media   Computer

Proposal

Media costs

Media

Timing

Agency evaluation — No

Yes

Plans board

Client evaluation — No

Yes

Agency presentation team
client

Implementation

Media

Figure 3.1 Planning sequence for large advertising campaign

are being developed, will be taken into account. Creative requirements likely to have a critical effect on the media plan are clearly those of movement and colour. It is likely at this stage that the account team will be in fairly constant touch with both the creative and media departments. Indeed Stephen King has argued very eloquently that there really can be no chicken and egg in the creative-media situation; both have to evolve together. From this view has sprung the title of Campaign Planner, although the function he fulfils varies from agency to agency. Media planning, at least in broad brush strokes, is always part of his assignment; and he may also be concerned with account handling, research and the creative input.

From these vital deliberations will flow draft media and creative strategies. These will be submitted to the client for his approval and it is usual for those who have been involved in their creation to be present to argue their case. Once these basic strategies have been approved, detailed work can commence. At this stage it is still very necessary for media and creative personnel to work closely together, since a vital factor for discussion will be the size of space, or length of time which is required to carry the advertising message. The bulk of the media planner's task is now concerned with the accumulation and analysis of data. The way in which he deals with the various inputs is discussed in later chapters. It is sufficient to say here that whether a model is used to assist in the production of a plan or not, similar procedures have to be gone through. The principal differences arise because the computer is able to consider many more variables at one time than the planner can without its assistance. For the use of a media model, all judgements have to be quantified.

From a computer print-out, or from his own calculations, the planner will now have a series of media vehicles, together with numbers of insertions in each of them. To turn this into a schedule, he needs to consider the spread of the campaign over time; he will then embody the whole of his thinking into a proposal, of the type which will be seen later in the chapter, for submission to the agency plans board. When this hurdle has been cleared, the total package, usually in the form of a document containing the full campaign plan, marketing, media and creative, together with ancillary recommendations for perhaps research and merchandising, will be presented to the client. The agency presentation team will usually include agency management, together with all senior personnel who have been responsible for creating the plan. Once it is agreed, the schedule is returned to the media department for buying.

Of course, if at any stage during the development of the plan there is a rejection, then the re-cycling process has to start and everyone has to try again. The advantage of obtaining client approval of strategies is that the problem is broken down into manageable portions. If the client sees nothing until he sees the final plan, he may well find himself in disagreement with the original marketing strategy, and much time will have been wasted.

3.2 Media briefs

The procedure outlined above shows the involvement of media personnel at every stage of the plan's development. If, under any circumstances, this does not happen, it becomes very necessary for the account team to supply the media department with a media brief. The form and content of these vary considerably, and an attempt to produce an authoritative version was made at the Esomar seminar on Media Planning held in May 1969. This is printed below in its entirety.

It should be noted that the contents of the brief, that is to say the questions asked by the media department of other people in the agency, is usually covered under the section headed 'strategy'. 'Outline recommendations' and 'media buying/negotiations' consist of questions which the media planner has to ask himself or has to ask other members of the media department. Some of the questions are asked for self-evident reasons. The use the media planner makes of the answers to others will be covered in one part or another of this book.

STRATEGY
Product, competition and objectives
What is the product, its uses, pack, price, method of distribution, level of distribution, type of outlet and seasonal rate of consumption?
What are competitive products and details, as for our own product?
What is the recent product sales and advertising history, including media effectiveness measurements?
What is a similar history for competitors?
What is the product and client company position relative to competitive products and companies?
What are the marketing, advertising and communication objectives and strategy?

Budget
Is there a media budget (excluding production costs) and, if so, what is it?
Or is there to be a recommendation on this?
If there is a budget, does it break down separately for theme, scheme and trade advertising?
What degree of flexibility is there in the budget?
Can provision be made for tactical reserves?
Does the advertiser qualify for additional discounts from other products?

Timetable
When will the campaign start?
When will it finish?
What are the relevant cancellation and copy dates?
Do these rule out any medium?
When will firm decisions be made on commercial length, colour, etc?
When is the media plan to be presented?
When will the advertiser's approval be obtained?
What are promotional plans/sales cycles?

Target
Who is the advertising aimed at? What is the demographic profile of the target market?

Is this target definition contained in the data to be used in planning? In buying? In post-campaign evaluation?

If not, what definitions should be used?

What value in response terms have repetition and domination of the target as against cover of the target?

What is the initial evaluation of matching or avoiding competitors?

Regionality

How are sales, or outlets, or expansion opportunities distributed over the country?

How should advertising be spread over regions?

Seasonality

How should advertising be spread over the weeks or months of the campaign?

Within this, should advertising be evenly spread or in bursts?

Are special days or times important? How much more valuable are they?

Creative

What are the communication objectives in terms of type of communication, e.g. demonstration, mood.

What are the creative possibilities arising from communication objectives, and how do the media available compare in creative potential related to the communication objectives?

OUTLINE RECOMMENDATIONS

Possible media

Which media are feasible on objective grounds, given the type of product, timetable, availability situation, regionality requirements?

Do we already have options on time or space?

What is the availability situation? Does this rule out any medium?

What cover of the target do different media give?

What are the costs of exposing advertisements in each medium given:

— the target definition

— realistic costs

— advertisement/page/break factors?

Have we authority to take options? To make firm bookings?

If not, when will this be obtained?

Can media be told now what the product is? If not, when can they be told?

What qualitative or other factors should be taken into account as well as the cost of exposing advertisements to the target?

What is the effect of media choice expected to be on the trade?

Are there other services offered by media which would be useful?

Research

What data is available on the past performance of the advertising?

What evidence exists of the effectiveness of given advertisements in different media in the markets under discussion?

What agency or client data is available on concept testing, image testing, post testing?
What market or creative research is planned? What pre- and post-campaign evaluation is planned?
Can media evaluation be built into the research?

Media choice
What is to be the main media group (*is* there to be a main medium)?
What would be the result of spending all the budget in the main media group?
Would it weaken the campaign seriously to spend less?
Would a campaign in this media group alone leave serious gaps?
Should other media groups be used — at what level of expenditure?
What criteria are to be used in constructing schedules?

MEDIA BUYING/NEGOTIATION

Have media owners' representatives been contacted to establish minimum rates and maximum value obtainable, for selected media, and for possible alternatives?
Are all discounts available to advertiser known, taking into account his full range of expenditure in each medium concerned?
Has full use been made of marketing flexibility in the media timing plan to ensure optimum use of media availabilities?
Is there sufficient flexibility in the timing plan to ensure maximum value through negotiations with media owners?

3.3 The media recommendation

The media man is often jealous of his creative counterpart who can sometimes put an advertisement on the table in front of a meeting and say 'There, I think that speaks for itself'. No media man would be allowed to do that with a schedule. Although the media recommendation must, of course, include a detailed schedule, its main purpose is to explain why this particular schedule has been arrived at. It should include most of the answers to most of the questions which appear in the media brief unless, as frequently happens, the media recommendation is a part of a larger document containing the agency's total campaign recommendations. In this case, reference will be made to the other relevant sections.

It will contain a full explanation of why the selected media have been selected: it will also cover other media that might have been used, and say why they have not been preferred. There will normally be a number of analyses of different types, some financial and some showing how the target market is actually covered by the planned campaign.

The recommendation which follows, and which is reproduced with the kind co-operation of Gallaher Limited and their advertising agency, Erwin Wasey (as they were then called), was included in the first edition of this book, and is now very dated in its detail. It appears here because the approach remains impeccable, and because this degree of thoroughness is not easy to come by today.

Since advertising for cigarettes is not permitted on commercial television, this medium has not been mentioned in the course of the recommendation. Nevertheless, the reader will see that this does not reduce the scale of the recommendation by any marked extent. The problem set was a peculiar one (as all media problems are) and centres around the need economically to cover a region of the country with a large appropriation. The final use of regional editions of national newspapers should be noted. Since the time the recommendation was written this ability to regionalise has been very considerably extended. Indeed, an interesting example of the influence which good buying can have on the planning stage is that the agency had been able to negotiate special splits for the purpose of this very campaign. Had this not been possible, the efficiency of the campaign would have been considerably impaired.

GALLAHER LIMITED
PARK DRIVE PLAIN
Media Recommendation
July–December, 1967

Background

1 PERIOD
   July–December 1967

2 BUDGET
a *Main Theme Advertising*

Budget for 1967	£235,000
Expenditure per quarter:	
January–March	£70,000
April–June	£70,000
Total 1st 6 months	£140,000
Less agreed cancellations (June)	£17,000
	£123,000 (committed)
Documented Budget available	
July/December	£95,000
Plus savings from above	£17,000
Total working budget	
July/December 1967	£112,000

b *Outdoor Advertising*

Annual Budget for 1967 is	£70,000
Working Budget for the period	
July–December 1967 is	£30,000

c *Production*

Estimated Budget July–December 1967:

Main Theme	£4,000
Outdoor	£4,000
Promotion	£10,000
Total	£18,000

3 TARGET MARKET

a Existing smokers of Park Drive Plain who are considering switching to another brand:

Profile

Age	:	66% are 35+
Sex	:	68% are male
Class	:	88% are C2DE

b Smokers of Woodbine Plain:

Profile

Age	:	80% are 35+ (stronger 45+ bias than Park Drive)
Sex	:	70% are male
Class	:	90% are C2DE (stronger DE bias than Park Drive)

c Area

Advertising is to be confined to the Manchester, Sheffield and Belfast Gallaher Branch Areas.

4 MARKETING STRATEGY

Objective Long-Term

To extend for as long as possible the profitable life of Park Drive Plain.

a To slow down the declining sales trend and recover market share.

b To convert more Woodbine Plain smokers to Park Drive Plain.

c To achieve a level of advertising spending consistent with the brand's market share and competition.

d To maximise the effectiveness of the brand's advertising and promotions by:

    (*i*) concentration in areas of greatest sales strength and potential

    (*ii*) imaginative use of media facilities

    (*iii*) more impactful and persuasive advertising

e To improve distribution in areas of strength and growth potential.

5 COPY STRATEGY

a Objective—to convince smokers of Park Drive Plain that, for real flavour, and full smoking satisfaction at 2/1d for 10, Park Drive Plain is today's best choice of cigarette.

b Image—Park Drive Plain will be seen as the straightforward cigarette which is enjoyed by men who really appreciate a good smoke.

6 CREATIVE

a Main Theme Advertising

Creative requirements are for full pages black and white in tabloid size newspapers and magazines, and half pages black and white in broadsheet size media.

b Outdoor

Creative requirements are for colour in the 16 sheet and 48 sheet size.

7 COMPETITIVE ACTIVITY

In Appendix G we set out estimated competitive press expenditure for 1967 based on Legion figures for the January–April 1967 period.

Media Objectives

1 To cover Manchester, Sheffield and Belfast Branch Areas.
2 To obtain maximum coverage/frequency on all adult smokers but with a strong emphasis on men aged 35–64 (but not excluding 16–34 age groups) in the C2DE socio-economic groups.
3 To achieve a continuous campaign (excluding Wakes weeks).
4 In reaching the Target Market, to achieve maximum cost efficiency.
5 To give extra advertising weight to specific prime and secondary towns which are listed in Appendix A.

Media Selection

The following main media are available for direct advertising on an area basis:
1 Regionalised editions of national newspapers and magazines.
2 Provincial daily morning and evening newspapers.
3 Local weekly newspapers.
4 Poster advertising.
5 Cinema advertising.
6 Pirate radio advertising.
7 Trade Press on a national basis.

The following media are recommended:

a *Main Theme Advertising*
On the budget level of £112,000 we recommend the use of national newspapers and magazines to provide broadscale coverage and frequency of the target market over the Manchester, Sheffield and Belfast Branch Areas.
Recommended Plan is shown as Schedule 1.

b *Outdoor Advertising*
We recommend the Outdoor Budget of £30,000 be used to give added emphasis to the towns listed in Appendix A, and the prime and secondary sales areas which are within the Manchester and Sheffield Branch Areas.

The following media are rejected

a *Cinema*
b *Pirate Radio*
c *Trade Press*

Reasons

1 MAIN THEME ADVERTISING

A. SELECTION OF NATIONAL PRESS

i As a Media Group
This media group is preferred for broadscale advertising as we consider it the most effective medium in terms of coverage and economy.
In Appendix B we demonstrate this point by comparing a selection of national newspapers and magazines with provincial daily newspapers over C2DE men and male cigarette smokers over the Northern ITV area. In Appendix C we compare provincial evening newspapers with local weekly newspapers owned by the four major provincial newspaper proprietors.
Due to lack of research information on local weekly newspapers we are compelled to compare these media in terms of circulation and cost only. In view of the previous comparison in Appendix B it is, of course, readily

apparent that national media would be far more economic and effective than local weekly newspapers.

The results of the inter-media comparisons made in Appendices B and C are that in broad terms whilst an equivalent coverage is obtainable by the sole use of nationals or provincial dailies or provincial weeklies—in terms of economy national newspapers are vastly superior over the other two media groups and are therefore preferred for Park Drive Plain advertising.

ii Specific Publications Selected

We have selected those newspapers or magazines which offer the best buy in terms of coverage and/or economy over C2DE male smokers in the three Gallaher areas.

The readership figures shown will be obtained by taking regionalised editions or implementing a special copy split with another Gallaher brand. This information is contained in Appendix D.

From this Appendix, we have compiled a list of media which we consider suitable to carry Park Drive Plain advertising.

They are:

	PUBLICATION	EDITION BOUGHT
a	*Daily Mirror*	Northern edition only
b	*The Sun*	Specially negotiated editions
c	*News of the World*	Specially negotiated editions
d	*The People*	Specially negotiated editions
e	*Sunday Mirror*	Specially negotiated editions
f	ITV Publications	Northern, Midlands, and Ulster editions
g	*Weekly News*	English and Ulster editions
h	*Reveille*	Specially negotiated editions.

a Daily Mirror—is selected as it offers an effective level of coverage and good economy.

The Northern Edition may be bought separately without any matching Brands in other editions thus enhancing flexibility and we feel that its use will lend authority to the schedule in that it is the leading national morning newspaper in the UK.

b The Sun—is recommended due to its excellent economy.

It is, in fact, the most economical publication for reaching our target market.

c, d and *e, News of the World, The People* and *Sunday Mirror* offer a high level of coverage with good economy and have the added advantage that (provided another Gallaher brand can be used) they will split copy so as to obtain a geographical blanket coverage over the three Gallaher areas.

f, g and *h*, ITV Publications, *Weekly News* and *Reveille* will again offer good coverage and economy, and can offer geographical blanket coverage over the three areas.

iii Rejection of Provincial Press

We have considered the possibility of using provincial evening newspapers to cover the list of prime and secondary towns, and with this in mind we have prepared an alternative schedule which deletes the *People* and *Sunday Mirror* and includes Provincial Evening Newspapers (where published) over the specified towns.

This alternative Plan is shown in Appendix E.

It can be seen that by comparing the evaluation of both schedules that using nationals only is superior in terms of coverage, frequency and economy and further, in the context of advertising weight, is 15% more efficient.

B. SELECTION OF OUTDOOR ADVERTISING

The advantages of Outdoor Advertising in the context of this particular campaign are:

  (i) Creative—colour and broad canvas

  (ii) Economy in terms of both capital cost and cost per '000 O.T.S.

  (iii) Good sites once obtained will be a permanent part of the overall campaign.

We recommend Outdoor to give concentrated support to the primary and secondary towns as it can be bought on a local basis without any sacrifice to coverage/cost efficiency (as opposed to provincial newspapers).

Media not recommended

It is a company policy that Pirate Radio should not be used; however, we feel it is also relevant to supply good media reasons for its exclusion.

a Cinema

Reasons for this medium's exclusion are the contents of an Agency document TPL/pmt dated 13.4.67.

Briefly re-stated they are that an extremely low coverage is obtainable—only 20% of all men visit the cinema regularly or occasionally, and the profile of the male cinema audience is contrary to the Park Drive Target Market (75% of male cinema goers are in the 16–35 age group).

b Radio

The two stations covering the Park Drive Areas are Radio Caroline (N), and Radio 270.

This medium is not recommended as a very low coverage is obtainable and profile of the audience is opposed to the Park Drive Target Market. (See Appendix F).

c Trade Press

This medium will not be used unless a major reformulation of the product such as a re-designed pack or price changes were to take place.

Schedule 1 (Main theme advertising)

Recommended Media Plan (Press)

Publication	Size	Cost £	No.	Total £	Jul.	Aug.	Sep.	Oct.	Nov.	Dec.
Daily Mirror	Page	765	12	9,180	XXX	XX	XX	XX	XX	X
The Sun	½ Page	380	12	4,560	XXX	XX	XX	XX	XX	X
TV Times (Nthn. edn.)	Page	840	12	10,080	XXX	XX	XX	XX	XX	X
TV World	Page	540	12	6,480	XXX	XX	XX	XX	XX	X
TV Post	Page	130	12	1,560	XXX	XX	XX	XX	XX	X
News of the World	½ Page	2,027	12	24,324	XXX	XX	XX	XX	XX	X
People	½ Page	2,128	12	25,536	XXX	XX	XX	XX	XX	X
Sunday Mirror	Page	1,456	12	17,472	XXX	XX	XX	XX	XX	X
Weekly News	Page	450	12	5,400	XXX	XX	XX	XX	XX	X
Reveille	Page	567	12	6,804	XXX	XX	XX	XX	XX	X
				£111,396						

Monthly Breakdown of Expenditure

	Total £	July £	August £	September £	October £	November £	December £
Press	111,396	27,849	18,566	18,566	18,566	18,566	9,283
Outdoor	30,000	5,000	5,000	5,000	5,000	5,000	5,000
Total	£141,396	32,849	23,566	23,566	23,566	23,566	14,283

Note: Detailed Outdoor Schedule will be supplied by Walter Hill & Co. Ltd.

Evaluation

Target Market—male C2DE smokers

	Coverage	Frequency (OTS)	CPT
	95%	38·0	19/-

Coverage	*All Men*	*16–34*	*35+*	*All Women*	*16–34*	*35+*
	91%	93%	91%	89%	93%	94%

Coverage	*All Men M/c Branch*	*Sheffield Branch*	*Belfast Branch*	*All Women M/c Branch*	*Sheffield Branch*	*Belfast Branch*
	90%	93%	89%	89%	89%	88%

Profile of advertising weight:

	Achieved	*Required*
Manchester	56%	55%
Sheffield	40%	42%
Belfast	4%	3%

APPENDIX A

Manchester Branch Area	Sheffield Branch Area
Primary Towns	*Primary Towns*
Blackpool	Hull
Oldham	Grimsby
Manchester	Scunthorpe
Rochdale	Doncaster
Stockport	Barnsley
Potteries	Sheffield
Wolverhampton	Chesterfield
Birmingham	Lincoln
Stourbridge	Leicester
Coventry	Derby
Kidderminster	Nottingham
	Loughborough
Secondary Towns	*Secondary Towns*
Isle of Man	Ripon
Anglesey	York
Colwyn Bay	Scarborough
Rhyl	Bridlington
Prestatyn	Skegness
Rugby	Hornsea
Burnley	
Stourport	

22

APPENDIX B National newspapers and magazines vs provincial evening and morning newspapers. Sample taken over the Northern (Lancs. and Yorks.) ITV Area—C2DE men and men cigarette smokers

Media	Cost Full page/half page, £	C2DE Men			Male cigarette smokers		
		%	Gross readership, '000	CPT	%	Gross readership, '000	CPT
Provincial Press (20 newspapers)	3,580	65	2,587	26/9	67	2,248	32/-
National Press Daily Mirror The Sun People Sunday Mirror	3,645*	65	6,075	12/-	67	5,207	14/-

Profiles:	All Men	C2DE Smokers	Male Smokers	All Adults	Men	Women
Provincials	100%	74%	63%	100%	51%	49%
Nationals	100%	82%	66%	100%	53%	47%

* Rates based on taking Northern editions only.
Source: Erwin Wasey estimate based on ENAB Readership Surveys over ITV Areas.
Due to lack of research information it is not possible to evaluate provincial newspapers over C2DE male smokers.

APPENDIX C Comparison of provincial evening newspapers vs local weekly newspapers

	½ Page cost, £	Combined circulation	CPT £
Westminster Press Group			
Provincial evenings (9 Newspapers)	753	574,287	1·31
Local weeklies (24 Newspapers)	1,136	503,638	2·26
Northcliffe Newspapers Group			
Provincial evenings (8 Newspapers)	782	603,000	1·30
Local weeklies (6 Newspapers)	270	103,000	2·62
Thomson Provincial Group			
Provincial evenings (9 Newspapers)	1,810	1,091,280	1·66
Local weeklies (20 Newspapers)	802	300,910	2·66
United Newspapers			
Provincial evenings (4 Newspapers)	716	481,116	1·49
Local weeklies (10 Newspapers)	570	242,229	2·35

APPENDIX D National newspapers and magazines. Coverage and Economy of Northern Editions within the Gallaher Manchester, Sheffield and Belfast Branch Areas

Publication	Cost Full page/half page, £	Estimated Universe (C2DE male smokers) 100% = 3,225,000			All men average noting, %	CPT after noting	
		%	'000	CPT			
Daily Mirror	765	27	880	17/6	33	52/6	Recommended
Daily Express	900	23	749	24/-	27	88/9	
Daily Mail	990	13	428	46/6	27	172/-	
Daily Sketch	250	6	196	25/6	32	79/-	
The Sun	532	25	799	13/4	27	48/6	Recommended
News of the World†	2,027	54	1741	23/-	26	87/4	Recommended
People†	2,128	55	1770	24/-	26	91/-	Recommended
Sunday Mirror†	1,456	33	1057	28/-	32	86/9	Recommended
ITV Publications*	1,510	37	1183	25/6	28	91/9	Recommended
Weekly News*	450	12	379	23/6	30	77/-	Recommended
Reveille†	567	23	732	15/6	30	51/-	Recommended
	£11,423		9718 average	23/-	29	78/-	

ITV Publications—*TV Times* (Northern Edition), *TV World, TV Post.*

* Geographic Blanket coverage of the three Gallaher Branch Areas is obtainable without other brands having to participate although it should be noted that an advantageous rate is negotiable with *TV Times* if another brand can take all other editions.

† Geographic Blanket Coverage over the three Gallaher Branch Areas is obtainable via the regionalised editions of these publications provided other Gallaher brands will take remaining editions.

Source: Erwin Wasey estimate based on a simulated IPA Card Run on Male Smokers and Agencies Research Consortium on Noting

APPENDIX E Alternative Media Plan (Not recommended)

Publication	Size	Cost £	No.	Total £
Daily Mirror	Full page	765	12	9,180
The Sun	Half page	380	12	4,560
TV Times (Nthn. Edn.)	Full page	840	12	10,608
TV World	Full page	540	12	6,480
TV Post	Full page	130	12	1,560
Weekly News	Full page	450	12	5,400
Reveille	Full page	472	12	6,804
News of the World	Half page	2,207	12	24,324
Selected provincial evening newspapers*	Full page/half page	3,617	12	43,404
				£111,720

* See overleaf for complete list of newspapers

Evaluation

	Coverage	Frequency (OTS)	Messages '000	CPT
Male C2DE smokers	85%	34·0	93,194	£1 4 0
Schedule 1	95%	38·0	113,217	19 0

26

APPENDIX E (Cont'd.)

Provincial Evening Newspapers

Publication	Size	Cost, £	Branch
Blackpool–West Lancs. Evening Gazette	page	120	
Oldham Evening Chronicle	page	75	
Manchester Evening News	half page	650	
Stoke–Staffs. Evening Sentinel	half page	165	
Wolverhampton Express & Star	page	312	
Birmingham Mail	half page	674	Manchester
Coventry Evening Telegraph	page	180	Total Cost: £2,176
Hull Daily Mail	half page	180	
Grimsby Evening Telegraph	half page	85	
Doncaster Evening Post	half page	75	
Sheffield Star	half page	321	
Lincoln–Lincs. Echo	half page	60	
Leicester Mercury	page	254	
Derby Evening Telegraph	page	126	
Nottingham Evening Post	half page	242	Sheffield
York–Yorks. Evening Press	half page	88	Total Cost: £1,441

APPENDIX F Male listenership of Radio Caroline

Percentage of adult males listening to Radio Caroline by age and class

All	16–24	25–34	35–44	45–54	55–64	65+	AB	C1	C2	DE
17	37	23	16	15	9	6	12	15	19	20

Profile of males listening compared with Target Market

	16–34	35+	ABC1	C2DE
Radio Caroline	52%	48%	26%	74%
Park Drive Smokers	34%	66%	12%	88%
Woodbine Plain	20%	80%	10%	90%

Note. No research information is available for Radio 270.

Source: NOP Survey on Pirate Radio

APPENDIX G Competitive expenditure January–April, 1967

	Total cigarette expenditure	£2,000,000	=	100%
	Total 'A' class expenditure	£695,000	=	35%

Expenditure by 'A' Class Products

Product	Percentage of total 'A' class expenditure	National Expenditure		Expenditure within M/c and Sheffield Branch Areas		
		Jan–Apr '67 £	Jan–Dec '67 £	Jan–Apr '67 £		Jan–Dec '67 £
Park Drive	10%	67,660	255,000	67,660	= 100%	255,000
Woodbine	23%	156,587	470,000	50,445	= 32%	151,000
Cadets	20%	144,528	435,000	51,978	= 36%	155,000
Weights	13%	89,620	270,000	26,515	= 30%	80,000
Players No. 6	25%	172,658	520,000	62,770	= 36%	190,000
Escort	9%	63,860	190,000	23,152	= 36%	70,000
Buckingham		—	—	—		
Regent		—	—	—		
Total competitive Expenditure:		£627,253	£1,900,000	£214,860	= 34%	£646,000

Source: Legion and Agency estimates (Press only)

29

Stephen King, *Inter-media decisions*, Admap Third World Advertising Workshop (1969).

4 Budget setting

4.1 Responsibility of the media planner

This subject was not covered in the first edition because, in the overwhelming majority of cases, the media planner has to work to a budget set by someone else, normally in the client organisation. Even if this is still true, it is helpful to know the processes which should have occurred in the preparation of the budget, and it is also possible that his advice will be sought, which makes it imperative.

4.2 Reasonable approaches

The objective is to set the media budget at such a level that to spend either more, or less, would result in an inferior profit return to the advertiser. This is illustrated in Figures 4.1 and 4.2. Figure 4.1 shows the connection between advertising expenditure (on the horizontal axis) and sales response (on the vertical axis). In the time period under consideration (usually a financial year), if we are planning for an established brand it is likely that we shall sell a significant quantity (OA) even if we do not advertise at all. This will be due to consumer loyalty, which takes time to erode, and the product remaining in distribution, reminding purchasers of its existence by on-shelf display. It is likely, however, that the *rate* of sale will decline as we progress through the year, and that the quantity OA for subsequent years would steadily decrease. Indeed, for most competitive markets, we would eventually lose distribution to the point at which OA would reduce to zero.

If advertising is confined to one 30-second spot on a Sunday morning in July, we would not be surprised to discover that little extra product was sold. In general, there is a level of advertising below which response is very slow: most people do not see enough to be motivated by it. This is point C in Figure 4.1. Looking at Figure 4.2 it will be seen that advertising expenditure in the range AC actually *reduces* profit, since the incremental sales are insufficient to offset the incremental expenditure.

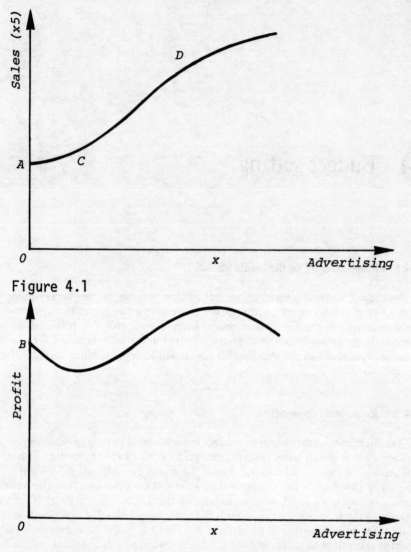

Figure 4.1

Figure 4.2

From C to D there is a good sales response to advertising, and profit rises continuously. Then the ability of extra advertising to generate extra sales dimin-
ishes: we are reaching the position at which it is increasingly difficult to persuade additional consumers to buy more of our brand, or to switch from their
existing brands, or to come into the market, or some combination of these possibilities. The amount of additional profit for each additional advertising pound
spent decreases, and eventually disappears. The point X (Figure 4.2) shows
where spending either more, or less, on advertising, reduces profit. This, then,
sets the optimal budget level.

In real life the relationships, particularly between sales and profits before advertising, are much more complex than is suggested here. In fact, the way accountants can produce different profit figures according to different ways of considering the figures is a subject in itself. Nevertheless, the principle is close enough to reality to follow as far as is possible.

How do we know when we have arrived at X? 'Know' is a strong word; but even if we do not 'know', there are several ways of getting sensible estimates.

4.2.1 Quantified models

The nearest we can get to certainty is by the construction of a mathematical model which we believe explains the interactions of the various marketing forces sufficiently well to be used predictively. If we have access to such a model, e.g. OR/MS Dialogue's STAB, it will tell us not only where X is, but many other things besides. (Possibly the most general model describes profit as a function of the 4Ps: product, place, promotion and price. The classic economist's solution was put forward by Dorfman and Steiner, but this approach has never been marketed for management use.)

The general form of such a model is:

Share in next period = Decay factor x share in this period +
Lagged advertising effect +
Lagged promotional effect +
Price effect +
Distribution effect +
Residual error

It is commonly observed that the best predictor of next month's share is this month's share; but, as we have described above, most products in competitive markets will decline if marketing activity is not applied to sustain them. This is the meaning of the 'decay factor'.

It is also well established that the effect of advertising is not necessarily instantaneous; more often it is spread out over time. This is why we have to 'lag' the advertising input. The same is true for promotions, although the extent of the spread of promotional effect is generally expected to be smaller, but may be negative in a period after that in which the promotion takes place. This happens if the promotion does not increase sales of the brand, but brings them forward in time.

The price at which our product is placed on the shelves, in relation to those of its direct competitors, may be critical. If there is much variation in the relationship from period to period, the fact is bound to play a part in the equation.

Similarly with distribution; a serious out-of-stock position can damage a brand's sales considerably, unless there is sufficient brand loyalty to make shoppers work hard to find it. (Most unusual!)

Competitive activity in general is often considered critical to our brand's sales; and yet analysis shows that it is, in practical terms, not so. The way it seems to work is this: the total level of competitive marketing sets an upper bound for our development, at least in the short term. Equally, however inept we may be, if we have an established brand it will sell some minimum amount during the year. What happens between these extremes is dependent on our own activities, save launches of new brands and major economic upset. Since these cannot be predicted, there is really no excuse for abdicating our responsibilities to others. Nevertheless, extraneous forces are bound to effect us in small and unpredictable ways. The latter are collected together in the 'residual error' term. If the model is to be useful, these errors must be small, randomly distributed over time and average zero. Then we may state that our brand share in a particular period, given the marketing inputs, will be of such a size, knowing the accuracy of this estimate, and that it is accurate enough to be useful.

Given this situation, the computer will assess for us the consequences of different levels of expenditure, and, in fact, draw Figures 4.1 and 4.2 for us.

4.2.2   Subjective models

Failing analysis of this rigour, it is nevertheless very useful to pursue our discussions as far as we can along the same lines. Managers take decisions according to models which they have in their heads. They may not know this; and if they do, they may not have worked out the models as carefully as they could.

John D. Little has shown how a systematic approach can be used with subjective inputs, taking us as close as possible to the position outlined in the previous section. This is his advertising budgeting model ADBUDG.

To get the inputs for this model, managers are asked four questions.

1   If advertising is cut to zero in this time period, what is the minimum level to which we could imagine brand share falling?
2   If we had saturation advertising in this period, what is the maximum level to which we could imagine brand share rising?
3   What advertising rate do we believe necessary to *maintain* our existing share?
4   What effect on share do we believe increasing this maintenance rate by 50 per cent would have?

Given these four figures an advertising-sales curve can be fitted, as shown in Figure 4.3.

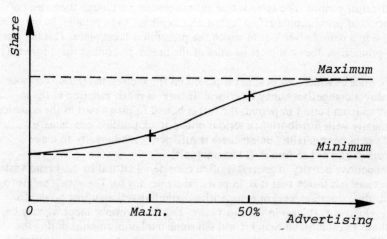

Figure 4.3

Forcing managers to quantify their judgements in this way is a salutary exer- *35*
cise for them, as well as others. It is likely to yield more rational decisions than
might otherwise be available, and points up areas in which research may be most
profitably applied. A development of this model, called BRANDAID, allows the
incorporation of any inputs which can be readily quantified. It is available for
use in an interactive way, so that the manager can test the effects of different
courses of action.

There are dangers, however. Whilst in the majority of cases, commonsense
and experience will have led to the correct area for advertising expenditure,
there are other cases in which this has not happened. It is possible for sales to
decline with increased advertising expenditure and to increase with reduced advertising expenditure. It is even possible, let it be whispered, that a particular
ad campaign has no effect on sales at all. The quantified model will uncover such
areas; subjective models are unlikely to do so.

4.2.3   Setting objectives

Another method is to monitor the approach to the correct budget level by setting objectives for the campaign, and see how well the objectives are attained.
Where good data on sales and profits are not available, this may be the only way
to proceed. Even if they are, the approach may be more understandable, and
therefore acceptable, than formal model building.

With this procedure the structure is reversed. A given level of profit is tar-
getted, implying levels of sales and advertising. Awareness, and often attitude
rating, targets are then set to achieve the sales level; and media targets are set
appropriately. All these measurements are then checked during the course of
the campaign, and necessary adjustments may be made. Over the course of time
such studies should aid decision taking, and will certainly give management
actionable information.

Problems may arise if the measurements do not move as expected. For a
mature brand, with high awareness, it is quite possible for this measurement to
reduce while sales increase; it is particularly easy for research to suggest that the
figure is reducing while sales increase. A successful brand may have an awareness
of 80 per cent, yet be bought in one year by no more than 5 per cent of consumers. Increasing the latter figure to 6 per cent will be very worthwhile, but a
reduction from 80 to 77 per cent may not be statistically significant, and is very
unlikely to be significant in business terms.

4.3   What happens in practice?

The most popular method of setting budgets is still to take a percentage of sales,
or forecast sales, as it was in the 'thirties. Only if we know that we are at X is
this justified; anywhere else it is less than optimal. Other methods may be even
cruder: brand managers who are short of their profit targets on first estimates
have been known to correct this by increasing sales budgets and reducing promotional budgets. Experience of objective setting may restrict this practice,
as it may be possible to demonstrate, on past figures, the low chances of success.

In discussion with other members of the planning team, the media planner will be more likely to influence decisions in a valuable way if he bears in mind the underlying structure of the problem, however far he may be from being able to measure it.

4.4   Related reading

D. Bloom, 'Consumer behaviour and the timing of advertising effects', *Admap* (September 1976).

John D. Little, 'Models and managers: concepts of a decision calculus', *Management Science* (April 1970).

Ambar G. Rao, *Quantitative theories in advertising*, John Wiley (1970).

R. Douglas Wells, 'An empirical model of television advertising awareness', *Journal of the Market Research Society* (October 1975).

5   Basic strategic decisions

5.1   Inter-media comparisons

One of the main paradoxes of media planning is that it is generally agreed that
there is no real basis for inter-media choice—and yet these choices are made
every day. Whilst it is possible to calculate within reasonable limits of precision
how many and what type of people will be exposed how frequently to the advertising by different media schedules, there is no way of determining whether one
exposure in medium A is more or less effective than one exposure in medium B.
Clearly there can never be a general answer since the creative content of the advertisement of one product in medium A may differ substantially in relation to
its counterpart for medium B, or for the same brand in a different year. Whilst
acknowledging the absence of a general answer, most planners would be absolutely delighted with the presence of a specific one. Ideally one would like to
use pre-testing techniques to measure the relative efficiency of a press advertisement and a television advertisement for the same campaign, building these values
into media assessments. This has, in fact, been done in one or two cases, but confidence in pre-testing techniques is not strong enough for its general adoption.

Study should be made of the major published works in this area. Two things
should be borne in mind when reading them. Firstly, many are commissioned
by media owners, who are clearly likely to study cases in which they believe
that they are likely to have the advantage. Secondly, if one medium does turn
out 'best', it does not necessarily mean that it should be used exclusively.

The only way at present to make an objective inter-media choice is to try
alternatives, and carefully measure the results. This subject is dealt with in
Chapter 27.

Most media plans are concerned with going brands. That is to say, the plans produced will run for a given period, usually a financial year, and the brand is currently being advertised and sold and probably has been advertised and sold for some years previously. The biggest single question on any media plan is that of the main medium and whether, in fact, there are going to be any other media in support of it. If an existing campaign is judged to be successful, then it is usually extremely difficult for the media planner to instigate a change of the main medium. This may seem very natural, but it should be remembered that the most difficult thing a creative man can do is to maintain a campaign which is judged to be successful. Quite simply, although people do not get tired of reading the *Daily Express* they would clearly very quickly get tired of reading the same *Daily Express* every day.

Mention of creative work raises one fundamental reason for a change of main medium, which is that a new creative campaign demands it. It may be, for example, that a toiletry product previously sold in only one variety is now going to be manufactured in several, and that the different varieties will be colour coded. If it is felt essential to show the new packs in their colours, and television has been the choice before, the limited penetration of colour sets may force reconsideration. Alternatively, it may be that a consumer durable which has been advertised successfully in the press has some modification made to it which clearly cries out for demonstration. In this case there will be a strong preference for television, and thus the change is made. Both of these examples demand a change in the product itself before a change in creative strategy. It is, however, sometimes possible for such a change to occur without a change in the product itself, and for agreement to be reached that the new creative treatment is so much superior to the old that a change in medium is justified.

Another important source of main medium changes is a dramatic change of budget. Clearly the more money one has, the more media one can use. It is equally true to say that there is a tendency for large-budget advertisers to appear principally in television and for small-budget advertisers to appear principally in the Press. Hence a dramatic upward change will usually involve at least close consideration of a switch from press to television and a dramatic downward change the reverse. This is such a well established pattern that one is forced to think that there may be something in it. Both media groups have sought to combat the effect, television in an attempt to bring in small advertisers and the Press in an attempt not to lose the larger ones. It appears to defy logic since most advertisers making this kind of change would say that television was the more efficient of the two media for their particular product. Nevertheless, there is a widespread feeling that for television to be effective it needs to be used with greater frequency than the press medium and therefore calls for larger budgets. To some extent the way in which the two media are used justifies the action. Figure 5.1 shows the response generated by press and television schedules, at different budget levels, given the same set of objectives. In this example, the Press appears more effective than television at all levels, but a small change in the relative effectiveness of the two media would produce'a cross-over effect.

The reason for this is quite simple. In the Press, the use of computers has forced planners into the logic of starting with more economical media and add-

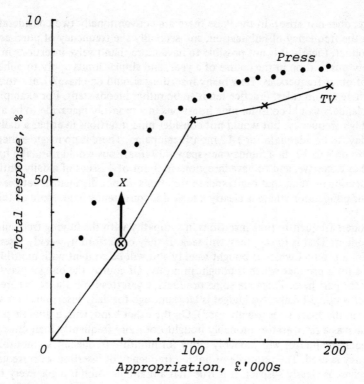

Figure 5.1

ing the less economical as more money becomes available. This is one reason for the levelling off of the Press curve. In television, on the other hand, if insufficient money is available to buy campaigns in all areas, it is usually the most cost-efficient which are dropped, and the least cost-efficient which are retained. In Figure 5.1 the X at £50,000 can be moved, as indicated by the arrow, by changing this policy. The higher figure is obtained by planning the television campaign as a press campaign, and buying low cost-per-thousand breaks across the network. This results, of course, in 'weak' campaigns in all areas, but a greater response nationally.

Thus, whilst current practice has logic at one stage, the underlying logic is seriously open to question.

5.3 Frequency

5.3.1 In the Press

The question of how frequently the advertisement should be put before the target market is for most media the critical one (in the case of outdoor the question, happily, does not arise). In the Press there are conventionally two considerations. Firstly the frequency of publication, and secondly the frequency of purchase of the product. Clearly it is not possible to have more than twelve insertions in a monthly publication in the course of a year, and similar limits apply to publications of other frequencies. How many insertions should one have? Unfortunately there are no rules. Practice tends to be rather inconsistent. For example, most planners would consider nine insertions in a monthly magazine to be a fairly high frequency, but would not consider nine insertions in either a daily, or a Sunday, to be adequate for a 12 month campaign. There is no magic either in the ratio of 9 to 12. In a Sunday newspaper 39 insertions would normally be regarded as excessive, and to have insertions in 3 out of 4 issues of a daily unthinkable. Bearing in mind that our response functions do not distinguish between types of publication, there is clearly a logical inconsistency here. More of this later.

Planners frequently time insertions in sympathy with the buying frequency of the product. That is to say, they will seek, if they can afford it, weekly insertions for a product which is bought weekly and will be content with monthly insertions for a product which is bought monthly. Of course, the budget plays an important part here. There are some products, cigarettes for instance, where the product is bought daily. No budget is large enough for daily insertions in many media (in the space sizes usually used). On the other hand, with a durable product such as a refrigerator, probably bought not more frequently than once in five years, the budget will probably allow for monthly frequency, so monthly frequency is used. The rationale of linking frequency of insertion with frequency of purchase is clearly suspect. It is true that a brand decision is made every time that a purchase is made and, therefore, the more opportunities we have for influencing that brand decision, the better chance we stand. In spite of this, it is certain that the effect of advertising is generally a long-term one and linked inextricably with product experience. At the point of purchase the consumer brings into play, however unconsciously, all that he, or she, has learnt about the brand and its competitors over his, or her, total buying experience of the product field. For this reason it is almost certainly better to plan insertions so as to obtain the maximum over-all effect, rather than slavishly attempt to match a pattern of purchase. In any case, in most consumer fields different consumers have very different patterns of purchasing and what one is talking about is merely mean frequency.

5.3.2 In television

In this case frequency is usually felt to be of paramount importance. Most television advertisers feel uncomfortable if a considerable proportion of their target market do not have the opportunity of seeing their commercial at least four times during a four-week period. In order to achieve such a frequency it is necessary to have two to three peak spots, or an equivalent amount of rating points in other segments, each week. In order to achieve such a frequency on any but the highest budgets it is necessary to curtail advertising to fairly short periods. How far one can take this curtailment, or conversely for how long one can afford to be without any advertising at all, is very much a matter of judgement.

At least one advertiser has built brand leadership in a competitive field by advertising on television at this frequency for two nine-week periods during the course
of the year. On the other hand, some years ago Phyllosan achieved a spectacular
sales growth by transmitting one 60-second commercial once a fortnight over a
six-month period.

5.3.3   In other media

In radio the frequency argument is carried still further. The first reason for this
is that audiences to any particular programme are very low and therefore to
build cumulative coverage it is necessary to have spots in many programmes.
Secondly, most people listen to radio whilst doing a number of other things.
Attention values are therefore low, and it is again felt that repetition helps to
overcome this problem. Again, the cost of radio is extremely low, and a high frequency of insertion can be afforded. 'High' in this context will probably mean at
least five spots per week, and these may all be grouped on a single night. It could
mean more than this. Some advertisers have used 30 to 50 spots during the
course of a week over a continuing campaign.

Frequency in the cinema medium is largely dictated by the pattern of usage.
One buys a week's campaign in a given cinema and during the course of that
week one's commercial is transmitted as many times as there are programmes.
(This varies around an average of 13 from 7 to 20.) The most common purchases
of cinema are either in continuous weekly patterns, i.e. the same cinema is
booked continuously for however many weeks the campaign is going to run, or
in alternate weeks, which may be, for instance, 13 out of 26. In general, because
of the low frequency of attendance at the cinema, it is best to have as continuous a pattern as is possible on the budget in order to reach the maximum number of people.

Frequency in direct mail is a particularly vexed question. Many advertisers
when using direct mail think of it as a one-shot medium. There is some justification for this when it is being used to do a specific job, such as a mailing to retailers to advise them of the introduction of a new campaign. On the other hand,
if direct mail is being used as a straightforward advertising medium, then there is
no reason to believe that frequency is any less important here than elsewhere.

5.4   Bursts versus continuous campaigns

Much has been spoken and written about the rival merits of the 'steady drip' versus the 'concentrated push' deployment of the advertising budget. Only recently
has it been realised that, whilst most answers to marketing questions are brand-
specific, the answer to this one is brand-*and appropriation*-specific.

Consider Figure 5.2 and the accompanying Table. The figures on the vertical
axis show the sales response (measured in extra sales dollars per thousand population per year) to advertising expenditure, (measured in dollars per thousand
population per year) on the horizontal axis. In this (actual) case, a high 'threshold' was encountered (see Section 4.2). The sales were measured in Nielsen bi-
monthly periods, and the two patterns of advertising evaluated were: an even

spread over the six periods; and a concentration, with one period having double weight, and the next nothing. Because of the 'threshold', spreading the lowest level evenly had no effect on sales whatsoever. Consequently, all the advertising money spent was lost. The 'burst' pattern meant that, while the advertising was happening, we were moving into a useful part of the response curve. The gain here was not entirely lost in the gaps, and the net effect, over the year, was a sales gain. This was not sufficient to completely cover the cost of advertising, but was a big improvement on the steady pattern.

Raising the appropriation to $10 per thousand helped both situations in sales terms, and produced a profit from the 'burst' pattern. Doubling it, to $14, produced a significant profit from the burst pattern, and came near to profit with continuous advertising.

Finally, raising the budget to $22 per thousand pushes burst expenditure up to the top of the curve, so that the new increase in sales is only $1 per thousand, and results in a net loss. However, at this level the constant pattern is very efficient, and results in incremental sales of $33 per thousand, and a resultant profit of $11, the highest shown. In actual practice, both series of profit outcomes

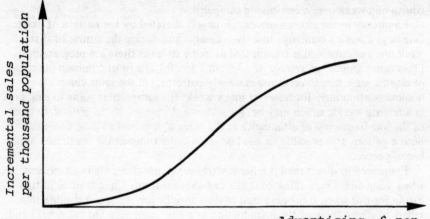

M_t	Incremental sales		Outcome	
	Constant rate	Bimonthly bursts	Constant	Bursts
7	0	5.5	(7)	(1.5)
10	3	12.0	(7)	2.0
14	11	19.0	(3)	5.0
22	33	20.0	11	(2.0)

Figure 5.2

would be graphed and the highest profit accruing would indicate both the budget and the correct tactics.

There is nothing magical about the Nielsen bi-monthly period, either for determining the length of a burst or the length of a 'holiday'. However, it must be borne in mind that we can only determine the effects of patterns which we can measure.

Again, we must answer the question: suppose we have not estimated the sales response function, what should we do? First, let us consider whether we are talking about repeat-purchases, i.e. non-durable products, or not.

For durables, consumers actively seek information before purchase and we should capitalise on that fact. The degree of search varies; many car-owners continually discuss developments with their friends, and read new model reviews as eagerly as others read theatre reviews. More typically, interest in the product wanes in the intervals between purchase, and rises to a peak immediately pre-purchase. In most durable markets there are a small number of media which contain many ads for the product field—they are virtually catalogues. First deployment of the appropriation should be towards continuous presence in them, so that the seeker for information may be rewarded.

Durables may then be divided into branded and non-branded. Cars, again, are the best example of branded products: no-one has any doubt as to the make or model he possesses. In such a case the remainder of the appropriation can safely be concentrated into a few bursts (possibly one) and used for special events—such as the introduction of new models.

At the other extreme, it is very difficult to ascertain the brand name of a wall-covering, once it has been pasted. The same is true for fitted carpets and many furnishing products. In these cases, since there is no other way of sustaining brand awareness, this must be an important task for advertising. Such a task calls for the maximum attainable continuity.

With repeat purchase products, the main consideration must be the degree of consumer satisfaction offered by our brand. If this is high, then the number of consumers switching out of the brand in any period will be compensated by a roughly equal number switching in. In this case, our advertising should be concentrated into big enough lumps to persuade a new group to try the brand.

On the other hand, if consumer satisfaction is low, then repeat purchase will not be enough to sustain the brand. We must advertise as continuously as possible, to keep topping-up our pool of current users. (We should also persuade our client to improve his product.)

5.5   Related reading

Jacques Durand, *Advertising and time: growth and decay,* Marcel Dassault Jours de France Awards (1969).

Readers Digest, *Look at Life: A major advertiser tests the effectiveness of general magazines and TV* (1970).

S. Segnit and S. Broadbent, 'Area tests and consumer surveys to measure advertising effectiveness, ESOMAR Congress (1970).

Nicolas Steinberg, *Forecasting results of an advertising campaign,* Media Research Group (1967).

44   J.B. Stewart, *Repetitive advertising in newspapers,* Harvard (1964).

E.W. Whitley, 'The media mix: some considerations', *Admap* (January 1975).

Ambar G. Rao and James R. Adams, 'The measurement and meaning of marketing inputs', MRS Conference (1977).

6 Basic calculations

Two basic criteria on which the planner will select media are cost-effectiveness and coverage. Each term is related to the target audience for the campaign and will be modified as described in later chapters.

6.1 How to look at the target market

Suppose our market research shows us that 50 per cent of the buyers of our product are ABC1. Since we know that the ABC1s only account for 34 per cent of the total population, we may say that each ABC1 is worth two C2DE's. What flows from this finding depends on the marketing strategy. It may be decided to concentrate on strength, or alternatively to attack the weak area. Suppose we take the view that we must support our existing franchise. Then we could, and in the past probably would, forget the C2DEs altogether, and devise a schedule to reach ABC1s. It will surprise no one that for equivalent space sizes the *Daily Telegraph* is more economical in reaching ABC1 adults than the *Daily Mirror*.

But we should consider all of the purchasing power, not only that which is most concentrated. The way we do this is to weight each sub-group in population according to the marketing objectives; that is, in our present case, we give each ABC1 a weighting of 100 and each C2DE a weighting of 50. The effect on media choice is quite dramatic. Using these weights, the *Daily Mirror* becomes a very much more attractive buy than the *Daily Telegraph*. Advertising messages delivered to members of the population outside the prime prospect group used to be described as 'wastage'. Using the weighting method converts them into 'bonus'.

Of course, in the great majority of markets, there are many more weights used than two. In the typical case, which is discussed further below, the weights used were:

Men	50	16-24	50
Women	100	25-34	100
AB	100	35-44	100
C1	100	45-54	80
C2	70	55-64	50
DE	20	65+	20

Note that the use of weights ranging from 0 to 100 is purely a convenience; what matters are the relationships between them.

6.2   Cost-effectiveness

It is not all that long ago that the only guide to the relative value of different media, other than the planner's own judgement, was the relative cost of buying 1000 circulation in each. This was extended, when readership figures became available, to cost-per-thousand adults. This has in turn been extended by the use of marketing weights, such as we have just discussed, and also media weights. To calculate the cost effectiveness of any particular medium today involves multiplying its audience in each defined cell by the appropriate marketing weight; adding these results together; multiplying the resulting number by the appropriate media weight; and then comparing the end product with the cost of an insertion. If the audience figure is divided into the cost, you may have today's version of cost-per-thousand. If the sum is done the other way round, we get 'impacts per pound', which many people prefer.

Clearly it is not even possible, let alone desirable, to carry out such calculations on a desk calculator. With the use of a computer terminal it is possible to access programs kept on-line by a number of computer bureaux for this kind of work. Alternatively, we may commission the bureau to carry out the analysis themselves.

All the analyses in this Chapter, and also Chapter 26, were carried out by Comshare Limited.

Table 6.1 shows the way the program calculated the relative cost-effectiveness of a number of press media, using the target market given above, rate card costs for a colour page, and media weights as shown. This list would be expected to include the *Telegraph Magazine*, but, at the time of writing, it was in process of transfer from the *Daily* to the *Sunday*, and any data shown might have been misleading. It will be noted that another of the useful things the computer does is to sort the list of publications into rank order. Normally, one would expect the schedule to contain publications from the top of this list.

6.3   Coverage

6.3.1   By vehicle

The other important parameter in choosing individual media vehicles is the per-

TABLE 6.1

Rank	Name	Media weight	Cost per thousand
1	*Good Housekeeping*	1.00	1.13
2	*My Weekly*	0.75	1.22
3	*Reader's Digest*	0.85	1.24
4	*She*	0.90	1.35
5	*Ideal Home*	1.00	1.42
6	*Homes & Gardens*	1.00	1.46
7	*Family Circle*	0.90	1.54
8	*Living*	0.90	1.73
9	*House & Garden*	1.00	1.75
10	*Woman & Home*	0.85	1.77
11	*Annabel*	0.80	1.82
12	*Woman's Weekly*	0.90	1.83
13	*Home-Freezer Digest*	0.85	1.84
14	*Do-It-Yourself*	0.75	1.93
15	*Cosmopolitan*	0.85	2.07
16	*Woman's Realm*	0.90	2.11
17	*Woman*	0.90	2.14
18	*Woman's Own*	0.90	2.14
19	*TV Times*	0.80	2.21
20	*Woman's Journal*	0.90	2.37
21	*Sunday Times Magazine*	0.90	2.51
22	*Radio Times*	0.80	2.53
23	*Observer Magazine*	0.90	2.74
24	*Practical Householder*	0.75	2.79
25	*Punch*	0.80	2.91
26	*Homemaker*	0.75	3.05

Source: National Readership Survey, October 1975 to March 1976

centage of the weighted target market exposed to the vehicle. It is quite common to find highly cost-effective media which are not seen by many people. This is true in some off-peak periods in television and also in the case of some of the smaller press media.

The specific marketing weights applied will reduce the total audiences to a vehicle by varying degrees, depending how rich the original audience was in members of the target group. Table 6.2 shows the same publications which we have already considered in relation to the same market, comparing their coverage of the weighted market with their coverage of all adults.

The planner has chosen many publications in which the coverage of the

TABLE 6.2

Rank	Name	Average readership	
		as % of target market	as % of all adults
1	*Good Housekeeping*	9.2	6.4
2	*My Weekly*	8.5	8.0
3	*Reader's Digest*	21.7	20.7
4	*She*	7.4	5.0
5	*Ideal Home*	7.4	5.9
6	*Homes & Gardens*	6.0	4.6
7	*Family Circle*	13.8	10.2
8	*Living*	6.9	4.8
9	*House & Garden*	4.8	3.6
10	*Woman & Home*	11.6	8.1
11	*Annabel*	2.5	2.1
12	*Woman's Weekly*	14.9	12.8
13	*Home-Freezer Digest*	5.3	3.0
14	*Do-It-Yourself*	4.6	5.0
15	*Cosmopolitan*	6.2	4.9
16	*Woman's Realm*	11.2	10.5
17	*Woman*	21.3	17.3
18	*Woman's Own*	22.0	18.3
19	*TV Times*	24.9	25.3
20	*Woman's Journal*	2.9	2.2
21	*Sunday Times Magazine*	13.9	10.2
22	*Radio Times*	26.3	24.0
23	*Observer Magazine*	8.6	7.0
24	*Practical Householder*	3.7	3.9
25	*Punch*	2.7	2.4
26	*Homemaker*	2.3	2.4

Source: National Readership Survey, October 1975 to March 1976

weighted market is higher, and sometimes considerably higher, than the coverage of all adults. Note that this does not necessarily place the publication high in the cost-effectiveness table.

6.3.2 *By media group*

Before the planner approaches the problem of selecting individual publications,

or time slots, or whatever, he may well have to consider the effective coverage
he can obtain through the medium, or the media group. This is particularly true
of cinema and radio which have relatively restricted audiences. There are also a
number of groups within the press medium which may offer low coverage of certain target groups.

The coverage of the second most cost-effective medium, *My Weekly*, is almost
identical amongst the target market and the total adult population. On the other
hand, the *Sunday Times Magazine*, which does nearly 40 per cent better in the
target market, comes near the bottom of the ranking. The main point of this
table is to show that in order to build economical coverage, a large number of
magazines would have to be used. It takes the top seven to give a two-thirds
coverage in terms of average readership, without taking into account duplication.

6.4 Frequency distributions

Another analysis which has an important bearing on schedule construction is the
distribution of different numbers of opportunities-to-see the advertising across
the population under consideration. Originally the National Readership Survey
showed respondents either being readers of a publication, or not. That is to say
they were either counted as seeing all issues, or none.

This led to a situation in which a schedule comprising eight insertions in each
of two publications would give rise to a frequency distribution in which the

TABLE 6.3

Opportunities-to-see	%	Cumulative coverage
0	40.4	
1	5.8	59.6
2	4.1	53.4
3	3.3	49.3
4	3.2	46.0
5	3.3	42.8
6	3.9	39.5
7	5.5	35.6
8	22.7	30.1
9	1.8	7.4
10	1.1	5.6
11	0.8	4.5
12	0.7	3.7
13	0.6	3.0
14	0.6	2.4
15	0.6	1.8
16	1.2	1.2

section of the population not classified as seeing either would have no exposures, those seeing one or other, but not both, would have eight exposures and
those seeing both publications would have sixteen.

Today respondents are assessed on the frequency of their exposure to different media, as well as whether they see them or not. This gives rise to the kind of
frequency distribution shown in Table 6.3. This distribution is calculated on a
weighted base in which living in a home with central heating plays an important
part. The schedule consists of eight insertions in each of the *Daily Express* and
the *Daily Mirror* and, not surprisingly, the largest group in this weighted population (with the exception of those not covered at all) is the group with eight
opportunities-to-see. The important point to note is the spread from one to sixteen and the fact that the weight of the distribution lies towards the lightly
covered end. Only half of the population who are covered at all are covered at
the level of eight opportunities-to-see.

It should also be noted that the introduction of a media weight which might
be used to convert opportunities-to-see the medium into opportunities-to-see the
advertising would push the distribution very much towards this lighter-covered
end.

6.5   How selective can we be?

It is not uncommon to hear agency men, when talking competitively, giving the
impression that they can deliver an entire budget against the target audience,
even when that target audience is only 20 per cent of the total population. It is
unfortunately true that, in general, media selection is a fairly blunt instrument.
It is not very difficult to concentrate the appropriation against the key section
of a target market, but it is very difficult to get high coverage of the target market without high coverage of all adults. Table 6.4 is reproduced from the first
edition of the book, since we have not been able to find a current example
which shows this degree of divergence. In 1968, the date of the information,
only about a quarter of adults lived in homes with telephones, and they were
markedly biased up-market. The table shows the cumulative coverage of adults
in telephone-owning homes, and adults in non-telephone owning homes, by the
National Daily and Sunday papers. The coverage is built up by taking the richest
medium first and then downward in progressive order.

Whilst it will be seen that, using the ten best newspapers it is possible to reach
two-thirds of the telephone owners, whilst reaching only one-third of non-telephone owners, to get nearly 90 per cent of owners it is necessary to reach nearly
80 per cent of non-owners.

In the majority of markets today, it is not possible to get high coverage of the
target group with even this degree of selectivity.

6.6   How much better is better?

Having made the point that almost any analysis is today too complicated to do
without the aid of a computer, and having also illustrated the serious limit to the
extent that the media planner can selectively reach his target audience, the

reader may be wondering whether it is worth bothering at all. At this point it has to be admitted that many media plans are prepared without rigorous preliminary work, and that certain simple combinations of media have established the reputation of being a good general answer to almost any problem.

To illustrate the extent to which the most sophisticated methods lead the simplest, we have produced two schedules via Comshare's Meteor optimisation program, and compared the results with those of two popular 'top-of-mind' schedules.

The first was devised from the analysis shown in Sections 6.1 - 6.3. The only additional data required were response weights, and these are shown for interest, although they are not discussed in detail until Chapter 24.

TABLE 6.4

Newspaper	Adults in telephone-owning homes	Adults in non-telephone-owning homes
A	3.1	0.6
+B	8.7	1.7
+C	11.6	2.4
+D	26.0	6.2
+E	35.5	9.8
+F	37.7	11.0
+G	42.0	12.9
+H	44.8	15.2
+I	64.1	30.7
+J	67.5	33.6
+K	71.3	40.1
+L	77.3	51.9
+M	80.1	57.2
+N	81.8	61.3
+O	81.9	61.6
+P	89.2	78.0
+Q	89.3	78.1
+R	92.3	87.2
+S	94.1	91.4
+T	95.0	94.3

Cumulative response weights

0	0
1	25
2	50
3	70
4	83
5	92
6	98
7 and above	100

The schedule produced was this:

Publication	Number of insertions
Good Housekeeping	3
My Weekly	5
Reader's Digest	5
She	4
Family Circle	2
Ideal Home	4
TV Times	2
Woman's Weekly	2
Woman's Own	1
Sunday Times Magazine	1

The total response generated by this schedule was 52.4. The maximum possible value, 100, is achieved by giving seven exposures to every member of the weighted target audience. Thus this 'best' schedule gets about half way to that goal. (Which suggests either that the response function was wrongly specified, or that the budget was insufficient for the task in hand.)

As an alternative, we spent the same money in six insertions in each of *Woman* and *Woman's Own* — a simple and popular combination. The response generated by this schedule was 33.7.

Thus the advantage of the optimised schedule over the simple schedule was, in this case, 55 per cent.

The comparison is clearly open to the objection that selection of publications halfway down the cost ranking is unlikely to produce good results. In practice, strong arguments are often produced for high coverage media even with this degree of cost disadvantage, particularly when six insertions can be placed in each, compared with the range of insertion frequencies shown in the optimised schedule. Understanding that people read a number of publications, and that it may be more efficient to reach them three times in one, and three times in another, than six times in a third, is not universal.

A second comparison uses the central heating data previously referred to.
Market weights were:

Men	100	AB	100
Women	85	C1	100
15-24	100	C2	90
25-34	100	DE	70
35-44	100	With central heating	100
45-54	100	Without central heating	25
55-64	100		
65+	48		

The cumulative response weights were:

0	0
1	6
2	26
3	62
4	76
5	86
6	91
7	95
8	97
9	99
10 and over	100

The candidate media list consisted of the National Dailies and Sundays, and the London Evenings, and the budget was £84,000. The optimisation produced the following schedule:

Publication	Number of insertions
Sunday Post	6
Sun	6
News of the World	4
Sunday Mirror	3
Daily Express	1

The response of this schedule was 56.8. With the same money it was possible to buy eight insertions in the *Daily Express* and eight insertions in the *Daily Mirror* – an even more popular combination. The response produced by this pairing was 46.9, and the advantage for the optimised schedule 21 per cent. This, although less than in the first example, is clearly substantial.

7 Specific marketing considerations

7.1 Size and direction of market, and brand share

The media plan will be affected by the size and direction both of the market and the brand share of the product for which the plan is being written. The size of the market will normally place a restriction on the budget (because it is unusual, although possible, for a brand plan to involve radical increase of market size). The size of the market normally sets the top limit to the potential for a brand and therefore conditions the company's profit expectations. We have previously discussed the effect of budget on media selection.

Another important aspect of market size is the degree of segmentation that exists. The total market for a product class may well be divided psychologically, or in other ways, so that our brand is not really competing in the whole market but only in a segment of it. In this case it is important to know how big that segment is and how near the brand is to filling it.

If the market is expanding then brand policy would normally be aggressive, aiming to bring in the new users before other brands could do so. On the other hand, in a declining market, the ambition of every brand would be to maintain its franchise for as long as possible.

The size of the brand share in the market is likely to influence the profile of the target market. If one has a large share then the profile of the brand is inevitably similar to the profile of the market as a whole. If the brand share is small, and the profile is different, then one has the choice of trying to capitalise on this difference, and attract more people of this type to the brand, or alternatively to match the profile of the market, or more particularly of the brand leader, in an endeavour to make share in that way.

With an expanding brand share one is normally looking for new users. It is important to ensure that the brief includes in the statement of marketing policy where these new users are to come from. If the total market is not expanding, then clearly they must come from some other brand, and it is usually possible to nominate which brand is most vulnerable. If this is done it may be good policy to use media currently used by that brand.

With a declining brand-share position, most of the advertising effort will be

spent on maintaining the 'loyal' users. Research can isolate who they are and an
endeavour will be made by the use of maximum possible frequency to keep
them with the brand.

7.2 Nature of the product

Differences are likely to emerge between media plans for, say, Granada Ghia
Motor Cars, Spangles, Andrex Toilet Tissues and a book on media planning,
both through the definition of the target market and the creative considerations.
In addition to these factors there is the question of suitability. Although this is
dealt with at length in Chapter 10, it is worth mentioning here as it does come
from a basic piece of marketing information. Most planners feel that it is wise to
place the advertising message before the prospect in a time and place which
seems appropriate. Whatever the figures were for the cinema attendance of lava-
tory paper buyers, one would hesitate to use the cinema medium, which is primarily an entertainment medium, for the sale of such a product. On the other
hand in the women's magazines which are devoted largely to the interests of the
woman in her role as a housewife, the subject seems entirely appropriate. Similarly, whilst readers of the *Financial Times* could be an excellent market for acid
drops, few planners would recommend such a medium for such a product. It is
simply that one expects to make rather weightier decisions when reading the
Financial Times than a brand decision of this nature.

7.3 Method and level of distribution

The majority of mass-selling consumer goods are sold through every retail outlet
that is available. Many durable goods, however, and also a number of toiletries
and other categories have deliberately restricted distribution. A small number of
dealers in any particular town are appointed as stockists and no invitation is extended to other retailers in the town. This situation should clearly be distinguished from that in which the manufacturer is unable to get his product into
more than a small number of outlets, although he wishes to cover the entire
field. The differences in media terms relate to the object of getting the customer
in touch with the product with the minimum amount of pain. Where the product is distributed almost everywhere the consumer would expect to find it,
there is little point in discussing the subject. If, on the other hand, the consumer
will have to look carefully for the product then something does have to be done.
It may be necessary, for instance, to issue a list of stockists to consumers who re-
quest one. Alternatively, the would-be consumer may be referred to an existing
listing published elsewhere, as for instance in the Yellow Pages in the telephone
directory; or a list may be published within the advertisement itself. Failing all
these alternatives, it is possible subtly to indicate to the consumer that he, or
she, will have a lot of trouble finding the product but that it will be well worth
his while looking.

Wherever distribution is restricted, it may well be advisable to run local campaigns in support of the dealers. Television is rarely used these days for such a
purpose, since the area of coverage is very large and the rates are usually too

high. However, local press media, posters, radio and cinema can all be used to advantage. It is often possible to enlist the support of the dealer financially in such advertising and, indeed, such participation can extend the advertising budget to a significant degree. The Evening Newspaper Advertising Bureau has organised a scheme to do just this.

If the distribution is inadequate, rather than restricted, then the media choice will usually be made with an eye on influencing more retailers into the fold. This has very often appeared in media recommendations as a reason for using television. Other media try very hard to use the same lever, and will make substantial efforts to assist the manufacturer to use their medium to increase distribution.

7.4 Seasonal patterns

Few products are sold at a uniform rate through 12 months of the year. Few advertising budgets allow for adequate frequency across 12 months of the year. The combination of these two facts leads to seasonal patterns of sales and advertising which sometimes affect each other adversely.

In general the advertiser seeks to place the weight of his advertising where brand decisions can be influenced most readily, that is to say when most purchasing decisions are being taken. It is for this reason that advertising for all brands in a product field tends to coincide with seasonal peaks in the product field sales. Inevitably, if the advertising is at all effective the likelihood is that the seasonal peaks will be increased. Since almost all production is most economic when spread uniformly through a year, the effect of this build-up is not wholly desirable. Since, moreover, a great many products tend to peak in spring and autumn, media become least available at these times and prices, therefore, rise. Thus many advertisers combine uneconomic production with uneconomic media buying. Nevertheless, it would be a bold media planner whose recommendation to his client was that he should advertise only in his slack sales months. Like most other dilemmas of this kind it can only be satisfactorily resolved by trying an experiement in the field. The classic example of success is that of Walls Ice Cream, once sold almost exclusively in the summer, and now purchased on a year round basis. This change in habit was only brought about by a sustained and relatively heavy level of expenditure.

7.5 Area differences

Very few brands with national distribution in this country have the same level of sales per head, or of brand share, throughout the country. These differences may arise through genuine differences of palate or habit in different parts of the country, but are very often due to geographical accidents in the location of the company's factory or warehouse. For a variety of human reasons most manufacturers' sales tend to be strongest in the immediate vicinity of their headquarters.

The question of allocation of the budget across different areas is really one which should start with the marketing planners but very often lands in the lap of the media planner. As with seasonal differences, the main question is whether one should support strength or weakness, although the considerations are different. 'Success breeds success' is a familiar motto in the advertising business, and there is the powerful stimulus of the advertising/sales ratio to contend with. This means that the advertising appropriation is calculated as a given fraction of the sales achieved. Therefore, in an area where high sales are achieved a high advertising budget is produced, and conversely. Slavish application of this formula usually results in a regional brand, which may be a perfectly satisfactory solution. Indeed, many advertisers waste a great deal of money trying to establish their brands in areas where they are very unlikely ever to be acceptable. On the other hand there are many advantages which stem from being truly national, and there is often a good case to be made for 'milking' the strong areas, in order to try to bring weaker areas up to par.

A factor of critical importance in many marketing decisions today is the stocking pattern of many supermarket chains. This consists of a policy to stock the brand leader, the brand number two, one or more house brands and a 'cheap' brand. To obtain good distribution for a quality product which is number three or four in the market is extremely difficult. It may, therefore, be sensible to confine advertising to those areas where there is probability of succeeding in becoming one or two in the market, and ignoring, for the time being at any rate, areas where this is not possible.

The media planner should always be aware that the decision to suspend advertising in one or more areas of the country will often raise substantial human problems, in the reaction of the sales force.

Again, the Company is in a strong position if it has estimated the Sales Response function by area. Consider Figure 7.1. Area 1 is a more successful area for the brand in every way; more product is sold there, and the A/S ratio is lower there than in Area 2. Yet, if the Sales Response curves are as shown, it will be profitable to transfer expenditure from Area 1 to Area 2.

The reason for this is that the *marginal* return, not the *average* return, is what matters. Having reached the top of the curve in Area 1, extra money spent will result in hardly any extra sales. In Area 2, by contrast, extra expenditure will

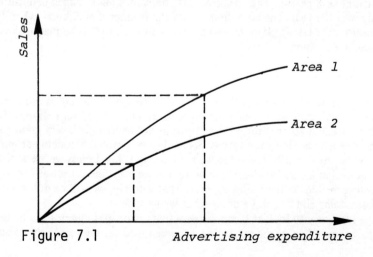

Figure 7.1   Advertising expenditure

give a considerable return. The effect of moving both Areas closer to the average position will be to reduce sales in Area 1, but to more than compensate by the increase in Area 2. It can be shown mathematically that the most profitable allocation occurs where the fraction

$$\frac{\text{Marginal gain in sales}}{\text{Marginal advertising expenditure}}$$

is equal for all areas.

Of course, this discussion has assumed that consumers respond to advertising *expenditure*. In truth, they respond (if at all) to advertising *exposure*. Hence, if the cost of advertising varies between areas, this will need to be taken into account. If the variation is not constant over time, the planner will be left busy trying to maintain the optimum allocation, and must keep in close contact with his buyer.

The logic of area allocation, where one has a medium truly flexible in area terms, is similar to that of allocation over time (see Section 5.4.1). Small budgets will only reach the profitable part of the sales response curve by concentrating on small and responsive areas. When enough money is available to make a large area viable, money should be concentrated in it. Only when all the areas can be covered at the profitable part of the curve should a national campaign be recommended.

7.6 Promotion

There are many and varied types of promotion available to the manufacturer as aids to increase his sales. They tend to be regarded as complementary to advertising and to have short term, rather than long term, aims. Indeed, it is probably true that some of them which produce large, short-term sales increases may do long-term sales harm.

Some of them, for instance competitions, will require media support. For those which do not, it is often an advantage to appear in gaps in the advertising. This has the advantage of allowing the planner to get high frequency when his advertising is appearing, and to spread the company's marketing expenditure evenly over the year. The vital thing is that the planner should know when the promotions are taking place, and what their nature is, so that he may make an appropriate decision.

7.7 Competition

Competitive activity is one of the major influences on all aspects of most marketing campaigns. This is usually wrong for a number of different reasons. Firstly, what our competitor is doing today is not necessarily a very good guide to what he may be doing tomorrow. Secondly, he is probably looking at our activity with just as much interest as we are looking at his. Unless we are absolutely convinced that he is a lot smarter than we are, we may find ourselves occupying opposite positions in the following year. That is to say, we will be doing what he has been doing and he will be doing what we have been.

The ideal way to look at competitive activity is to try to learn from it. By careful examination of the marketing campaign, and the sales and other results which have flowed from it, it may be possible to telescope the amount of testing that one undertakes on one's own behalf. This does require a sophisticated information-gathering procedure and may mean that somebody is building a marketing model. Often it is difficult enough to get sufficient data to relate one's own performance to one's own activities: with a competitor it inevitably involves getting copies of their advertisements and carrying out copy tests on them.

Since media choice plays a relatively small part in the total marketing mix, it would be very rash to assume that to change one's media pattern to that of the successful competitor would necessarily bring success.

7.8 Client status

When a brand is produced by a relatively small and unknown company it may be difficult to establish a foothold, especially in a competitive business. The media planner can sometimes help by giving the client and the brand an appearance of bigness, where it does not in fact exist. This may be a reason, for instance, for using large spaces, whole pages for example, where the budget does not really run to them. There is, undoubtedly, some association in the public mind between large advertisements and large companies. Alternative ways of achieving the same effect may be area concentration and domination of a medium. It is important to distinguish between these two ways of achieving higher repetition on a limited coverage.

Most planners faced with an appropriation which would normally not be considered of national weight, would recommend concentrating the appropriation in a particular area. In the case of a development brand, where it is hoped that success in the limited area will lead to expansion into further areas and the eventual establishment of a national brand, this is almost certainly correct. If the advertiser's promotional resources are limited, then probably his sales and distribution resources are equally limited. In an area he can compete on equal terms with the 'big boys', whereas on a national basis he would be lost.

However, some products are unlikely ever to appeal to a very large range of consumers or to achieve a very high sale. If the consumers are spread thinly on the ground then it is probably essential to reach them wherever in the country they may reside. If enough is known about them, it will usually be possible to select one or more press media which will contain amongst their readership a significantly higher proportion of this target than a general campaign would produce. Concentration of this type may also be necessary for a perfectly normal product which, for some reason, has to be in national distribution but whose budget is nevertheless limited. It may be better, and in some cases has been shown to be, to be a very big brand in the minds of, say, *Woman's Own* readers than to be a medium-sized brand in the minds of the readers of all the women's weeklies.

7.9 Related reading

P. Kotler, *Marketing decision-making: a model building approach,* Holt, Rinehart & Winston (1971).

8 Special situations

Two media plans likely to cause the planner particular concern are those for test towns and for test areas. We will deal with the test area, which is the easier of the two, first.

8.1 Test areas

8.1.1 Purpose

The function of the test area is to enable management to arrive at a decision as to action that should be taken on a national basis, without risking national investment. It may, of course, be for the launch of a new product, a subject with which we deal separately later in the chapter. It may, however, be for any one of a number of different reasons; different copy for example, the introduction of a different pack perhaps, a promotion, or even a media test.

8.1.2 Dangers

The planner should have two facts indelibly stamped on his mind when he comes to the consideration of test areas. The first is that no test area in this country is typical of the nation.

So much propaganda is issued concerning the complete demographic match of areas of the country with the nation as a whole that we must exaggerate in order to make the point that areas do not represent the country. The best possible education for the media planner in this context is personally to visit and to stay in as many different parts of the country as he can at an early stage of his work. This is one instance where subjective information is more helpful than objective.

The second is that in employing one test area only he will have no information as to whether changes which occur are due to the change in treatment which is being applied, or whether they are due to other circumstances peculiar to the test area. For both these reasons, it is most seriously recommended that at least two areas should be used for any test whenever it is conceivably possible.

These two areas should encompass, as far as it is possible, the spread of probabilities with regard to the particular product. For instance, where the product has different acceptance in the south and the north, one area should be from each part. Where a product is particularly successful in one area and particularly unsuccessful in another, then both should be included, if possible. (This is not to suggest that one would normally gamble one's best area in a test; test areas are usually small and each will probably not represent more than 10 per cent of the total market.)

Nothing we have said should be taken as meaning that a test area should be selected where the advertising treatment is not likely to have any influence on the results. For instance there would be no point in carrying out a media test in an area where the client has no distribution.

Again if a quantified marketing model is available it will greatly increase the sensitivity with which area tests can be read.

8.1.3   Media factors

When we talk of test areas we almost inevitably mean television areas. Not only are these clearly defined, and on the whole sensible marketing areas, but most research organisations are currently geared to their use. No test would be of any value if we could not measure the results. Television, cinema, radio and outdoor advertising can all be bought within this definition, but national press media are difficult to handle, and need special negotiation where any facilities are available. Another important factor is that of cost. In general, national press media offering regional splits charge a premium for so doing, in some cases a very substantial one. If a group of regional press media are used as an alternative to editions of national media, their standard rates normally represent a substantial premium over national rates. On the other hand, it is common for television contractors to offer incentives, either in the form of discounts direct, or other forms of subsidy, to encourage advertisers to use their particular region. In the case of cinema and outdoor, there is no premium on the space cost since the space units are bought individually, but production costs may be very high in relation to the space cost. There is no film equivalent to the video-tape commercial which may be used in television, and the full cost of producing a colour film may impose a high penalty on the advertiser wishing to test cinema. A similar situation exists in outdoor. The capital cost of printing 500 posters may not be very much less than the cost of printing 5000, and so the test area production budget may need to be very nearly as high as that for a national campaign.

One media group that requires particular care, perhaps surprisingly, is the regional evening press. Coverage by television area is quite variable. The fact that the 'National' mornings are so London-biased makes the London evenings weak, relative to their regional counterparts. There is low coverage also in the Harlech and Central Scottish TV areas.

A problem that is common to test areas and to test towns is the allocation of budget. The test area will be no more typical of the nation in terms of the availability and cost-effectiveness of different media, than in any other way. The cost-per-thousand obtained on television, for example, varies widely from one area to another. What allowance, therefore, does one make in planning the budget?

The best solution we can offer is to draw up the national plan which it is hoped to reproduce and calculate the coverage and frequency on the target group in the media under consideration. This pattern should then be reproduced in the test area as closely as possible, regardless of the cost of doing so. Care should be taken in distinguishing between frequency of exposure and frequency of insertion. If, for instance, one has to use regional evening newspapers to reproduce the effect of national dailies in an area, then the insertion rate in them is likely to be considerably higher than that in the national dailies, simply because these duplicate considerably amongst themselves, whilst in evening newspapers there is practically no duplication.

Another danger carefully to be watched is the generosity of TV contractors. In gratitude for being given a test market, it has been known for a station to over-run the budgetted TVRs to such an extent as to make a test unreadable. Care will have to be taken in explaining to the time-buyer that this is not a desirable result, since it will be alien to his nature and training to discourage overdelivery.

8.2   Test towns

Most of what has been said concerning the selection of test areas applies also, but with even greater force, to the selection of test towns. We believe it imperative that not only should the same treatment be applied in at least two towns, but at least two further towns should be used as controls with no treatment supplied at all. Where such an exercise is carried out, it is not in the least uncommon to find that sales gains in one of the untreated towns is greater than in either of the treated towns. This fact usually leads to some caution in the interpretation of the results of the test.

In the selection of test towns much greater attention has to be paid to media availability than in the case of the areas. The coverage afforded and indeed the availability of various media on a local basis does vary considerably. It is important to see that the media suggested for use do have something like national characteristics in the town under consideration. It is very important too to see that the effective boundaries of the media used are clearly understood and followed, both for research and distribution objectives.

Although it is not directly in the media planner's province, he should take all steps that he can to ensure that the research which is intended to measure the results of the test is adequate to do so. No company maintains regular panels of a satisfactory nature in test towns, although some media owners, notably Westminster Press and the Thomson Organisation, do all they can to help in this respect. A chastening discipline is to run the chosen research tool in the towns

selected for six months before the commencement of whatever the test may be.
Comparison of the variations in results may well lead to the use of test areas,
rather than test towns. This is usually the correct decision.

Where test towns have to be used the other important criterion is that they
should be reasonably self-contained as marketing areas. There is little point in
carrying out a heavy campaign for, say, a refrigerator, in a particular town when
people from that town commonly go to a nearby city to buy their refrigerators.
The fact that so few British towns meet these various criteria has meant that a
great deal of testing has gone on in the classic towns like Swindon, Oxford,
York, etc. This may in itself set an uncomfortable background for a new test.

8.3   Launches

8.3.1   *Purpose*

The launch of any new brand is fraught with difficulty as the various (but all
high) figures for failure demonstrate. The prime function of the advertising campaign and, indeed, of the marketing campaign, is to get the highest possible level
of trial. Although there are a variety of techniques available to assist in the re-
tention of tryers as regular buyers, there is no doubt that the most important influence at this stage is the perceived performance of the product itself. The
media planner's task is to ensure that the widest possible coverage is given to the
target market, provided that the coverage is in sufficient depth.

In the case of a test launch (and all launches should start with a test) it is even
more important than usual for the media planner to ensure that he understands
the exact purpose of the campaign. Is it, for instance, intended that there should
be an attempt to project the results of a test market up to a national figure? Or
is it intended that the test area, if successful, should form a first phase of a
national roll out? Critical profit decisions have to be made on the planner's
assessment of the cost of reproducing nationally the advertising campaign which
he has planned in the test area. Whilst every advantage should be taken of the
discounts offered by various media (particularly the television contractors) for
test marketing exercises, it should be remembered that these will not be earned
nationally, or possibly in extension areas.

8.3.2   *Timing*

We have referred previously to the problem of defining average frequency of purchase since the interval about the average is so large. Nevertheless, in any product field it is possible to determine the normal 'greatest length' which occurs
between any two purchasing occasions. The most intense portion of the launch
campaign should, wherever possible, continue for this length of time, so that
every consumer likely to be in the market is reached at the time of purchase by
the heaviest possible campaign. In this way, of course, the second purchase, and
sometimes the third purchase of the heavier buyers will also have been covered.
For this reason the second purchase cycle can be at a lighter weight, serving

mainly to remind those who have tried the product to repurchase. What follows from then depends very largely on the nature of the product and the size of the available budget.

8.3.3   Size of space/length of time

We show below the importance of advertising quality: it is essential to allow the creative man enough scope. This is not to say that some creative messages which do a first class job in 45 seconds, do not do an indifferent one in 60 seconds. Rather it is to say that one compelling whole page in colour is more than a match for two uncompelling half pages.

Once the critical introductory period is over it is usually fairly easy to reduce the size of space or length of the commercial in order to accommodate the follow-up message.

8.3.4   Choice of media

In 1955 when commercial television was introduced to this country, people who could see it had firstly to be sufficiently affluent to pay up the money for the set, or the conversion thereof, and secondly to be of a disposition to be attracted by new commercial ideas. This made the audience for commercial television a very soft target for new brand introductions. Apart from this special situation, television did, of course, have many advantages over its competitors. The classic ones were vision, plus sound, plus movement, together in the home. Two further factors were important in 1955: the salesman was tickled pink by the thought of his brand being advertised in this new medium and the retailer was very impressed by the promise of television support.

The combination of all these factors meant that it was hardly surprising that there were some startling success stories for new brand introductions on television. Today the inherent advantages of the medium remain, and the memory of those early days means that television is still a good talking point to most salesmen and to most retailers. At the same time both have become more sophisticated, and are far less impressed by meaningless numbers of commerical exposures produced by the agency media research department. The research services and other forms of support offered by the television contractors are often very useful adjuncts to a test launch, but the retailers' studio party, once a telling weapon, is unlikely to carry much weight today.

All these virtues are so well known to the young media planner that he is often tempted to forget that new products were successfully introduced before commercial television arrived. Even today there are some product fields, particularly durables, in which the brunt of the new product introduction falls upon the press. Cigarettes too, which are currently denied the use of the television medium, have seen the introduction of several highly successful new brands with the press spearheading the media pattern. The problem of the area test launch remains, and although, as we have said above, many press media are available in regional breaks, it is still quite difficult adequately to cover the particular region required.

Cinema offers the greatest creative opportunities of any medium and provided that the product under test is fitted to the cinema audience there is no reason why the cinema should not be used for launch purposes, provided that the high cost of production does not militate against it. It can be localised to any desired area and dealer support can be achieved with considerable precision. Cinema owners do, of course, use the medium themselves for promoting the sales of different refreshments from the tray service girls. It is hoped that one day they will tell the rest of the world the most effective ways they have discovered for using the medium for this purpose.

Radio is seldom used as a launch medium except in a supporting role. Perhaps its easiest use is to popularise a jingle which carries the advertising message. High repetition of this, which can be achieved very economically, can greatly strengthen a television campaign.

The paramount advantage of the outdoor medium for launching new products is its ability to carry a very much enlarged version of the pack in its true colours. Clearly, where, as is the case with many fast-moving items, pack recognition plays an important part in the purchase decision, this is a considerable advantage. On the other hand, outdoors is seldom able to carry the burden of a new product introduction simply because the essence of the poster medium is a short copy message. If a new product is worth introducing there is almost inevitably a story to tell about it, and a story is one thing the outdoor medium, with very few exceptions, cannot carry. Of course, in financial terms, cigarette launches are very important, and these are often mounted on posters.

8.4 One medium or more?

There are two aspects to this question. Firstly, do we have enough money to do an adequate job in more than one medium? Secondly, will the gain in the use of the second medium be sufficient to offset the additional costs of using it? Neither question is pertinent only to the launch situation, but to all media plans. Nevertheless, the ways in which they are answered differ from a launch to a campaign for an on-going brand.

What is an 'adequate job'? Carrying the message to the target market, in the first buying cycle, with enough repetition to establish it, is the essential preliminary. Given that trial is a function of awareness, the earlier the awareness, the earlier the trial, the earlier the shelf-movement, with encouragement to retailer and client sales-force, and the greater the amount of repeat-purchase.

But there are many aspects to this question which must be considered in detail.

8.4.1 The relationship between advertising quality and weight, forgetting and awareness

Many factors contribute to the success of a new brand, and word-of-mouth publicity is often important. What follows is a discussion of the advertising contribution only, and, although simplified, should help the reader to understand broadly the part it plays.

The general presumption is that, in the first period of advertising, the following relationship holds.

$$\text{New awareness} = (\text{Maximum awareness} - \text{Initial awareness}) \text{ x}$$
$$1 - \left[\frac{1}{2.718^{\,(\text{Ad quality x Media weight})}} \right]$$

where:

1   *New awareness* is the percentage of consumers who were not aware at the beginning of the period, but were at the end.

2   *Maximum awareness* is the limit of awareness growth; this is often almost 100 per cent, but there are some product fields, of low interest to some consumers, where it does not seem possible, however hard one tries, to reach this figure.

3   *Initial awareness* is the percentage claiming to know of the brand before advertising commences; they may have seen it on shelf, or may merely have confused it with a similar name.

The first bracket therefore represents the ground to be won: a perfect campaign would generate just this amount of awareness, so that, by the end of the first period, all who could be made aware, actually were.

In the fraction, 2.718 is an approximation for the natural constant 'e' (or exponential), which occurs in many mathematical relationships.

4   *Advertising quality* is a number representing the power of the ad to generate awareness.

5   *Media weight* is the number of *hundreds* of gross rating points delivered in the period. For example, if we had a four week period, and were using TV at a rate of 100 TVRs per week, the media weight would be 4.

The expression (advertising quality x media weight) is written above exponential, because it is raising it to a power. Thus, if advertising quality = 0.5, and media weight = 4, 0.5 x 4 = 2, and the fraction becomes $1/e^2$ (or about 0.135).

It will be seen that the smaller this fraction is, the nearer the bracket comes to equal 1, the number of the perfect campaign. The fraction gets smaller when either the advertising quality, or the media weight, or both, get larger.

Moreover, the two act in exactly the same way: twice as good an ad will produce the same result as twice the media weight (although the higher media weight will cost about twice as much as the lower, and the better ad may cost no more than the inferior one).

In practice, it has been found that 50 per cent of ads for new products which one particular company investigated have values between 0.056 and 0.105 (which range is nearly 1:2). At the lower end, this means that a launch weight of 400 gross rating points will produce a 20 per cent awareness at the end of the first period, assuming no initial awareness, and 100 per cent maximum awareness.

An ad at the upper end of the range would produce a 35 per cent awareness, with other factors remaining the same.

Now we have to consider 'forgetting'. Many have concluded that people generally forget new brands at a pretty steady rate. A good approximation seems to be that if 100 people were aware at the beginning of a week, only 97 would be aware at the end, if there were no advertising (and no other means of reminder). At the end of a month, the figure will fall to 91 (97% of 97% of 97%).

This means that we need continuous advertising merely to *maintain* awareness. It can be shown that, if awareness has reached 50 per cent, on the assumtions made above, at the lower figure for advertising quality, 150 gross rating points per period will be needed to keep it there.

At the higher figure for advertising quality, the same media weight will give *continued growth* of about 4 percentage points per period.

Thus we get the curves for different creative treatments, as in Figure 8.1.

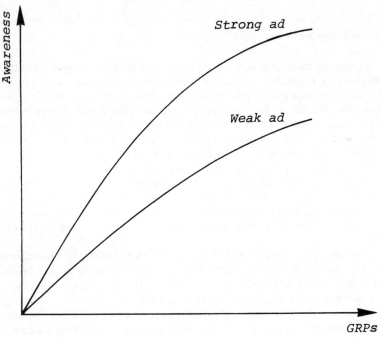

Figure 8.1

8.4.2   *The effect of loyalty*

Awareness leads to trial, trial leads to repeat purchase (or should). The percentage of trialists who buy the product again may be regarded as a measure of the degree to which the consumer has been satisfied that the promise on which she based her trial has been fulfilled by the product in use. Note that this is not the same thing as how well the product performs the claims made for it. (It should do this perfectly.) She may not have perceived the promise as it was intended; and she may misuse the product. Nevertheless, this is how repeat purchase actually does, or does not, happen.

But even after the first repeat the manufacturer is not home and dry. The manufacturer of whatever was bought previously will be making strenuous efforts to regain the consumer's custom, and habit will be pulling in the same direction. If these forces are strong enough, our early trial will rapidly be dissipated, and the brand will die if we do not support it.

The general rule is, the stronger the loyalty, the more front-loaded the campaign should be, and vice versa. The perfect example is part-works. The levels of trial vary considerably, depending on the subject, and its presentation; but of the half of trialists that normally buy a second issue, the great majority buy almost all succeeding issues. The pattern of media spending employed by the publishers, generally 70 per cent in the first week, and 30 per cent in the second, is correct for such a high loyalty, but an unthinkable plan for most launches.

8.4.3   Distribution

All the foregoing assumes that the product is available to be bought when the campaign starts. In this sense, available means that the consumer who wants to try it can find it during the course of a shopping trip. It is not a term definable precisely, like Nielsen sterling distribution (although this figure is often substituted) because people's patterns of shopping vary considerably, and the strength of desire for the product will affect how hard the consumer looks for it. (It is also possible for the brand to be stocked by an outlet shopped at, but not to be seen, because of poor pack design, bad display, etc.)

If the product is not fully available at the launch date (and many are not) it is potentially damaging to create demand which cannot be satisfied. This is true in the short-term, as a wasted opportunity; and may be true also in the long-term, since a consumer once frustrated may not purchase when she does get the opportunity.

These facts suggest that instead of the normal front loading to a launch campaign, there should be a steady build up as distribution is built up. The problem with this logic is that retailers who *do* stock initially, and even the manufacturer's own sales force, may feel that the brand lacks impetus. Experience offers two suggestions. First, get the most realistic possible estimate of distribution build-up. (What happened the last three times the company launched a new brand?) Second, steer a careful compromise course between the logic and the emotion.

8.4.4   Additional media

Hopefully, the reader is now in a position to know whether he has enough to do an 'adequate job' in his first medium of choice. But, to make it even clearer, let us put some numbers to it. Suppose we target to reach 50 per cent awareness as soon as possible, and then will be content to remain at this level. Suppose also that we have the better ad (referred to above) to help us. Then we will be able to achieve our awareness objectives by deploying 400 gross rating points in the first period, 300 in the second, and 100 per period thereafter. The cost of buying this pattern on television (if 100 adult TVRs cost £32,500) is £553,000. Not many launches have that much money behind them, but more will have to, in these inflationary times.

However, is 100 TVRs per four-week period a pattern we will be happy with, assuming a television weight of 700 TVRs in the first eight weeks is acceptable?

Possibly not. Certainly we should consider the use of a second medium, particularly if it is more economical. The criteria must be: can we buy this medium as cheaply as TV? Will the ad sustain awareness, as we have calculated the commercial will? Will exposure in a second medium add something useful to our campaign?

The last question is the most important, and the most difficult to answer. Given helpful creative people, it is always possible to convert a commercial into an ad suitable for another medium. But this may be quite the wrong way to do it; certainly press, radio and outdoor have contributions of their own to make, which may deepen understanding, suggest new uses, or create better pack recognition, besides keeping awareness alive. The media man may have a problem selling this aspect of his plan, but it is a vital element in the difference between passable and good.

8.5   Examples

8.5.1   A toiletry launch

We are very grateful to L'Oreal, and their advertising agency, Beverley Fowler Maslin Oxlade & Starkey Limited, for the case history of a successful test launch using women's magazines.

The market was hair conditioners and cream rinses, and had been thoroughly researched. TCPI data showed volume as well as sterling growth, with cream rinses accounting for about two-thirds of total sales. Nevertheless, penetration of the heaviest using group (the 16-24s) was only two-fifths, so that it was felt that considerable potential remained.

Brand shares were generally small, with Alberto Balsam showing the greatest growth. This was achieved with an advertising budget which, although less than £200,000 (all in TV), was probably at an A/S ratio above 50 per cent. The brand had an average cost per c.c., and a high trade margin. L'Oreal's new product, called Elseve Balsam, had already proved successful in several other European countries, and consumer tests in the UK promised well. In order to minimise the financial risk involved in a launch, it was decided to assess the market-place reaction through area tests.

Judgmentally, it was believed that the French advertising, which had been very successful in France, would work well, in translation, in this country. As it took the form of colour pages in women's magazines, the options for testing in the same medium in this country were examined. IPC are currently offering such facilities in some 30 areas (basically towns).

Within a clearly defined circulation area, test ads may be 'tipped-in' to all or any of the four IPC women's weeklies. 'Tipping-in' means the addition of a leaf, or four page insert, to regular copies of the magazines, distributed through the normal channels. Thus any ad size up to four pages, colour or black and white, can be accommodated. IPC offer assistance with a full range of research services.

In this particular case two test areas were chosen: Swindon and York. Both are 'classic' test towns, having the desirable qualities of good retail outlets, and considerable separation from other shopping centres. Three of the four magazines were used, *Women's Realm* being excluded (see Figure 8.2).

As will be seen, approximately 50 per cent of the launch money was spent in the initial burst, covering a four-week period. The other 50 per cent was spread over a further seventeen weeks, with the insertions arranged so that no two ads appeared in the same week, and there was no period of more than two weeks without an ad appearing at all. To buy this amount of space nationally, at rate card rates, would cost about £130,000.

An important part of the launch plan was sampling; getting the product into the hands of potential buyers is always to be recommended. Advantage was taken of the four-page insert, and a sachet of Elseve Balsam was attached to the fourth page in each copy.

Consumer and trade research was carried out, with very encouraging results. By the end of the test, 24 per cent of women interviewed were aware of the brand. Most importantly, 50 per cent of those had purchased the product at least once. This average awareness-to-trial ratio of 50 per cent is very high, and the subsequent repeat purchase rate of 40 per cent is also satisfactory. On the basis of these figures it was decided to launch nationally in 1976.

In the meantime, the client and agency had developed a television idea which it was felt would prove even more successful than the press campaign had been. Accordingly, plans for the national launch were made on the basis of a television schedule.

The normal patterns of media usage have been followed in the national campaign; the television weight is even more concentrated at the beginning of the campaign than was the press, and the number of advertising weeks has been reduced from ten to six. Coverage has been reduced in the sense that areas other than London, Midlands, Granada, Trident and Southern receive only token support. At the same time the appropriation has been increased to around £250,000, and, clearly, this will considerably raise the coverage of women in the main areas (see Figure 8.3).

Since there is no consumer press advertising, a new vehicle has had to be found for the distribution of samples. This has taken the form of a card, with a small sample bottle attached, and also a 5p coupon redeemable against the first purchase. These cards (4 million of them) are being distributed door-to-door in the areas receiving major TV support. The drop is in two phases, the greater part being distributed with the first TV burst, and the remainder at the time of the autumn burst.

It will be seen that the overall promotional pattern of the national launch bears little resemblance to that of the test areas, although this was judged to be successful. This is not in the least uncommon, for many other considerations often intervene. In this case there was no attempt to project the test experience to national level. The purpose of the test was to see whether women would buy the product in the shops, and, having bought it, whether they would be sufficiently satisfied with it to buy it again. Having established this, the purpose of the national plan was to give the brand the best possible chance of success, with total freedom of options.

In the event, the pack conformation and pricing were also significantly changed, so that there was not a close relationship to the test market in many ways. However, the principle of carrying out waves of research, so as to monitor consumer reaction at all stages, was strictly observed.

1975	April	May					June				July				August					September	
W/e Saturday	26	3	10	17	24	31	7	14	21	28	5	12	19	26	2	9	16	23	30	6	13
Woman																					
4 consecutive pages	x																				
Double page spreads		x					x								x						
Woman's Own																					
4 consecutive pages	x																				
Double page spreads			x						x									x			
Woman's Weekly																					
Double page spreads				x								x								x	

Figure 8.2

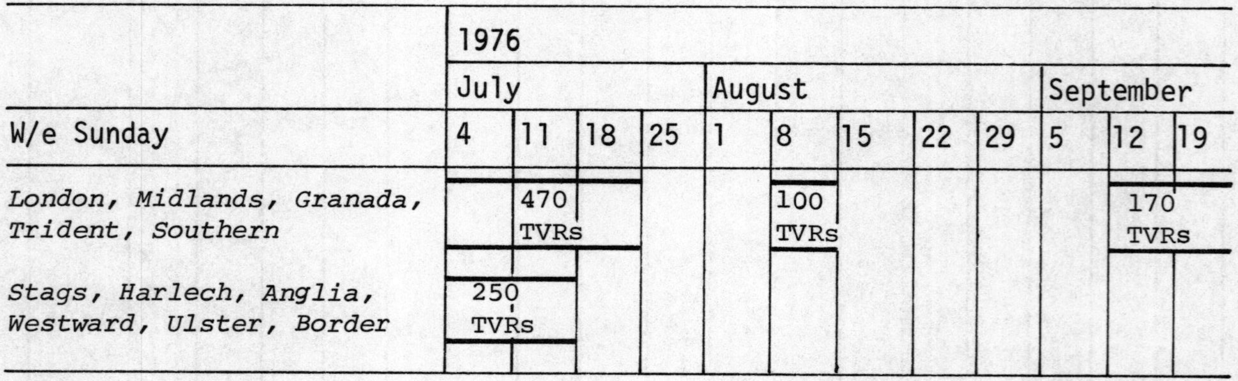

1976	July				August					September		
W/e Sunday	4	11	18	25	1	8	15	22	29	5	12	19
London, Midlands, Granada, Trident, Southern		470 TVRs				100 TVRs					170 TVRs	
Stags, Harlech, Anglia, Westward, Ulster, Border	250 TVRs											

Figure 8.3

Week starting Monday	1974															
	August		September					October				November				December
	19	26	2	9	16	23	30	7	14	21	28	4	11	18	25	2
Newcastle Evening Chronicle Half page colour	x		x		x		x									
Woman Colour insert 264 x 199												x		x		x
Woman's Own Colour insert 264 x 199												x	x		x	
Woman's Realm Colour insert 264 x 199												x	x	x		x
Tyne Tees Television 30-sec spots									x	x	x	x	x	x	x	x

428 TVRs

ESTIMATED COMBINED ACHIEVEMENT   90 per cent cover; 6.4 OTS

Figure 8.4

Another launch provides an interesting example of the incorporation of a media test, which was of considerable importance. For this case we are indebted to Playtex Limited and their agency, BBDO.

In 1974 the Company had established a very strong position in the UK market, having, in a few years from entry, come to a dominating position in the branded sector of both bra and girdle markets. This success was largely due to classic marketing methods, including the (virtually sole) use of TV, backing very well made products.

However, there was an important sector of the bra market, technically known as the half-cup sector, in which the company was not represented. Gossard, with the Wonderbra, had a near-monopoly. Apart from the profit potential, this type of bra was worn mainly by young women, and was therefore important in the establishment of brand habits. This younger group of women was also where Playtex had its lowest brand share.

After a considerable amount of development work Playtex succeeded in producing a product, which they called Body Language, which was preferred to the Wonderbra in consumer tests. BBDO were asked to prepare a launch campaign, which would begin with an area test in Tyne Tees.

The agency were convinced that the normal choice of TV should be reconsidered for this launch. Playtex set media targets for launch campaigns in terms of coverage and frequency achieved on the target market. On the budget available for this launch, with the agreed TV cost projections for the launch period, it was clear that these targets could not be met.

The reason was simple. The targets were set in relation to the usual targets for Playtex products, ladies of 25 years and upwards. Those in the Body Language market, 15-34, weighted towards 15-24, were lighter viewers of TV, and therefore more expensive, and more difficult to reach.

On the other hand, they could be reached more economically through women's magazines. To contrast the relative efficiencies of the two media against the two markets the agency produced the following estimates:

	All women	*15-34 women*
Whole-page colour, women's magazines	60p	121p
30-sec, network TV	80p	363p
TV premium	+33%	+300%

In view of past sales successes, the company were prepared to view a 33 per cent premium with equanimity; a 300 per cent premium clearly presented problems.

In the event, Playtex accepted BBDO's recommendation that the launch budget should be divided 80 TV/20 press for the following reasons:
1   This was the minimum press proportion which allowed for the launch targets to be met.
2   It was felt, on judgement, to provide a viable campaign in each medium.
3   It allowed for the use of the intrusive nature of TV, felt to be of particular value in new product launches.

It provided a low level of 'risk' in the introduction of an untried medium.

In order to simulate the launch campaign in the Tyne Tees area, use was made of three IPC women's weeklies, *Woman, Woman's Own* and *Woman's Realm*. Since it was too large an area to cover with 'tip-ins', loose inserts were used.

For trade reasons, it became necessary to get some reading of consumer response some weeks before the area campaign was due to commence. It was not possible to sell-in anywhere outside the test area, and so it was decided to use Newcastle as a forerunner. The only medium which could provide colour facilities within the time was the *Newcastle Evening Chronicle*: the gnat of women's magazines immediately followed by the camel of a regional evening! Figure 8.4 shows the test area schedule.

A considerably inhibiting factor on the use of the press for area tests is the premium local facilities carry — in contrast to discounts on television time. In this particular case the 80:20 national split which the test was designed to replicate became 52:48 in the test area (not including the *Evening Chronicle*).

Everything, particularly sales, went extremely well. It was decided to implement the national plan in the summer of 1975, and this echoed the test campaign, with only two variations. The optimised press schedule which was used was considerably longer than that in the test area, and labour relations problems put the ITV contractors off the air in the launch week.

8.6   Related reading

J.H. Parfitt and B.J. Collins, 'The use of consumer panels for brand share prediction', *Journal of Marketing Research* (May 1968).

R.A. Wachsler, *NEWS*, Batten, Barton, Durstine and Osborn Inc. (1970).

9 Quantitative media factors

9.1 Audience size

In essence the media planner is dealing with two numbers. The first represents
the size of the useful audience which the medium offers him, and the second represents the cost of the appropriate space unit in that medium.

The second of these two numbers rarely represents a problem; the first invariably does. Even supposing that the target market is explicitly described, then the
chance that the media audience is comparably described is slender. The best
hope comes from a product/media survey, which we shall be discussing in Chapter 21.

In many cases we will be relying on other measures, which we will weight in
various ways, to give what we think is a reasonable approximation to the target
market audience. Where readership figures do not exist for a publication, clearly
we have to look at circulation to provide us with some sort of guide. When we
are dealing with very similar publications, then it may be quite a useful guide. A
cautionary note is needed though, since if we did not have readership figures for
Woman's Weekly and *Woman's Realm* surely we would expect their readerships
to be in proportion to their circulations. In fact, the National Readership Survey
shows that there is a significant disproportion.

One way in which circulation figures can usefully be used to modify readership data is in making projections. It is common to plan for a schedule which is
starting six months ahead, on readership data which refers to a year which ended
three months ago. Since circulations are easier to forecast than readerships, it is
common to adjust the readership figure by the projected circulation.

Except for the National Readership Survey, there is no industry measurement
that offers up to date sub-divisions of the market suitable for target definition.
In television, this is deliberate. It has been found that further break-downs in the
audience beyond adults, men, women, housewives and children, do not produce
better information. Nevertheless, the media planner is constantly faced with a
situation in which he has to take some other measure than the measure he would
like to take for his calculations. An interesting real-life example of how this
problem may be solved follows. It is drawn from a media recommendation made

also reproduced from the first edition, so that the detail is out of date. However, the approach remains sound.

The use of posters is proposed for a number of reasons. Firstly, the outdoor medium is particularly suited to the creative approach envisaged, offering a large display area in colour. Secondly, the outdoor medium offers excellent regional flexibility, and can be used tactically to support sales outlets. Thirdly, by careful selection a campaign can be built up giving weight to areas with a suitable higher class profile. Fourthly, it is understood that in Scotland particularly Carlsberg have built up a campaign of good sites, an investment which should not be lost. A budget of £35,000 is proposed for the poster medium.

Reasonable research data (the National Readership Survey 1967) enables us to make an assessment of the relative costs of contacting the defined target audience using different media.

Using the marketing weights given in section 3 each individual in the population (or survey sample) can be given a relative value reflecting the probability of his consuming Carlsberg. (The method of arriving at this is explained in Appendix A).

The readers, viewers or listeners of each possible medium, e.g. average peak time TV, *Daily Express*, were then examined (in a computer) and each given their marketing values. These values were then added together to arrive at the total marketing value of the readers offered by each medium. This value was then divided by the cost of using the medium to arrive at a rating of the economy of each medium. At the same time the coverage of the target market was calculated. The broad results, indicating the positions of media groups, are as follows: fuller results are given in Appendix B for press media and Appendix C for other media.

RESULTS

	Number of advertising contacts per £ spent	Coverage of target market, %	Space unit
Radio Luxembourg	5,180	5·8	30 sec
Scottish Newspapers	1,608–2,289	5·6–14·6	½ page b/w
Reader's Digest	1,481	23·2	½ page b/w
Daily Mirror	1,341	35·5	½ page b/w
Other national dailies and Sundays	340–675	7·4–33·8	½ page b/w
Television	369·0	26·6	30 sec
Cinema	138·5	15·0	30 sec
National dailies and Sundays	51·1–361·6	7·4–30·3	w/p colour

Contact costs were then examined in relation to the 'qualitative' aspects of each medium, particularly the way the media are read or looked at, their atmosphere, their creative scope, and in relation to the total budget available.

Radio Luxembourg, even with its particularly low contact cost, was rejected because of current creative requirements. It lacks the visual dimension, stature and permanency.

It was considered that at this point in time the extra dimension of television did not make up the contact cost differential with the most economic newspapers. Further within the total budget available we did not consider it possible to use both press and television and to buy viable campaigns in both media. For the same reasons the cinema medium was excluded. The exclusion of television and cinema is by no means permanent. The life of the creative campaign which is proposed can be very much extended by presenting it to the public through different media. Television and cinema could therefore play a most important role in the future.

The proposed allocation of the budget between media is therefore as follows:

National and Scottish newspapers and magazines	£100,000
Poster	£35,000
Trade	£5,000
Production	£10,000
	£150,000

In this allocation magazines and newspapers are seen as the prime media. In order to achieve a really good coverage of the target market and maintain a good frequency of advertising using colour as well as black and white, a budget of £100,000 is considered necessary. The poster medium is used as support in the major towns where £35,000 will provide a good display of 16 sheets and 4 sheets, for three months (twelve months in Scotland).

APPENDIX A

METHOD OF ASSESSING MEDIA EFFICIENCY

Not all persons in the population are of equal value in marketing terms, i.e. some persons are more likely to buy Carlsberg Lager than others.

If we can make a statement of the relative differences between people in the population of buying or consuming Carlsberg, we can then make a realistic assessment of media efficiency.

This statement of relative differences between people was made in Section 3 of Part 3 of this document. For the purpose of this explanation we will assume only two characteristics are predictive of purchasing Carlsberg—sex and age. We will further assume the differences in the probability of purchase for individuals in the following sub-groups are:

Men	100	18–34	100
Women	50	34+	50

By a multiplicative process we can arrive at the following values for each type of person:

	Type of Person		
a	Men —18–34	$(100 \times 100\%)$	=100
b	Women—18–34	$(50 \times 100\%)$	= 50
c	Men —34+	$(100 \times 50\%)$	= 50
d	Women—34+	$(50 \times 50\%)$	= 25

If we then examine the readers/viewers of each medium in which we are interested, we can attach their relative marketing value. By adding together the marketing values of each of the individuals reading or viewing we can arrive at a realistic assessment of the value offered by the medium. This can then be related to the price of using the medium. For example, a readership study might provide the following information about the readers of two publications:

Publication A		Publication B	
	Value		*Value*
10 (*a*) readers	1,000	25 (*a*) readers	2,500
15 (*b*) readers	750	15 (*b*) readers	750
25 (*c*) readers	1,250	15 (*c*) readers	750
50 (*d*) readers	1,250	10 (*d*) readers	250
Total value	4,250		4,250
Unit cost	£200		£175
Valued readers for each £ spent	212·5		243·0

This is the basic method of media comparison used. These comparisons are then subjected to judgement about the qualitative aspects of each medium, both in media and creative terms.

APPENDIX B

SHORT-LISTED PUBLICATIONS

	Number of valued readers per £1 spent	Coverage of target media, %	Comparative space unit
Glasgow Sunday Post	2,284·2 (*s*)	14·6	½ page b/w
Glasgow Sunday Mail	1,608·1	8·3	½ page b/w
Reader's Digest	1,481·2 (*s*)	23·2	w/p b/w
Daily Mirror	1,341·0 (*s*)	35·5	quad. col b/w
Reader's Digest	1,243·1 (*s*)	23·2	w/p colour
Daily Sketch	1,120·7	7·3	quad. col b/w
Sunday Mirror	1,013·3	34·4	quad. col b/w
People	675·4	33·8	½ page b/w
Radio Times	675·1 (*s*)	32·4	w/p b/w
Daily Express	648·8 (*s*)	30·3	½ page b/w
TV Times	624·2	23·3	w/p b/w
Punch	600·2	3·2	w/p b/w
Daily Mail	570·9 (*s*)	14·7	½ page b/w
Sun	554·4	7·4	½ page b/w
Daily Telegraph	460·8 (*s*)	11·9	½ page b/w
Sunday Times	420·6	14·8	½ page b/w
Evening Standard	397·5	4·8	quad. col b/w
TV Times	388·4	23·3	colour page
Observer	384·2	8·6	½ page b/w
Evening News	382·0	9·2	w/p b/w

Radio Times	373·9 (s)	32·4	w/p colour
Sunday Telegraph	369·6	6·5	½ page b/w
Observer Colour Magazine	361·6	10·0	w/p colour
Guardian	359·1	3·4	½ page b/w
Punch	343·0	3·2	w/p colour
Sunday Times Magazine	325·0	14·8	w/p colour
Daily Telegraph Magazine	299·4 (s)	11·9	w/p colour
The Times	260·2	3·7	½ page b/w
Daily Mail	170·0 (s)	14·7	w/p colour
Daily Express	133·6 (s)	30·3	w/p colour
Evening News	83·4	9·2	w/p colour
Evening Standard	51·1	4·8	2 page col.

(s)—included in proposed schedule

APPENDIX C

METHOD OF ARRIVING AT CONTACT COSTS FOR NON-PRESS MEDIA

The 1967 National Readership survey asked certain questions about frequency of exposure to Radio Luxembourg, Cinema and ITV. The results of these questions were tabulated for the target audience in which we are interested. From these results it is possible to apply a probability of being exposed to an advertisement transmitted during peak time for radio and ITV or for a week in the case of the cinema. The resulting number of valued persons could then be related to cost to establish (as for press media) the number of valued contacts delivered for each pound spent.

Listening to *Radio Luxembourg* YESTERDAY for

	'000 valued audience	Estimated percentage exposed to peak advert	Estimated number exposed, '000
½ hr	354·6	0·085	30·0
½–1 hr	467·8	0·125	58·25
1–1½ hr	247·4	0·21	51·75
1½–2 hr	196·3	0·29	56·7
2–2½ hr	108·3	0·375	40·5
2½ hr or more	455·6	0·50	227·8
			465·00

	Cost per 30-sec spot	Number of contacts per £	'000 valued listeners
Radio Luxembourg	£90	5,180	465·0

	'000 valued audience	Number of exposures to advert	Estimated number exposed
1	852·8	1·0	852·8
2	89·8	2·0	179·6
3	5·5	3·0	16·5
4	0·7	4·0	2·8
5	0·6	5·0	3·0
6+	9·7	7·0	68·6
			1,125·3

	1 week cost per 30-sec spot	Number of contacts per £	Valued audience
Cinema	£8,074	138·5	1,125·3

Television Number viewing YESTERDAY

	'000 valued audience	Estimated percentage exposed to advert	Estimated number exposed
Under ½ hr	420·0	0·12	50·4
½–1½ hr	1,377·0	0·25	344·0
1½–2½ hr	1,186·0	0·50	593·0
2½–3½ hr	637·7	0·75	479·0
3½–4½ hr	287·1	1·00	287·1
Over 4½ hr	243·5	1·00	243·5
			1,997·0

	1 peak 30-sec spot cost	Number of contacts per £	Valued audience
ITV	£5,400	369·0	1,997·0

The only questions which arise under this heading are as follows. Firstly, have we the right costs? Secondly, are we comparing like with like? The first question is purely a matter of planner/buyer liaison and is discussed further in Chapter 10. The second is more complex and concerns the nature of equivalence. The reader will have noted that in the Carlsberg example a number of different sizes of space and lengths of time are treated as being equal. In general terms a whole page black and white in a large-size newspaper is treated as being equal to a whole page in a magazine, or four columns in a tabloid newspaper. (The colour spaces are obviously not intended to be equal to the black and white spaces.) In radio, cinema and television the unit for calculations is a 30-second commercial.

There is no point in arguing about these decisions (unless you have a direct involvement in the campaign planned!) but their choice clearly presents the planner with a considerable problem. Had he chosen different spaces and lengths of time the answers would very likely have been different.

The only guide which we can offer is to suggest that the planner takes the size or length that the creative department would require if that medium were to be the medium of choice. This is, in fact, not a very simple solution, since creative work can always be changed to fit different possibilities. Nevertheless, the question is best put to the creative department, and if its purpose is explained it is probable that a helpful answer will be obtained. Clearly the basic problem in arriving at equivalence is the variety of meanings which are attached to measurements of audience for different media.

9.3   Measurement differences

Let us begin by spelling out the qualification used in arriving at the audience for each of the principal media (see Table 9.1).

It is important to realise that these differences are not only of degree, but also of kind. At what is probably the lowest end, the fact that someone has passed a poster site does not give him a very high chance of having actually seen one of the posters on that site. Clearly though, for sites of the same type, there is probably a fairly direct relationship between the numbers of passages and the number of actual sightings. In the application of poster research there is a further qualification in that we are not actually talking about passages past any particular site, but the patterns of movements in towns and the effect of these movements on the probability of people seeing average campaigns.

In the case of the press medium, we are talking about specific publications; nevertheless, the chance of someone looking at an average issue of any publication is not a very direct measurement of the chances of their having been exposed to our advertisement in a particular issue of it.

With both radio and television we are concerned with a pretty short time interval surrounding the exposure of our actual commercial. For television, there is a very strong chance that someone being in the room in which the set sits whilst the commercial is being transmitted, will get something from that transmission. The only problem here concerns the fact that one may be counted as being in the room when one is in fact absent for the commercial break. A good deal of

TABLE 9.1

Medium	Research	Qualification
Press	National Readership Survey	Looked at any copy in (qualifying period)*
Television	JICTAR Surveys[+]	Being present in the room in which TV set is on for 8 or more min out of 15
Outdoor (Posters)	IPA Poster Audience Surveys	Passing location of poster
Radio	JICRAR Surveys[+]	Listening to quarter/half-hour periods
Cinema	National Readership Surveys	Visiting a cinema

*The National Readership Survey also asks questions concerning frequency of readership. However, for practical purposes, the average audience figure is the one most widely used.

[+]Some information available from National Readership Survey

work has been done in trying to bridge this gap, so far without success. That the radio qualification is less precise means that the problem is slightly more difficult and, of course, the way in which the medium is received means that the value of the opportunity must be less.

Clearly most people sitting in a cinema when the commercials are screened are likely to pay a good deal of attention to them. Although it is true that a number of people (including probably most readers of this book) will manage to get into the cinema just before the main feature starts, and after the commercials have been screened, this is a very atypical behaviour. The chief problem with a cinema measurement is that, like the poster measurement, it is referring to average exposure to average campaigns and tells us very little about the actual audience to our campaign.

The one thing that is common to all the media measurements is that they are designed to produce the maximum possible audiences. This state of affairs is likely to continue as long as media owners are called upon to bear the largest part of the costs of the surveys.

9.4 Audience break-downs

The National Readership Survey publishes over 200 separate pieces of information concerning the readership of each publication that it covers. This figure excludes readership profiles, re-calculations of other pieces of data and frequency data. The number can be greatly expanded through special analysis.

In comparison with this figure, the 21 breaks available for the television audience seem meagre, and it is to be remembered that these are not supplied on a frequent basis. The regular weekly data has only five sub-divisions. Of course, the audience to Independent Television programmes can be described in a great deal of detail through the National Readership Survey figures and through special analyses. This is true also of Cinema and Radio Luxembourg. Local radio audiences are classified into 17 different groups.

This leaves outdoor, where the only industry information refers to one figure for all adults. TGI figures show very large variations about the average, in line with commonsense expectations. Clearly, different groups of the population spend different proportions of their time travelling and are therefore exposed to outdoor advertising to different degrees. The highest indices are achieved by 25-34 males, and 20-24 females, in the AB socio-economic group. Lowest indices are for state pensioners; area variations are less extreme, but the East of England region leads.

Thus, given a precise definition of his target market, the planner will have very different degrees of success in calculating the proportion of the *total* audience reached by different media which fall within it.

10 Qualitative factors

This chapter is devoted to the considerations that influence media selection beyond those of cost-per-thousand. They are qualitative in the sense that no generally accepted research is available to enable numbers to be attached to them. In spite of this, one of the media planner's most onerous tasks today is that he has to put a number to all of them in order to be able to use a media model.

10.1 The value of the opportunity

In Chapter 9 we discussed the wide differences that exist in the definition of the total audience to different media. These definitions bear very directly on the differences between the value of 'opportunities to see' in the different media. Attempts to find a number which can be used to modify the basic audience measurement so that it more accurately represents the probability of exposure to an advertisement, have been going on for very many years. It is now clear that most measures, beyond media audiences, are heavily dependent on the creative quality, and inherent product interest, of the ads concerned. Thus, no generalisable data are likely to be produced. There is more on this subject in Chapter 22.

One of the problems besetting the industry in relation to this area is the absence of explicit agreement as to the purpose of the research. This is not the place to discuss theories of advertising, but we would propose that the media planner really wishes to establish the relationship between inserting an advertisement into a given medium and the probability of that action resulting in sales motivation on the audience to the medium. Let us spell out what we mean by this.

It is virtually certain that a whole-page advertisement does not have twice the opportunity of being seen of a half-page advertisement, even though the cost relationship be two to one. However, if, as may well be the case, the whole page has more motivating effect on those who see it than does the half page on those that see that, then the opportunity of seeing the whole page must be more valuable than the opportunity of seeing the half page. Thus, whilst strict application of reading and noting data will direct the advertiser into smaller and smaller press spaces, direct response advertisers tend to use the largest spaces available.

If the attempts to measure attention values have currently not met with success and if the planner is faced with a problem which does not involve direct response, what does he do? We will discuss what we believe to be the only satisfactory answer to this in Chapter 27.

10.2   The nature of coverage

Clearly no one can be directly affected by an advertisement unless they are exposed to it. (In saying this we must not forget the important, but relatively unexplored, effects of word of mouth, shop display and product in use.) For this reason total schedule coverage is a dimension frequently given considerable importance. In recent years there has been some re-examination of the concept: what do we mean by coverage?

There was a time when this was regarded as being the total unduplicated number of people who had the opportunity of seeing at least one insertion on the schedule. This is only a useful definition if we believe that having one opportunity to see is likely to produce response. There has been a counter-movement towards concern with coverage at a stated frequency, which might be four a month, or any other number that can be pulled out of the air. The early days of television advertising convinced those involved that it could be profitable dramatically to reduce coverage in order to produce greater impact. The impact produced by television on the very small audiences which were then attainable had a greater sales effect than the widespread coverage which had been possible through the press medium. How high the frequency has to be and how low the coverage which could be tolerated, are questions which can only be answered in conjunction with the consideration of the shape of the response function (see Chapter 26).

It is useful to remember that the biggest brands are seldom bought by more than 20 per cent of the population and that large sums of money can be made by selling products to markets measured in hundreds of thousands. The difficulty is in covering the appropriate consumers without covering the population at large, and has been illustrated in Table 6.4.

10.3   Physical attributes

A picture normally communicates better than words, a moving picture normally communicates better than a still picture, a moving picture with the addition of sound is a further improvement, and a coloured moving picture with sound represents the present-day ultimate in communication-effectiveness. These dimensions are, therefore, very important measurements of the media we have under consideration.

So, too, is the degree of captivity of the audience. No one is trying to persuade us to look at a poster site (other than the advertiser) and there are many distractions; in any case we are usually only physically able to look at it for a few seconds. At the other extreme, in the cinema, it is difficult to walk about, it is difficult to look elsewhere than at the screen and the whole purpose of visiting the cinema is to look at the screen.

In addition to the inherent characteristics of the medium, its ability to convey the particular message with which we are concerned is clearly of importance, but it is difficult to know the degree. For instance, one of the cases in which this used to weigh most heavily was the use of colour for food advertising. The well-known phrase was 'appetite appeal'. In view of the very large volume of food advertising which appeared on TV in black and white, it is clear that this factor is not as important as might have been believed. Most of the arguments in fact revolve around the question of colour. Some press media are eschewed simply because the quality of their colour reproduction is not sufficiently high to convey successfully the proposed advertising message. Again, a note of caution is necessary. Few consumers have the expert critical faculty of the client, and if they are satisfied with editorial pictures of the same quality, they may well not notice the difference.

10.4   Proximity to purchase

People forget things. Exciting news that we give to consumers about our clients' brands is seldom particularly significant to them in relation to their total lives. There is, therefore, an argument for presenting our commercial message as close in time to the point of purchase as possible. This is why Thursdays and Fridays are so popular for advertising goods bought mainly on Fridays and Saturdays.

There are two caveats which should be made to any planner thinking of applying this thought as a general rule. Firstly, the fall-off in recall is very much more dramatic during the first 24 hours, than it is subsequently. Thus from the point of view of making a purchase on Saturday, what has been learnt on Monday may not be very different from what has been learnt on Thursday. Secondly, with most major products the consumer has acquired, over a period of perhaps years, a good deal of knowledge which she has learnt so well that she will not forget it quickly.

It is arguable that proximity of place is more important than proximity in time. Some of the best advertising success stories have come when the point of sale material has been well distributed and has clearly recalled the advertising theme. If an advertiser can produce a campaign which favourably influences the consumer, and can then produce recall of that campaign whilst the consumer is standing in front of the display shelves, then that campaign is likely to be successful.

This may help to account for the popularity of four-sheet poster sites, many of which are positioned in shopping precincts. Whilst display material is chronically difficult to get into supermarkets, the four-sheet poster just outside is probably the best available substitute.

10.5   Atmosphere, context and impact

These three words, once so important in media planning, have become less popular largely because of the difficulty of measuring them. It has been thought that advertisements benefitted from appearing in media which, whatever their audience characteristics might be, had the 'right' sort of editorial. Very often this was a way of saying that the advertiser wished to see his advertisements in the publications he read. Religious publications have been described by some advertisers as speaking 'with the voice of the pulpit'.

Another aspect of this thought which is perhaps better based is that advertisements should appear in a related editorial context. For instance, advertisements for baby products should appear alongside editorial concerning baby welfare. This is clearly a method of ensuring that the advertisement is put before the eye of the most interested readers. The alternative view is that greater impact is produced by putting advertisements out of context. This must clearly be true in one respect, in that there is a surprise element involved.

In some very specialised publications an advertisement which is quite irrelevant to the reader's frame of mind as she reads the publication, may achieve little or no attention. The figures show, for example, that *Do-It-Yourself* reaches about the same number of women at a substantially lower cost than does *Woman's Journal*. Nevertheless, few of the campaigns which appear in *Woman's Journal* would be likely to have a greater effect if placed in *Do-It-Yourself*.

Finally, it must be remembered that the consumer is in fact a number of different animals rolled into one, and the particular animal he is when exposing himself to a particular medium may be important. Perhaps the most important distinction to be drawn here is between work and play. The businessman may be prepared to read advertisements concerning his work with considerable avidity if they appear in the serious newspapers and the business press. On the other hand he may receive an advertisement for a computer appearing in *Penthouse* with nothing but irritation. In the case of the woman, she is concerned with her house-wifely duties for a very large amount of her time and any information, including advertisements, that will help her in her task is likely to be appreciated. When she is trying to escape from it all, as she probably is when she visits the cinema, it may be very inappropriate to remind her about it.

That this argument has to be used with caution, is clearly illustrated by the television medium. This is, on the whole, a medium of relaxation and yet can successfully carry serious messages for businessmen and for housewives.

10.6   Effect of qualitative factors

Although, as we have said, it is extremely difficult to measure these effects, one can make some deductions about them by the use of sensitivity tests in media models. This subject is covered in Chapter 23 but it is worth stating the general findings here. The general pattern of schedule evaluation shows that there are some media which are very cost-effective for a particular campaign, a large number that show small variations from each other but are some way behind the leaders, and then another batch a long way behind the average. Clearly it is not going to take a very large subjective (qualitative) weight to change the relative position of the mass in the middle, so that a particular medium is excluded, or included. On the other hand, a very substantial bias will have to be shown against one of the leaders to exclude it, and a very considerable bias in favour of one of the laggards will be needed to include it. In fact the extent of this bias can be simply demonstrated.

Bureau of Commercial Research, 'Qualitative media assessments', *TV Times* (1967).
H.A. Smith, 'Beyond vehicle audiences', ESOMAR Congress (1976).

11 Tactics

11.1 The importance of flexibility

It is very important not to get the impression that the media planner's task on a particular brand finishes when his recommendation for the year is accepted by the client. Acceptance may be as much as six months before the campaign actually commences, and in the eighteen months before it finishes there is opportunity for a great many changes to occur. The good media planner will keep his eye on all the campaigns under his control with a view to modifying them in the light of changed circumstances.

This is, of course, done as a matter of routine in the case of television schedules. Although it is normally the buyer's rather than the planner's responsibility to select specific times and days for the appearance of the commercials, the planner will suggest the balances of peak and off-peak, weekend and weekday time. If changes in ratings are of sufficient magnitude, these basic rules may need to be changed.

It is possible these days for similarly dramatic changes to occur in circulations, either upwards or downwards, and the planner should not be afraid of recommending a change in the middle of a campaign, in view of these circumstances.

Often new media opportunities will offer themselves. A new national publication offering regional facilities, for instance, or colour where colour was not available before, or perhaps a new medium altogether.

11.2 New media

New media present media planners with the biggest challenge they have. No media planner wishes to recommend a medium that does not succeed, and new media introductions are not markedly more successful than new product introductions in other fields. The owner of the medium is likely to be rather impatient of such caution and accuse the planners of conservatism. This charge is usually a true one, but that is the way the cards are stacked. Very seldom is an

advertiser going to get a marked advantage from being in at the beginning of a
new medium, and it is quite possible that he will catch a cold.

Apart from trying to invent (often with the assistance of the media owner) audience figures for the new medium on which he can make an objective comparison with existing media, the media planner also has to be a businessman in his assessment of the likelihood of the medium starting at all. Very many good ideas have failed simply because of the lack of capital resources of the originators.

On the other hand, some of the publishing giants have recently withdrawn a new medium before the launch simply because they have not attracted the target level of bookings, or because they have had disputes, either with unions or distributive channels, or whatever.

Nevertheless, the media planner must be prepared to back his judgement where he thinks that a new medium does offer a real opportunity for his client. He will add considerably to his reputation if he should prove to be right.

11.3   Brand performance

Another important source of information which the media planner should go out of his way to receive is the performance of the product itself. Media planners ought to receive Nielsen, TCA, or other continuing sales measures and wherever possible attend the presentations. Apart from monitoring any tests that he may have running, the general feel of the market which this kind of exposure generates is essential background for producing the optimum media plan.

11.4   Special offers

The planner should also be in a position to respond to buying opportunities. Quite often, for one reason or another, a media owner will come with the offer of space or time at a 'bargain' rate. Should the media planner disturb his schedule in order to take advantage of such an offer? The wise media planner will, wherever possible, maintain a tactical reserve on his budget for just such a purpose. However, this may have been committed in other directions, or it may not be sufficient for the opportunity offered. The key question always is: is this 'bargain' a better opportunity than those which I am currently buying? Some media, at half price, will not be a better buy for a particular brand than the media already scheduled at the full price. Any offer which is confined to a particular region should be checked carefully with the advertiser to see whether he has adequate distribution from stocks to meet additional demand in the areas, and whether in fact it is profitable for him to sell an additional quantity there.

It is also possible that disturbing the existing schedule may affect quantity or series discounts and thereby lose money in the long run. Finally it is worth examining which part of the target market is going to be affected by the new deal. If extra weight is going to be placed at the heaviest-exposed end of the distribution, this is likely to be far less valuable then extra pressure on the lightly exposed.

The question of the buyer's ability bears on the plan as far as it affects the rates charged. It is very important that the planner in constructing the schedule has the real rates which will be paid in front of him, rather than merely the rate cards. This is sometimes difficult since the rate which can be negotiated is likely to depend on the volume of bookings placed. In this situation the process normally adopted is for the buyer to make initial investigations as to what kind of deals may be offered, and the planner to include these in his considerations. When an optimum schedule at these rates has been generated, the buyers can then go back to the media and see whether they can be made firm. Alternatively, these days some media are quite pleased to be told what rate they would have to charge in order to appear on a schedule. Clearly there is a limit to the amount of such re-cycling that can go on, but it is almost always worth (the advertiser) the planner and buyer co-operating as far as they possibly can in this process.

12 The press

12.1 Characteristics of press media

As will be seen from Figure 12.1, the press medium attracts the greatest share of advertising revenue in this country. Although, as we have previously remarked, this figure is an exaggeration of the importance of the press to large national advertisers, it still remains the principal medium for some large, and many medium sized, appropriations. Its complexity is such that we will have to discuss it under a number of different headings, but we will begin by considering many of the common factors.

12.1.1 Coverage

Various forms of press media offer virtually total coverage of the adult population of the UK several times over. The great majority of people read one of the eight morning newspapers published from London (together with their editions published in Manchester and Glasgow). Most people read two of the newspapers published in London every Sunday. Four in every five adults in Scotland read the *Sunday Post* every week. Many adults read an evening newspaper, and most people across the country read a local weekly.

Every conceivable taste is catered for by one or other magazine. Programme publications, both for commercial television and the BBC, are read by about 10 million. The majority of women read a women's weekly magazine and, although the readerships of monthly magazines are lower, *Reader's Digest* is read by over 8 million adults and there are 12 titles in the women's monthly field with women readerships of more than a million.

12.1.2 Available information

Another characteristic of the press medium is how much we know about it. Indeed we know so much that it is almost incredible that we should want to know

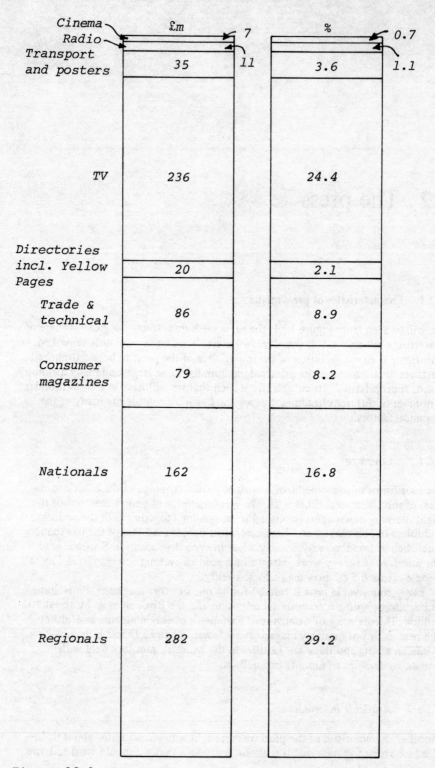

Figure 12.1 Breakdown of total advertising expenditure by media. (Source: Advertising Association 1975)

more. Readership data in tremendous detail is available from the National
Readership Survey on about 90 of our major publications. In addition we have
audited circulation figures for most of these. We have circulation figures too for
many of the publications not covered by the National Readership Survey, although this is an area in which further information can legitimately be deman-
ded. Apart from other large-scale quasi-industry surveys, which cover press
readership, the media owners themselves have commissioned a very large number of surveys into all aspects of their readerships.

12.1.3   Selectivity

One of the most important aspects of the press as a whole, for the media planner,
is his ability to choose widely contrasting vehicles for the advertising message.
(Perhaps we should here lament that we do put 'the advertising message' into
many different publications. Indeed, the effectiveness of campaigns could well
be markedly increased by putting different messages into different press media.
In the real world this is seldom done.)

Let us consider the contrast available between, for example, the *Daily Express* and *19*. The *Daily Express* is the third largest morning newspaper in the
country and the average issue is read by 21 per cent of all adults. The point
which is unique about this readership is that there is comparatively little variation across different demographic sub-divisions. Seventeen per cent of the 15-
24s read the paper; 16 per cent of the 25-34s; 21 per cent of the 35-44s; 23 per
cent of the 45-54s; 25 per cent of the 55-64s; and 23 per cent of the over 65s. In
the socio-economic grades, the coverage is 24 per cent in the As, 23 per cent in
the Bs, 25 per cent in the C1s, 20 per cent in the C2s, 17 per cent in the Ds, and
17 per cent in the Es. In the regions, we find 20 per cent coverage in London
and the South East, 17 per cent in the South West and Wales, 16 per cent in the
Midlands, 26 per cent in the North West, 17 per cent in the North East and
North and 33 per cent in Scotland. This last figure is exceptional, owing to the
position of the *Scottish Daily Express* which was, for years, printed in Glasgow.

More esoteric breaks still show a similar pattern. The paper is read by 22 per
cent of members of car-owning households, 24 per cent of members of two-car-
owning households; 23 per cent of those who left school at 15 or under; 22 per
cent who had some further education; 22 per cent of those with full central heating; 23 per cent of those with colour TV. There is a considerable difference between readership by men and women (24 per cent and 18 per cent, respectively),
as is usually the case for national dailies.

At the other extreme, consider IPC's *19*. This is read by 1 per cent of men,
but 4 per cent of women; by 10 per cent of 15-24s, and less than 1 per cent of
55+s; by 5 per cent of As, and less than 1 per cent of Es. True, its regional profile is remarkably even, either 2 or 3 per cent penetration in each area. However,
looking at marital status as well as age, we find that it is read by 23 per cent of
single women 15-24, but only 2 per cent of married women. (Figures from NRS
July 1974-June 1975.)

To round out the picture of differences which exist in the print medium, let
us contrast the *News of the World,* selling over 5 million copies every week and
reaching people with tremendously diverse interests with, for instance, *Coins and*

Medals selling 7000+ copies every month and reaching people with a common, but very narrow, bond. (There are doubtless many magazines in circulation with a smaller sale and narrower following, but we found none willing to admit the fact.)

12.1.4   Flexibility

The range of flexibility in the press medium is almost as great as the range in any other measurement of the medium. It is possible to place a classified advertisement by telephone in the morning and see it appear in the midday editions of the evening newspapers. For full-colour reproduction in monthly magazines, however, copy is frequently required nearly three months before the publication appears. Similarly with cancellation periods. A great deal of classified advertising may be officially cancelled at no more than two days notice. Some publishers still require six months cancellation notice for colour. The general tendency is towards greater flexibility and it is often possible to effect considerable advances on the official positions by special negotiation.

12.1.5   Production

Production costs can be kept to an extremely small portion of the budget. A direct response advertiser for a pension plan has carried the same copy unchanged for upwards of 20 years. At the other extreme, a fibre manufacturer illustrating a wide number of styles in a wide number of publications, can easily run up to 25 per cent of the advertising budget in production. Some remarkably effective advertisements have been typeset by the publication itself, and even more sophisticated advertisements may carry a low entrance fee into the medium.

With the speed of production which they entail, many newspapers and quite a number of other press media are not able to reproduce illustrations, and in particular half-tone illustrations, to the standard which many advertisers would desire. A similar statement could be made about the reproduction of colour in the high-speed gravure process. This point can be sufficiently important to have a bearing on media selection. It is difficult to justify it having more than a bearing though, since if the medium is correct for the target market, it must be possible to produce some form of effective advertisement which can be printed in it.

12.1.6   Sizes, shapes and colours

The basic unit of space in newspapers is the single column centimetre; most other spaces are built up from this size. In magazines the basic unit is the page and other spaces are either built up from or reduced from, this space. Shapes can vary widely, although most of them are rectangular. Recent years have seen something of a return to the pre-war concern with shapes other than rectangular.

Colour is playing an increasingly important role in the press, not only in advertising but also in editorial matter. We have seen great developments over the last ten years and more are coming, although the rate of change is slower than some people expected. Most press media are now able to offer full colour in some form or other.

Newspaper sizes   The most commonly used spaces by display advertisers in broadsheet newspapers are 200 mm across 2 columns; 280 mm across 3 or 4 columns; 330 mm across 5 columns; and 380 mm across 6 columns. Pages and half pages are also popular, and this is even more true in tabloids, which now account for the majority of UK newspapers. Smaller spaces in tabloids are often sold by the column, or fraction thereof.

One of the small but vexing problems facing the media planner and his colleagues is the question of what equivalent spaces should be used in tabloid newspapers. There are two popular approaches to this problem; the first is to take the equivalent proportion of the page in each newspaper. The difficulty with this approach is that the sheer amount of copy in the advertisement may mean that the fairly considerable physical reduction in size which results makes the advertisement look cramped and possibly difficult to read.

The other approach is to equate the physical area of the spaces as closely as possible. There is a good correspondence between a 380 mm across 6 columns in a broadsheet newspaper and a whole page in a tabloid. Several other sizes can be similarly matched. There is, however, no space in a tabloid which can really be equated with a half-page landscape in a large newspaper, and it is almost certain that if both sizes of newspapers are required on the same schedule, then an alternative layout will be needed.

As far as shapes in newspapers are concerned, it is quite difficult to depart by far from the conventional spaces, because of difficulties with layout. Many newspapers impose a restriction that the number of centimetres may not be less than the number of columns. The purpose of unusual spaces is usually to gain impact at a low cost, rather than to accommodate a particular creative problem. There is no doubt, for instance, that a 200 mm across 8 columns has very much the same impact as a half page, and costs proportionately less. This is one reason for the popularity of the 380 mm across 6 columns space. It normally appears solus on a page and is sufficiently big to dominate a page; indeed some people prefer this space to a whole page on the grounds that the editorial matter on the page is likely to produce a better chance of the advertisement being noticed than if it were by itself. The same argument can be applied to a three-quarter quin column in tabloids. The search for novelty has produced combinations of rectangles such as L shapes. None of these, however, have proved popular in the sense that they are often seen.

A very impressive way of using conventional spaces is to use a lot of them. On several occasions a single advertiser has taken every space in one issue of a newspaper. Using the usual variety of spaces and sizes, he has given individual treatment to very many aspects of his sales story. Obviously this is a very expensive exercise and can only be warranted by an occasion of particular importance. Equally obviously, on such an occasion it can make a tremendous impact on the readership of that newspaper.

Magazine sizes   Pages and sub-divisions down to sixteenths and multiples without number are the usual tools of the media planner. Although circular advertisements have occasionally appeared in magazines, unusual combinations of usual spaces are far more widely seen. Some magazine publishers, and particularly the IPC women's weekly group, have been stimulating the sale of such spaces.

Other unusual spaces, which are not available in newspapers, are the gatefold, and similar positions. By folding in a page, and inviting the reader to fold it out again, it is possible to get two pages where there should be only one. Of course, the effect of the gatefold can, nowadays, usually be equalled by having two double-page spreads in colour, consecutively. The advantage of a gatefold lies mostly in its novelty, but there is always the danger that the reader either will not understand it, and pass it by, or else purely not bother to undo it. Gatefolds are used to great effect in magazines like *Reader's Digest,* where it is possible to use the folded over portion as a tear off mail-in. By making this a pre-paid, pre-addressed postcard, a very economical cost per reply can be achieved. A variety of space units available in *Reader's Digest* is shown in Plate 1.

To buy all the spaces in most magazines would cost a very large sum of money indeed, but a similar effect to that mentioned with newspapers can be achieved by buying a number of them running consecutively. Again by using half pages, quarter pages, full pages, varying from black and white to full colour, a great deal of both variety and impact can be achieved.

Colour in newspapers   Because the newspaper medium is primarily a black and white one, it has long been felt that colour in a newspaper would carry far greater impact than colour in a magazine. But, with the exception of newspapers printed by the web-offset process, colour requires a special printing. This prompted some early pioneering work by what were then Odhams Newspapers, and led to the establishment of the Pre-Print Publishing Company whose sole concern was arranging for colour pages to be inserted into black and white newspapers.

The heart of this process is known as 'wallpaper'. It relies on reels of paper to be pre-printed gravure or litho at one of a number of printers, in full colour, and for these reels to be distributed to the newspaper, or newspapers, who are going to carry the advertisement. At the newspaper printing press it is run in with the remainder of the paper with ordinary black and white printing on the reverse side, and occasionally with special over-printing on the advertisement side. It is known as 'wallpaper' because the design is repeated continually and the portion which appears to the reader is a random cut-off, depending where the guillotine falls. It should be explained that the design is basically the same size as the newspaper in which it is to appear, but that the pre-printed reel usually shrinks somewhere along the line. The difference which results may be only one sixteenth of an inch per copy, but in the course of printing several thousand copies the design will slip right through and re-appear in the correct place. This process clearly calls for some skill in design, and it must be said that this is not always noticeable.

In an attempt to refine the basic crudity of this process, registered colour has made a good deal of headway. In this process register marks are included at regular intervals on the pre-printed reel and special electronic eyes are fitted to the printing machines. Their function is to maintain the relationship between the pre-printed reel and the ordinary newspaper pages, so that one design is centrally registered throughout. The problem with these machines is that they normally slow down the printing process. In view of the critical nature of time in relation to the distribution of newspapers, this may mean that the attempt has to be abandoned at some point in time during the run. From that point on either the reel is allowed to lapse back to wallpaper, or alternatively the run is completed with a black and white version of the colour advertisement.

Clearly the great advantage to the advertiser of getting registration is that once this is possible, spaces smaller than whole pages are possible. Some newspapers are already selling registered gravure colour in such smaller spaces at the moment. Again while costs are lower than those for a full page, some planners will argue that they are even more effective.

One way of avoiding the complication of register is to employ a process for printing the newspaper which is adaptable to colour in itself. The best available process is web off-set, and this is now used for the printing of many weekly and evening newspapers. Unfortunately the process is still too slow for large circulation newspapers to be printed on it, without employing printing presses in many different centres. Although this is the way that newspaper production was thought to be developing until recently, it now seems doubtful as to whether it will ever be economically possible to print in this way.

Clearly the easiest way to get colour into a newspaper is by including a colour magazine. The three weekend magazines, those of the *Sunday Times,* the *Observer* and the *Sunday Telegraph* have enjoyed very considerable success both in terms of circulation and also advertisement revenue.

Long before full-colour reproduction was available in newspapers, some advertisers had been making ingenious use of a second colour, printed letterpress. Over the years a few advertisers have refined this process into an effective way of advertising. It is much easier to do in the web off-set publication. An inferior way of doing the same thing is by use of the so called 'fudge' colour. The majority of newspaper presses have a 'fudge box' mounted on them, which enables them to carry either the title or the edition number and probably late news in red, or some other second colour. This can be adapted to run a certain limited amount of colour on an advertising space somewhere in the paper. Although it is very cheap, the limitations are such that it is not widely used.

Colour in magazines   The great majority of magazines are printed in full colour and so allow for full-colour advertising. Rotogravure and web off-set are commonly used, as is also high-quality letterpress. Occasionally two processes, usually gravure and letterpress, are included in different sections of the same publication. Since the standard of colour available may not be the same in the two sections, it is important for the planner to know and to agree with his creative department, just where the space is to appear.

There are technical difficulties involved in printing colour on both sides of the same sheet. This has led to a situation in which double-page spreads were easy, but two following pages of colour were impossible. Although most magazines now offer colour backing colour, the planner must be careful to ensure that this is true of magazines which he is considering if that is the creative requirement.

The time is not long past when the only way of reducing a rate published on a rate card for a British publication was to involve in some hard bargaining with the publication's representative. Since buyers and sellers varied considerably in skill, a variety of different rates were paid in the same publication for the same space. Although this does still go on to some extent, it has been reduced substantially by the introduction of published volume discounts and seasonal discounts.

Some newspapers offer different prices for different degrees of flexibility which the advertiser will allow. For example, the *Sun* currently has one rate for a 5-6 day option for insertion; asks about 5 per cent more for 2-4 day option; and about 2½ per cent on top of that for guaranteed day (other than Saturday).

Quite a number of press media have series discounts and some have new business discounts. This means that they will offer a discount to an advertiser whose expenditure in their medium is running at a higher rate than it was in the previous year.

The effect of this to the planner is quite significant. For example, if the planner is using a media model then by putting a publication in at a series discount rate it might well appear on the schedule with sufficient insertions to justify the discount. On the other hand, if he puts it in at the full rate then it might never appear at all. A simpler situation arises when by moving an insertion date by a week, a considerable sum of money can be saved, probably without any adverse effect.

12.3 The functions of different classes of press media

The vast field of publications can be sub-divided in a number of different ways. The bulk of those published in this country come under the general heading of trade and technical publications, and these we are going to deal with separately in a different chapter. The easiest division to follow is the production division, and that is how we are going to tackle the problem. This division corresponds with another major division, that between information and entertainment. On the whole, newspapers tend to be informative and magazines tend to be entertainment media. However, there are so many cases in which this rule is reversed that one would not wish to be dogmatic about it.

Very important to the planner are the differences in audience which the different publications can provide. This is the way we started the chapter. Also likely to be very important to him are the differences in timing. For a campaign that demands high frequency he has to use the daily or Sunday press; monthlies just do not come out frequently enough. Another major difference between the two types of media is that the readership of the daily is almost entirely achieved during the day of issue; with a monthly magazine, readership can build up for as long as five months after the cover date. Which of these alternatives is preferable depends entirely on the campaign in question. It is an important consideration when there is any seasonality involved in selling.

Over the course of time some publications have been positively identified with a particular type of advertising and this may be an excellent reason for placing that type of advertising in them. When people are setting out to obtain new furniture, or new domestic appliances, they will often turn to one of the publications carrying advertising and editorial on such subjects, for example, *House & Garden.* Women looking for fashion ideas often turn to the great fashion publications such as *Vogue,* or, if they are in the right age group, *19.* The classified columns of some national newspapers are renowned for some subjects and there are occasions when the national advertiser of branded goods can usefully use them. Advertisers wishing to convey a message to top businessmen frequently use the 'quality' newspapers and in particular, for instance, the *Financial Times.* The planner should never consider such precedents as binding, but he should always pay particular attention to the ready-made market which exists in such publications.

12.4　Patterns of usage

Under this heading we are grouping a number of established ways of buying press media which the student could observe by systematic reading. We are not suggesting that the practices described should be followed either slavishly, or indeed at all. Indeed, all of them have been broken with conspicuous success. Nevertheless they do tend to represent some consensus of opinion of how things should be done.

Firstly, it is common practice to think in terms of groups within press media as possible alternatives. For instance one may have a newspaper schedule, or one may have a magazine schedule. It is usually possible to find an acceptable reason for not mixing the two. Some would go even further and propose a daily newspaper schedule, or a Sunday newspaper schedule; a weekly magazine schedule, or a monthly magazine schedule. However, the use of the media model makes this difficult, unless one restricts the candidate list entirely to one particular type of vehicle.

There is some feeling that advertisements of a newsy nature look best in newspapers and clearly this is valid in so far as the combination of copy dates and reading times may mean that news in a magazine will be several months old.

Days of insertion are sometimes related to different classes of goods. In the case of newspapers, convenience goods, for example, are often advertised only in the daily newspapers on the theory that the advertisement should appear close to the time of purchase. This has a strong bearing on the fatness of Thursday and Friday newspapers compared with the rest of the week. Mail order advertisements appear largely on Saturdays and Sundays with the exception of the advertisements for department stores, particularly those concerned with fashion (usually seen on Mondays). On the other hand, Sunday is thought to be a particularly suitable day for selling consumer durables. The theory is that the purchase can then be discussed by the husband and wife who are available to look at the advertisement together.

12.5　Main divisions of press media

12.5.1　The nationals

This term is generally understood to mean the group of daily and Sunday newspapers published in London, plus the *Guardian.* They vary enormously each from the other, in terms of circulation, influence and content. Their dependence on advertising as a source of revenue also varies considerably, as does their economic viability; a subject media planners have sometimes been taxed with.

Daily Mirror and Sunday Mirror   The *Daily Mirror* and *Sunday Mirror* are owned by Mirror Group Newspapers and are similar in format, editorial style and readership. They both sell around 4 million copies each publishing day, and are successful. Not long ago, however, the figure was 5 million, and the trend gives rise to concern amongst advertisers, as well as the proprietors. They are both fundamentally tender-minded psychologically and left-wing in politics, are designed to be easy to read and have pictures which are designed to be easy to look at. Their readership is three quarters C2DE, less strongly biased towards the young, and towards the southern half of the country (both have companion newspapers published in Scotland). Rate structures are highly competitive with other newspapers, and the chief competitor of the *Sunday Mirror* is usually the *Daily Mirror.* Because of their high duplication, it is not common to see them both on the same schedule.

Daily Express and Sunday Express   The *Daily Express* and *Sunday Express* are far less alike than the *Daily Mirror* and *Sunday Mirror.* They share format, a circulation around 3 million (Daily less, Sunday more) and a strong right-wing political bias, but in other respects their editorial and readership is markedly different. As was noted at the beginning of this chapter, the readership of the *Daily Express* is drawn very evenly from all parts of the community. That of the *Sunday Express* is markedly skewed up-market. Of the adult readership of the *Daily Express,* 27 per cent comes from the DE group, compared with 15 per cent in the ABs. For the *Sunday Express* the figures are 19 per cent in the DEs and 23 per cent in the ABs.

In advertising terms the *Daily Express* has been in the forefront of a number of new developments, particularly that of colour. The half page on page 3 (a favourite position in itself for many advertisers) has often been used to considerable effect with a second colour over-printed. The paper has also carried a very large volume of pre-printed gravure colour—both wallpaper and in register form.

The *Sunday Express* is often criticised for the volume and make-up of the advertising in its pages, although this fact does not seem to stop advertisers trying to get in. In fact, the volume of advertising it carries is substantially lower than those of the three 'quality' Sundays, but their solid consecutive pages of classified advertising do not seem to be counted as such by the average consumer. The *Sunday Express* has a particular reputation as being successful with fashion advertising, and having a considerable effect on department store buyers.

The Times and the *Sunday Times*   The grouping of *The Times* and the *Sunday Times* may sound like sacrilege to some, but it is convenient since they are now in the same ownership. Although they both draw their readership primarily from the upper end of the socio-economic strata, they have little else in common.

The Times was established in 1785 and was run for many years by powerful families who established it as, perhaps, the most influential newspaper in the world. Even today it is read internationally, especially by politicians and journal-

ists. It is credited with having had a very considerable influence on British politics over the years.

It did not derive this influence from its circulation, which for many years was
of the order of a quarter of a million. After its acquisition by the Thomson
Organisation it rose to the 400,000 mark, and is now selling about 300,000. Its
influence is probably mainly derived still from a small fraction of this number. It
is considered a particularly important vehicle for placing an advertising message
before members of Parliament and the Civil Service and, to a lesser extent, the
heads of big business. The combination of its coverage and its cost-per-thousand
mean that one needs some special reason for including it on a schedule.

The *Sunday Times* is also relatively old-established, dating back to 1822, and
was for a number of years the proudest possession of Lord Kemsley, who sold it
to Lord Thomson (or Roy Thomson, as he then was) in 1959. Since then its circulation has almost doubled, and is running at nearly a million and a half copies
every Sunday. One of the chief reasons for this spectacular growth was the introduction of the colour magazine, which now has several imitators.

The readership of the *Sunday Times* is a prime target for many advertisers of
high-priced consumer and luxury goods. Its 31 per cent coverage of the AB
group is the highest of the quality papers, and the ability to use colour in the
magazine is an added attraction. Its right-wing stance has been equated by some
with materialism, with the suggestion that the readership is both rich and acqui-
sitive—an ideal combination from the advertisers' point of view. A further important development in the history of the *Sunday Times* has been the introduction of the *Business News Section*. Its quality of editorial has made it compul-
sory reading for the majority of businessmen and correspondingly an extremely
good medium for reaching them with advertising.

Daily Telegraph and Sunday Telegraph   The *Daily Telegraph* sells nearly twice
as many copies as the *Sunday Telegraph*—but then it had over a hundred years
start. The *Sunday Telegraph* is in fact the newest of the national newspapers, being launched in 1961 (this does not count re-vamps like the *Sun*). The *Daily
Telegraph* had for years a very strong appeal to the successful conservative family living predominantly in the South East. Whilst it attracted general advertising
likely to appeal to this group, it has had a tremendous strength in the area of
appointments advertising; indeed, it has been the first choice in many campaigns
aimed at recruiting managers.

For a long time the proprietors watched the ever increasing success of the
Sunday Times and *Observer* and finally decided that here was a growth market
that they should be in. The *Sunday Telegraph*, when it appeared, looked remarkably like the *Daily Telegraph*. The basic appeal on which it was launched was
that it was all in one piece, instead of sectionalised, as by now the *Observer* and
Sunday Times had become.

Once the *Sunday Times Colour Magazine* had become established it was clear
that the *Observer* and *Daily Telegraph* were likely to follow suit. In fact the
magazines appeared within a few weeks of each other, and the only surprising
thing as far as the industry was concerned was that the *Daily Telegraph* chose to
couple its colour magazine with the *Daily Telegraph* rather than with the *Sunday
Telegraph*. By publishing on Friday and calling the magazine the *Weekend Telegraph*, it may have been hoped to make a better bridge between the circulations

of the two newspapers. The *Magazine* was transferred to the *Sunday Telegraph* in the autumn of 1976.

Observer   Although it is under different ownership and sells over twice as many copies, the editorial of the *Observer* is closest to that of the *Guardian*. The second oldest of the nationals, being established in 1791, its management has been sufficiently forward-looking to enable it to survive without the benefit of a profitable sister paper, even in the economic jungle of present-day Fleet Street. Although it has come very near to the altar on a number of occasions in recent years, it now looks as though it will remain on its own, at least for the foreseeable future.

While its financial position hardly allows it to innovate, it has very successfully plagiarised the more successful introductions of other newspapers, particularly the *Sunday Times*, whose profile it closely matches.

Guardian   This is the only paper called National that originated outside London, although it is printed there (as well as in Manchester where it started in 1821). Its combination of a strong Liberal tradition and editorial which makes uncompromising demands on its readers' intelligence, may explain the reason for the circulation (just over 300,000) growing more slowly than some of its competitors. It may also lead to the educational profile of the *Guardian* being the highest of any national. Although the socio-economic profile of *Guardian* readers qualifies the paper for inclusion on luxury goods schedules, there are undoubtedly some advertisers who are deterred by the 'other world' image which *Guardian* readers tend to have.

Financial Times   The *Financial Times* is unique not only because it it printed on pink paper. With a circulation of only 175,000 (although this has grown rapidly in recent years) it is able to claim the top coverage of any newspaper amongst senior company officials, and in the City of London. A very carefully integrated advertising and editorial policy over the years has made it paramount as a medium for reaching industry. Even the recent successes of the Business News sections have not harmed its position.

It should not be overlooked that in addition to providing the widest coverage of financial, industrial and business news, it also has very good general news and feature columns. In spite of this fact it has few solus readers.

News of the World   The *News of the World* is, by a comfortable margin, the largest selling publication in this country. Although it suffered a long period of decline from its top circulation figure of about 8 million just after the war, it still sells 5 million today. This massive circulation naturally gives it a dominating position in the coverage of many target groups. Although its bias is down market, and towards men, it nevertheless covers more ABs than *The Times*, and more housewives than *Woman*.

Since its acquisition by Rupert Murdoch, the editional content has not undergone any fundamental change. Its traditional emphasis on items with a sexual flavour seems hardly remarkarkable today, but has in the past deterred some advertisers from taking space in the paper.

Sun   This has been the success story of Fleet Street in recent years. Acquired by Rupert Murdoch from IPC in 1969, almost as a favour, the paper was then selling just over 1 million copies daily.

Great vigour has been applied to all aspects of the paper's activities, and the brash style of editorial and promotion has brought some measure of criticism. It has also brought large circulation and advertising gains, and a strong threat to the *Daily Mirror*'s lead position. The appeal has been particularly strong to younger adults, and its coverage of 15-34s is already the highest of the national dailies.

Sunday People   Although the *Sunday People* is published by the International Publishing Corporation, it is very difficult to distinguish, in terms of editorial content, from the *News of the World*. Indeed these two newspapers are undoubtedly the most similar of any pair of Sundays. Although its circulation is between ½ and ¾ million behind that of the *News of the World*, it still provides massive coverage and its readership is slightly less down-market.

Daily Mail   Most regularly tipped for extinction, the *Daily Mail*, now selling about 1.7 million copies a day, looks remarkably vigorous. Its adoption of a tabloid format certainly did it no harm, and it appears to tread its tightrope of 'quality popular' quite firmly.

Whatever fortune may hold for it, newspaper publishing is not dictated purely by business economics and there is no question that the newspaper will continue to be published as long as the proprietors consider that it should.

12.5.2   Regional newspapers

With the honourable exception of the *Guardian,* newspapers originating outside the metropolis are classified as regional and primarily, of course, because they do not circulate nationally. The largest of them, the *Sunday Post,* has a circulation approaching 1½ million. The smallest weeklies have circulations in four figures. As they encompass evening and morning newspapers, in addition to Sundays and weeklies, it is clear that their range is extensive.

Nonetheless, from the point of view of the media planner, it is not unfair to group them together according to their time of publication.

Mornings   There are 18 morning papers published in England, Wales, Scotland and Northern Ireland, outside London, the great majority of them published as stable-mates to evening newspapers. The *Daily Record,* which is published in Glasgow, is a companion paper to the *Daily Mirror* and in fact in Scotland is quasi-national. The majority of the remainder are strongly oriented towards the businessmen in the communities they serve.

This fact is reflected in the relative weakness of *The Times* and *Financial Times* outside the South East. Schedules designed to reach businessmen on a national basis are likely to include a number of regional mornings.

Evenings   There are two evening newspapers published in London and 74 in the rest of the UK. The London evenings have long been treated, for instance in the National Readership Survey, as on a par with the national mornings, but this is to misunderstand their position.

The impression of their national distribution is fostered, for the traveller from London, by the fact that they are usually available at mainline railway bookstalls throughout the country. Nevertheless the vast bulk of their sales is concentrated in the Greater London area and of their readership in the London television area. To the media planner their great attraction is for local advertising, even though the locality concerned may be a very big one. One important difference between the London evening and the remainder, is that their coverage of the area they serve is very much lower. Taking only the greater London conurbation, the penetration amongst all adults of the *Evening News* is 25 per cent and of the *Evening Standard* 18 per cent. Many provincial evenings attain coverage of the order of 80 per cent and several reach virtually saturation figures.

The publishing of these 76 papers is concentrated in 74 of our larger cities and towns, and the circulation areas extend perhaps 30 miles around them. Because of their high penetration in a concentrated area, the readership profiles obviously conform closely to the population profiles. The *Belfast Telegraph* is perhaps a special case in that it is the largest selling newspaper in Northern Ireland, and is often used to supplement national morning schedules for this reason.

Evening newspapers are often used on mass consumer schedules where regional weight needs to be given for one reason or another. This may simply be a matter of distribution of money across the country; it may be a matter of supporting special sales drives in a particular area; perhaps of increasing or specially supporting a number of stockists; or making a special offer or some other kind of promotion which is localised to one area of the country. The reason that regional evenings (and regional newspapers in general) are not used for the majority of consumer campaigns is that the cost-per-thousand they offer is very much higher than that which can be obtained in the national dailies. Special justification is, therefore, necessary for their inclusion.

For a long time, especially after the establishment of the Evening Newspaper Advertising Bureau Limited, it was argued that the special affinity that these newspapers had with their readers made advertisements in them proportionately more valuable. However, no one ever succeeded in putting a cash value on this affinity. Although the proportion of national advertising is small (while increasing) the monopoly position they enjoy, and their undoubted value for local business, makes them very profitable.

Sundays   The largest selling newspaper published outside London, the *Sunday Post,* we have already mentioned. It provides a very even coverage of the Scottish market, reaching an almost incredible four out of five adults. It also has a readership of over a million outside Scotland, mostly in the North East and North. For this reason it tends to over-shadow the *Sunday Mail,* also published in Glasgow, which is the Scottish counterpart of the *Sunday Mirror,* or the Sunday counterpart of the *Daily Record.* This sells over ¾ million copies every Sunday and is read by over half of the adults in Scotland.

After this we have the *Sunday Sun* in Newcastle and the *Sunday Mercury* in Birmingham, each selling around ¼ million copies; the *Independent* in Plymouth and the *Sunday News* in Belfast, selling around 50,000, and the *Island Sun* in the Channel Islands, which does not provide an audited figure. The *Sunday Mercury* and the *Sunday Sun* were both started just after the First World War and have been quite successful. Nevertheless, with the blanket coverage afforded by the national Sundays, it is often difficult for the media planner to justify their inclusion, except for reasons specifically concerned with the areas of their circulation.

Weeklies   There are about 1200 weekly newspapers published in the United Kingdom and almost every community has one; few have two, but the circulation areas of adjacent publications often overlap. They tend to be strongest where other newspapers are weakest and, of course, provide almost the sole source of local news in many rural areas. If it is necessary to give blanket coverage to a particular part of the country, it is often done by using the evenings as far as possible and filling in the gaps with local weeklies.

This is about the only time that a national advertiser will approach them with any enthusiasm, since the cost-per-thousand problem, mentioned in relation to the regional dailies, is even more acute in the case of the weeklies. Additional problems concern lack of information on circulations and circulation areas; the variety of formats, make-ups and qualities of reproduction; and the frequent difficulty of arousing interest in national advertising amongst local managements.

Some years ago the Weekly Newspapers Advertising Bureau was started in an attempt to overcome some of these problems. The task of getting so many independent managements to move together with cohesion has always been a difficult one. It has also been established that the interests of the weekly newspapers can better be developed in other areas than national advertising.

12.5.3   Consumer magazines

For convenience we will divide consumer magazines into five groups—women's weeklies, women's monthlies, general weeklies, general monthlies and special publications. The first two groups are reasonably cohesive and self-descriptive; the others less so.

Women's weeklies   Four large women's weeklies, which form an extremely important media group, happen all to be in the ownership of the International Publishing Corporation. They have been organised in such a way that they may be bought as a group. No one quite knows why they appeal less to women than they used to, but the four titles were seven, and the circulation of *Woman, Woman's Own* and *Woman's Realm* have all declined quite sharply in recent years. The fourth, *Woman's Weekly,* has held up well.

It is very difficult, both for the publishers and for the readers, to distinguish between *Woman* and *Woman's Own* in meaningful terms; but there is a distinction. There used to be a marked distinction in circulation terms, but today each sells just under 1.5 million copies. In general they appeal to the woman as a woman, catering broadly for her concern with fashion, beauty, health and home; looking after her leisure with a considerable amount of fiction, astrology, readers' letters, problem pages, etc. The colour content, and the quality of reproduction, has increased dramatically in recent years and the number of pages the reader is offered has also increased steadily. ·

Woman's Realm does set out to cater more specifically for the housewife (although the resulting profile difference is marginal). It has a slightly smaller format than *Woman* and *Woman's Own* and sells about 800,000 copies, making it the fifth largest in the group.

It is easy to see the difference between *Woman's Weekly* and the other three. Its appeal is very specifically towards the more conservative, quieter, inward looking women, so much so that it did not even appear in colour for many years after its competitors. One of the considerable editorial achievements of IPC has been effecting the change to colour without losing the quality of the editorial. In fact its circulation has climbed steadily in recent years and it is now selling just under 1.7 million copies. There may be some clue here to the general trend of decline in the mass-selling weeklies. At one point in time it was felt that the only possible recipe for success was to produce magazines that were ahead of the latest trends in fashions and morals. It is possible that the number of readers seeking these qualities is limited, and smaller than was thought.

Support for this view may come from the fastest growing property in the women's weekly field, *My Weekly*. No one would apply a charge of being ahead of trends to this publication, but it has grown rapidly to approximately 870,000 copies, and has displaced *Woman's Realm* from fourth place. Whilst the readership of *My Weekly* is fairly evenly spread by age, class and region, that of its sister publication, *People's Friend*, is strongly biased towards Scotland and (although less so) to older women and lower socio-economic grades. Nevertheless, with a circulation approaching three-quarters of a million, it should be considered when women's weeklies are being used.

The women's weeklies as a whole usually represent the most severe challenge to television for the vast range of consumer goods bought by the housewife. IPC is also very concerned at giving the same quality of merchandising and research support which the contractors have long offered, and their efforts have succeeded in winning away from television significant advertising appropriations.

Women's monthlies   The National Readership Survey lists over 20 magazines under the heading of Women's Monthlies. Some of them tend to cover the same general range of women's interests as do the weeklies (for instance *She*) but many of them are quite specialised. Some of them have quite a high male readership. The 'home' publications, *Ideal Home, Homes & Gardens* and *House & Garden,* each have men for about one-third of their readers, and so does *Home & Freezer Digest.*

The size of the magazines covered by the National Readership Survey range in circulation terms from *Family Circle,* selling over 800,000 copies a month, to *Harper's and Queen,* selling just over 50,000. In terms of readership the range goes from a little over four million for *Family Circle,* down to less than 400,000 for *My Story.* A characteristic of the group is the discrepancy between readership and circulation. Each copy of *Vogue,* for instance, is read (within the NRS definition) by at least 18 people, whilst the figure for *Home & Freezer Digest* is less than three. This inevitably means that the readership figures have to be viewed (and hopefully used) with some circumspection. The widespread scepticism about them amongst media buyers received a severe jolt when Dr William Belson produced his famous study some years ago, which showed that readership of the monthly magazine tended on the whole to be under-estimated, rather than over-estimated. Clearly, the sheer permanence of their format means that they do lead a long life, and especially with those which are commonly used in waiting rooms, have a very high chance of exposure.

The fact that some are seen in public places and some are not does not wholly explain the discrepancies. Indeed some appear to be inexplicable. It seems quite credible though, that a publication like *Family Circle,* which is very specifically designed for the self-education of young housewives, should be retained for reference, rather than passed to anybody else.

In considering these readerships, the planner has to ask himself three questions. Firstly, is the format such that his advertisement stands a reasonably equal chance of being seen by 'flippers' and by thorough readers? Secondly, is the demographic profile of the total readership such that the editorial is likely to be directly meaningful to the sixth, twelfth or eighteenth reader? Thirdly, is his message of a kind which can stand being delayed by perhaps five months before the full value of the readership is accumulated?

It must be confessed that if he does not answer 'yes' to these questions, then he has a problem. To omit the publication altogether from the candidate media list is probably to under-rate it. On the other hand, to include it implies weighting the readership in some way, and this is frequently very difficult. It would clearly be easy to introduce subjective weights for the purchaser of the publication, for secondary readers within the household, for tertiary readers, and so on, if we had any way of knowing which of the readers they were. As it is, many planners will rely on other demographic weightings in the definition of the target audience, to single out those readers of the publication who are most likely to be, if not its primary readers, at least those most interested in his advertising in it.

One check on the value of the NRS readership figures is provided by direct response advertisers. *Ideal Home,* for example, which has an excellent pulling record, has over ten readers per copy. It may be, of course, that its pulling power is purely derived from the fact that when people are in the market for consumer durables they will tend to look at publications like *Ideal Home* as catalogues. However, to most advertisers it really matters little what the interaction of these two factors may be, provided that they get their results.

General weeklies   Many of the publications listed in the NRS under this heading are far from general. We shall consider two important groups here and deal with the remainder under the specialist heading. Firstly, there are the programme publications: the *TV Times* and the *Radio Times,* the first covering Independent Television programmes and selling about 3¼ million copies, and the second those of the BBC selling a little over 3½ million copies. In addition to the actual programme information, each carries a certain amount of general editorial. Each is read by over a quarter of the adults in the country, and each has a fairly even spread in terms of age and region.

The *Radio Times,* however, tends to be strongest in the South, and the *TV Times* in the North. The class differences are larger. Whilst the *TV Times* is almost classless, the *Radio Times* is strongly biased up-market, covering 42 per cent of As, but only 17 per cent of Es.

The second group consists of the four publications, *Reveille, Weekend, Weekly News* and *Tit-Bits.* All four are more popular with the younger age groups than the old, although the difference is very marked in the case of *Weekend* and marginal in the case of *Weekly News.* They are also strongly biased down market and have a fairly even regional profile, except in the case of the *Weekly News,* which has almost a third of its readers in Scotland, and relatively few in the southern half of the country.

General monthlies   Most monthlies listed under this heading in the NRS are 'general' only in the sense that they are not 'women's', The most important of these will be discussed under Specialist publications.

The outstanding exception is *Reader's Digest,* the British edition of a world-wide giant, selling in this country some 1.5 million copies per issue, with a readership of about 8.5 million. It is a publication about which it is difficult to be neutral; as a business it is (with its many spin-offs) highly successful. The peculiar editorial flavour (once described as comprising articles with titles like 'My Dog Taught Me To Pray') is not universally admired. The fairly even age and regional profiles of the readers, combined with its substantial up-market bias, and low cost-per-thousand, ensure its appearance on a large number of computer-optimised schedules. Its unusually small format presents a challenge to creative departments, and one which they are often anxious to decline. For all these reasons, the *Digest* tends to be heavily supported by those most concerned with value for money, the direct response advertisers. The publication has pioneered the use of reply-paid postcards and detachable gate-folds, and these have, on occasion, drawn very large numbers of replies at a very low cost.

Specialist publications   British Rate & Data lists some 40 classifications of different interests, but we shall deal here only with eight. These eight probably account for at least three-quarters of the total advertising expenditure.

1   FASHION AND BEAUTY   Although most of the magazines we shall be discussing under this heading have already been included in previous categories, and a number have been commented on, there is some point in discussing them as a group. Clearly much advertising money for fashion and beauty will be spent outside these publications – in the big women's weeklies and on television.

It is perhaps ironic that the titles should themselves be subject to the whims of fashion to no small extent. With the increasing pace of change in fashion trends, and the recent domination of the fashion scene by young people, the publishers have been hard put to it to keep up and have not, in every case, succeeded.

Whilst there is a lot or room for argument at the margins as to which publications should be included and which should be excluded from such a list, the brand leader is, without doubt, *Vogue.* Although subject to many challenges in recent years, and comfortably out-sold by many of its competitors, it maintains a handsome lead in the readership stakes, probably both amongst consumers and retailers. These figures appear to combine with the momentum gathered in over 50 years of publishing to make *Vogue* almost impossible to omit from a campaign in this area. Next in order of readership comes *Nineteen,* a monthly publication from IPC, the readership of which we have previously discussed. It is closely followed by its older and more fragile stable mate, *Honey,* which cannibalised *Vanity Fair. Over 21, Harper's* and *Queen,* attract a good deal of advertising support in this area, without really being specialised editorially, but then so do *She* and *Cosmopolitan.*

2   DO-IT-YOURSELF   In spite of social and economic trends, it is surprising that this sector is so much less healthy than it was twenty years ago. The market for publications covering it has not been sufficient to sustain all the titles which have been launched. Nevertheless it is large, different and fairly compact. The relative readerships of the three main publications have been somewhat questioned, owing to the brilliance of Link House Publications in adopting the title *Do-It-Yourself* for their own magazine. This is shown as having some 400,000 more readers than *Practical Householder,* although selling some 13,000 copies fewer.

Homemaker, whilst undoubtedly the smallest of the three, compares very unfavourably, with just over half the number of readers per copy attributed to *Do-It-Yourself.* In terms of selection these differences are probably unimportant, since many advertisers will go in the three magazines as a group. Nevertheless, the differences clearly have a bearing on the advertisements rates that can be charged.

3   HOME INTERESTS   There are three publications with a strong reputation as media for the advertising of consumer durables, furniture and furnishing. They are *Ideal Home, Homes & Gardens* and *House & Garden.* The first two publications have maintained circulations above 150,000, although only with a great deal of cannibalisation. Their reputation today must be based primarily on their titles, since the composition of their editorial is very similar to that of other monthly magazines, although their advertising pages tend to be far more specialised. *House & Garden* is a smaller publication, selling about 115,000 copies a month, but on the upward trend. All the magazines have readerships with a fairly even age and regional distribution, but are markedly up-market.

Outside these three there is a wide variety of choice, including *Good Housekeeping,* which swallowed *House Beautiful,* lately a fourth specialist publication. As its title implies, *Good Housekeeping* has a long and very successful reputation for concern with running the home, rather than establishing it.

4   HUMOUR   This classification is clearly different from others in the sense that hardly anyone is advertising products which are intended to have a humorous appeal.

Punch, in fact, lists itself as a general weekly and a lot of the writing in it is undoubtedly serious. On the other hand, it has a tradition of more than 125 years of offering cartoons and humorous articles, and it is known internationally for this. Its circulation has fallen to around 60,000 (UK) but a high readers-per-copy figure gives a total readership in excess of a million.

Advertisers who have not been mentioned in its pages may enjoy reading *Private Eye.* They are normally shyer of having their products featured in it. There have often been doubts as to whether publication could continue past the next libel action. These have led to distribution, and therefore circulation, difficulties. Nevertheless, the NBRS, July 1976, showed 30,000 'businessmen' readers, and for the brave media planner, with a brave client, it represents an economical way of reaching a desirable audience.

5   MEN'S MAGAZINES   The media planner wishing to reach a female audience with economical cover is embarrassed by choice. The planner with a male

audience has to struggle. Although there are a variety of media available, the great majority are bi-sexual and it is only a small section which caters predominantly for men.

Even in this permissive age, many advertisers regret that the only way of establishing a magazine as being directed at men, is to fill it with near-pornography. This fact also makes it extremely difficult to get accurate readership information. *Men Only* is a pre-war title, although the current magazine is absolutely nothing like the pre-war version, but age seems to have given it sufficient respectability for men to admit to reading it. The readers per copy figure of less than 4.5 for *Mayfair* and *Penthouse* seems very unlikely to be accurate.

New entrants are frequent in this field, and many succeed in business terms. Mostly they come from specialist publishing houses. IPC entered the area with *Club,* but was not successful; the magazine, sold to Paul Raymond and re-named *Club International,* is currently selling over 300,000 copies per month,although almost half of these are overseas.

6   MOTORING   One of the puzzling aspects of the media scene has been the way in which the growth in the ownership of private cars has been in no way paralleled by a corresponding upsurge in publications covering the subject. It is true that most motorists are not motoring enthusiasts, and that general media do give wide coverage of motoring matters. Nevertheless, when men congregate, motoring is a popular subject of conversation, and one would have thought there was a need.

It was hoped that *Drive* might satisfy that need. Started as a quarterly, published by *Reader's Digest* in association with the Automobile Association and issued free to members of the AA, it has now become a bi-monthly on general sale. It is clear that these changes will affect it considerably, but it is not yet clear what the end result will be.

After *Drive* comes a long list of publications which are really catering for the enthusiastic driver or car owner. They include *Practical Motorist, Car Mechanics, Motor Sport, Popular Motoring, Hot Car* and *Car and Car Conversions,* all of which are covered by the NRS and have readerships varying between 750,000 and 2 million. *Motor* and *Autocar,* respected names from the past, continue, and there are many others, some with ABC figures around the 100,000 mark. Unfortunately, many do not have either readership or audited circulation figures, which makes their value very difficult to assess.

In general it may be said that the magazines cover three separate categories: those who are interested in owning motor cars, those who are interested in maintaining motor cars and those who are interested in racing motor cars. It is important to establish the precise category which the advertiser wishes to reach before approaching the preparation of a schedule.

7   TEENAGE AND POP   This is another area with very blurred edges. The advertiser who wishes to reach a mass youth market through the press will find that a preponderance of the publications lean heavily towards young women, as distinct from young men, and that the pop publications, although substantially biased towards the younger market, do attract readers from other age groups. *Jackie,* published weekly by D.C. Thomson, is the most solid title, having maintained a sale of around 600,000 for many years. Other titles have been very

volatile in circulation, and many have been withdrawn.

Of the specialist publications, two weeklies, *New Musical Express* and *Melody Maker,* have readerships well over the million mark, primarily drawn from the 15-24 age group. The monthly *Film Review,* with more than three-quarters of a million, and the other weekly, *Sounds,* with over half a million, have similar profiles as far as age is concerned, although the first two named are slightly more up-market.

8   CONTROLLED CIRCULATION PUBLICATIONS   The maintenance of a publication purely by sales of advertising, without in any way relying on cover price, is not a new conception. Recent years have shown a very marked increase in its use. The criticism often levelled, that the audience will pay less attention to a medium for which they have not paid money, is countered by those who would say that if the editorial is good enough the readers will read it. They are able to point to Commercial Television in support of their argument.

By far the largest and most important controlled circulation consumer publication is *Shopping,* distributed three times a year to about 10 million homes in Great Britain. Space is purchased by television areas. Most advertisers are either offering cut-out cash coupons to tie in with merchandising schemes, or the introduction of new brands, or alternatively are soliciting direct response in terms of coupon offers of some sort.

One of the most rapid growth areas is that of local weekly newspapers, distributed on a house-to-house basis. It is argued that the primary reason for the purchase of local weekly newspapers is very often the advertising content, and, therefore, the free sheet should have comparable reading interest. Whether or not this is true, there is no doubt that the ones that have been published so far have attracted sufficient support from advertisers to enable them, in many cases, to expand into adjoining areas.

12.6   Related reading

Newspaper Press Directory, Benn Brothers (Annually).

13 Television

The television medium presents a challenge to both media planners and buyers, principally because the audience research provided by the industry insists that it should. The cost per thousand (homes, adults, housewives, etc.) is published weekly for each commercial slot, and, for 7.29 on Tuesday in London will vary considerably by week of the year; if the Thames programme changes; if the BBC1 or 2 programme changes; and often if there are no changes. Every time the audience is shown to be less than expected, and the cost per thousand there- fore greater, trouble will ensue for the agency and contractor. Since this is likely to happen at least 50 per cent of the time, there is scope for a lot of trouble.

As if this were not enough, other pieces of industry research, concerning levels of attention, the definition of area boundaries and the nature of viewing patterns in the overlap areas, for example, provide topics for disagreement. Pre- diction of rating performance is not easy for well-known-programmes; it is more difficult for new, and especially one-off shows; and even titles are often not known well in advance of transmission. Finally, TV rate cards tend to be ex- tremely complex, and to change frequently not only in level, but in format. For- tunately, there are important simplifications compared with Press: only twelve salesmen to see, and the fact that the most difficult audiences are best reached by the highest rated programmes.

Organisationally, television contractors run, in thirteen areas of the country, monopolies awarded and controlled by the Independent Broadcasting Authority, which is itself responsible to Parliament. In the fourteenth, London, two con- tractors share the contract. Thames Television operates from Monday to 7 pm on Friday, and London Weekend Television maintains the service from 7 pm on Friday to Sunday. The areas of reception, as can be seen from the map (Figure 13.1), derive from the physical location of the television transmitters and the limit of signal strength or the presence of natural barriers, such as mountains. For this reason they are roughly comparable in terms of area, but as Table 13.1 (data by courtesy of AGB Limited) shows are very different in terms of mar- keting opportunity. The pattern which exists at the moment was laid down to operate from 30 July 1968, and to run for six years. Any reorganisation would depend on Governmental action following the report of the Annan Committee.

Plate Section

Space Units

Run-of-paper spaces.

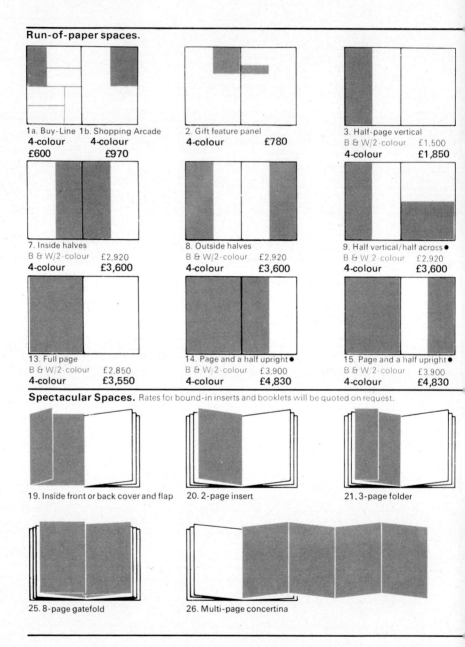

1a. Buy-Line 1b. Shopping Arcade
4-colour **4-colour**
£600 **£970**

2. Gift feature panel
4-colour **£780**

3. Half-page vertical
B & W/2-colour £1,500
4-colour **£1,850**

7. Inside halves
B & W/2-colour £2,920
4-colour **£3,600**

8. Outside halves
B & W/2-colour £2,920
4-colour **£3,600**

9. Half vertical/half across ●
B & W/2-colour £2,920
4-colour **£3,600**

13. Full page
B & W/2-colour £2,850
4-colour **£3,550**

14. Page and a half upright ●
B & W/2-colour £3,900
4-colour **£4,830**

15. Page and a half upright ●
B & W/2-colour £3,900
4-colour **£4,830**

Spectacular Spaces. Rates for bound-in inserts and booklets will be quoted on request.

19. Inside front or back cover and flap

20. 2-page insert

21. 3-page folder

25. 8-page gatefold

26. Multi-page concertina

In addition to regular run-of-paper space units, Reader's Digest offers advertisers exciting creative opportunities with a wide range of spaces.

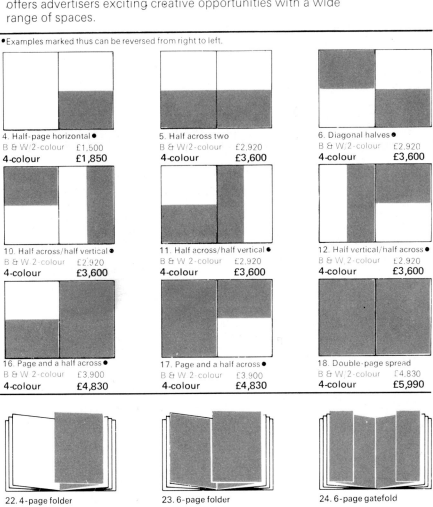

4. Half-page horizontal ●
B & W/2-colour   £1,500
4-colour   **£1,850**

5. Half across two
B & W/2-colour   £2,920
4-colour   **£3,600**

6. Diagonal halves ●
B & W/2-colour   £2,920
4-colour   **£3,600**

10. Half across/half vertical ●
B & W 2-colour   £2,920
4-colour   **£3,600**

11. Half across/half vertical ●
B & W/2-colour   £2,920
4-colour   **£3,600**

12. Half vertical/half across ●
B & W 2-colour   £2,920
4-colour   **£3,600**

16. Page and a half across ●
B & W 2-colour   £3,900
4-colour   **£4,830**

17. Page and a half across ●
B & W 2-colour   £3,900
4-colour   **£4,830**

18. Double-page spread
B & W/2-colour   £4,830
4-colour   **£5,990**

22. 4-page folder

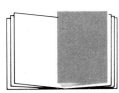

23. 6-page folder

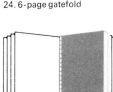

24. 6-page gatefold

27. Multi-page section

28. Reverse-bound booklet

29. Bracket-stripped booklet

A large gin and tonic.

Schweppes

Plate 2

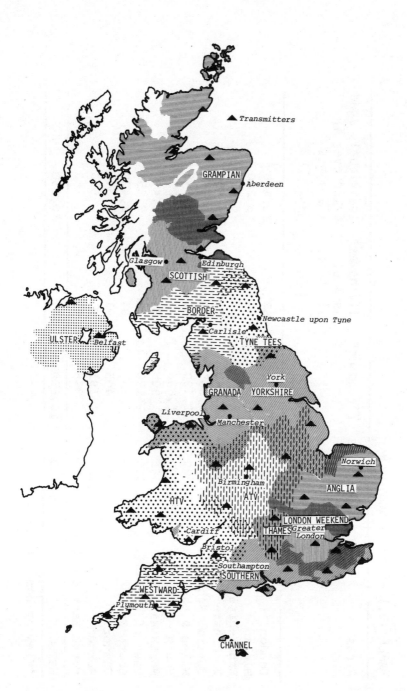

▲ Transmitters

GRAMPIAN
• Aberdeen

Glasgow • SCOTTISH • Edinburgh

BORDER

ULSTER • Belfast

• Carlisle
Newcastle upon Tyne

TYNE TEES

Liverpool • GRANADA • York
YORKSHIRE
Manchester

Norwich

Birmingham ATV ANGLIA

ATV

LONDON WEEKEND
Cardiff • THAMES • Greater London

Bristol •

Southampton
WESTWARD SOUTHERN

Plymouth

CHANNEL

TABLE 13.1 The ITV audience

Areas	All homes 000s	ITV homes* 000s	ITV homes* as % of all homes	Individuals aged 4 and over in ITV homes 000s
London	5,070	4,390	87	11,460
Midlands	3,530	3,060	87	8,280
Lancashire	2,900	2,570	89	6,920
Yorkshire	2,530	2,040	81	5,450
Central Scotland	1,375	1,265	92	3,655
Wales & the West	1,685	1,420	84	3,845
South	2,080	1,600	77	4,220
North East	965	925	96	2,490
East of England	1,530	1,190	78	3,253
South West	640	537	84	1,420
Ulster	443	405	91	1,345
Border	211	191	91	515
North East Scotland	423	348	82	960
NETWORK	19,350	18,680	97	50,250

*Viewing home transmitter

The anomaly of television taking less advertising revenue than the press, whilst accounting for between 70 per cent and 80 per cent of the billing of the largest advertising agencies, is not difficult to explain. The largest advertising budgets are devoted to the sale of mass convenience products. These appropriations are concentrated in the larger agencies, and for these products television is seen to have the greatest advantages over alternative media. Many media planners would consider that television's identification with convenience goods in this country under-estimates the breadth of its potential. Certainly in America it has been used with tremendous success to sell capital goods to businessmen. One of the best known examples of this has been the success of the Xerox Corporation. The popularity of Xerox shares, although undoubtedly attributable mainly to the profit growth record, may have been influenced by the rub-off of the television advertising on the general investor.

13.1 Rates

Television is sold in spots which are intervals of time of seven or fifteen seconds, or multiples of fifteen seconds. Nearly two-thirds of spots transmitted are in the 30-second category, and about one-quarter in the 15-second. The cost of any commercial length varies primarily according to the time and day of week when it is scheduled to be transmitted. Rate segments are classified broadly into peak and off-peak. The peak time band is normally the longest, as well as the most expensive on the rate card, and over the course of years it has been adjusted to be the period where the demand is heaviest. The fact that the size of the audience within the peak segment may vary by 100 per cent from one break to another, and for the same time by a similar amount from one week to another, gives television buying all its excitement. Although the broad general shape of the audience pattern is well established, these important fluctuations are based on the relative popularity of the competing programmes on BBC and ITV, and the skill of the buyer lies, therefore, in determining which juxtaposition is likely to be more favourable to him. His task is made considerably more difficult because it is frequently not known until shortly in advance of the programme what the programmes are actually going to be. Even when he knows this he may well not have seen the programme at all, or the particular episode in a series.

On either side of peak time there are a number of narrower bands at lower rates. Generally these produce smaller audiences at lower costs-per-thousand, but neither of these generalities may be true in a particular instance.

In addition to the price charged for a segment of air time, the advertiser can pay a surcharge, usually 15 per cent, in order to fix his commercial within a particular break in that segment. He can go even further and specify the actual position within the break (generally first or last commercial) and the further surcharge for this is 5 per cent.

There are a wide number of ways in which time may be bought more cheaply than at full rate-card prices. There is some variation from one contractor to another, and some variation within the same contractor over time, but the more important and generally applicable types of discounted spots are listed.

Pre-empt spots   The principle of pre-empting is fairly new to this country but has been popular in America for many years. Quite simply, the advertiser buys a spot in a particular segment at a discounted rate, the discount normally being of the order of 25 to 50 per cent. If, prior to transmission, another advertiser wishes to buy the same time at the full rate the pre-empt spot will be dropped. There are various types of option attached to pre-empt spots. Sometimes the spot is only pre-emptable up to a fixed period before transmission, of perhaps seven days; once this point has been passed the advertiser knows that he can no longer be pre-empted.

Guaranteed impressions   Under these schemes the advertiser does not buy specific breaks, but instead buys a guaranteed delivery of audience. The contractor will offer him a package of say, 2 million home impressions at a given cost-per-thousand, say 60p. The cost of this package would clearly be £1200. The contractor then transmits spots until the number of homes reached are shown by the TV ratings reports to have reached 2 million. Alternatively, the contractor may guarantee a level of ratings for the spot price. How good a bargain this is depends on a number of factors. Firstly, there is the relation between the guaranteed cost-per-thousand and that which could be achieved in ordinary spot buying. Secondly, there is the importance of the actual control of the times of transmission. GHI packages can sometimes run over a considerable period of time, or may be bunched in a way which the planner would not wish to bunch them. Thirdly, the planner is not trying to reach sets but people, and the composition of the audience in front of the set when GHIs are transmitted obviously varies. Since GHIs are normally offered in periods of low demand and low audience, the cost-per-thousand for the particular target group at which the advertising is being aimed may be considerably higher than the cost-per-thousand homes. Fourthly, the value obtained depends to a large extent on the skill of the programme contractor in anticipating his ratings. Where considerable care is not taken in the placing of the spots, it is possible to get a substantial over-run on the guaranteed delivery, thus substantially reducing the actual cost-per-thousand paid.

Run-of-week spots   With a run-of-week spot the contractor undertakes to transmit a given spot during a given week and usually between certain time limits, providing that the air time is available. The rate charged is suitably discounted to allow for all these uncertainties.

Support spots   These are usually similar to run-of-week spots with the exception that in order to qualify for them an advertiser must be booking a schedule of fully paid time running concurrently. Support spots provide a good opportunity for increasing frequency on a properly planned schedule, and at the same time reducing the over-all cost-per-thousand.

Local rates   If a retailer, say in Coventry, wishes to advertise on television, it is impossible for him not to advertise over the whole of the Midland region. At the same time it is clear that the bulk of his custom will come from the area around Coventry. In acknowledgement of this fact, the contractors usually offer to such retailers reductions on the rate card prices.

Short advertisements   A number of contractors offer the facility of running
several 7-second spots together as a package, the generic name of which used to
be 'Market Place'. These packages now run in breaks as time is available, and the
rate is usually a substantial discount on the standard 7-second rate.

Most contractors also offer the facility to transmit 5-second slides over which
the station announcer will read copy.

Seasonal rates   The television contractors over the years have endeared themselves to, and infuriated, advertisers alternately by their willingness to respond
to pressures of demand. This has meant a succession of price increases over the
years, but has also meant that when demand has fallen rate reductions have
followed quickly.

The regular manifestation of this fact has been the seasonal discounts usually
applying to the summer and immediate post-Christmas periods. The period, complexity and rates of discount vary from year to year and from contractor to contractor. In the summer the discounts are usually more than sufficient to compensate for the fall-off in viewing, whilst, of course, in the winter period there is no
fall-off in viewing, and time may be bought relatively cheaply.

Volume discounts   All the contractors offer volume discounts for total expenditure within a 52-week period. This is sometimes a calendar year, or sometimes
any period notified in advance. The discounts are quite substantial, usually going up to about 15 per cent but the structures are pitched so that there is not
usually more than one advertiser getting the top rate. Indeed, an advertiser has
to be a substantial user of television to get any volume discount.

13.2   Flexibility

The standard cancellation period for television time is eight weeks. The average
length of time for the production of a television commercial is about three
months. It is, however, not only possible, but happens, for a decision to be taken
on a particular morning to advertise on television, and for the advertisement to
appear that evening. The fact that television is the most flexible of all media
stems from the possibility of making an advertisement by sitting someone in
front of a camera and having him talk for 30 seconds. This is assisted by the contractors ability and willingness to agree to the transmission of advertisements of
this kind at very short notice.

The cancellation clause itself, although of average length in relation to other
media, is far less restrictive than those of most media. The reason for this is that,
subject to availability, the contractors will allow spots to be moved within the
eight-week period and usually from within to outside the eight-week period,
provided that the guarantee is given that the spots will not be subsequently cancelled. Contrary to this, however, is the considerable reluctance of contractors
to allow copy substitution. Many media, faced with a cancellation, would be
delighted to find any alternative to fill the gap. In television, it is not just a question of the same agency, nor yet the same client; allied, although different, products in the same product group from the same advertiser have been refused as
substitutes. To the advertiser, this is seen as a copy change, but the contractors

have claimed that, to them, it is unjustified loss of revenue.

Flexibility in geographical terms is reflected in the ability to purchase any one of the independent television regions separately, or in combination with any group of the others. The fact that the geographical boundaries of the transmitter cannot be changed to suit the advertiser's convenience has been of little importance in recent years, since the great majority of major advertisers have tailored their sales and marketing programmes to conform with the television boundaries or some reasonable approximation thereto.

13.3   Production

The range of times and costs for production is so wide that it is difficult to be helpful. Although live commercials are hardly ever used these days, it is possible to videotape a presenter commercial (as we mentioned above) very quickly and at a very low cost. It is equally possible to transmit a slide with voice-over for a very small sum. On the other hand a 60-second animated commercial, to say nothing of live action commercials including elephants, will take months from briefing to bulk prints, and will cost tens of thousands of pounds.

The proportion of the total appropriation which needs to be devoted to production would depend largely on the number of times which it is felt that one commercial can be transmitted. The best practice is to test run commercials from time to time during the course of the campaign against alternatives, to ascertain the point at which the running commercials have 'worn out' to such a degree that it is time to replace them. This counsel of perfection is seldom followed, firstly because few advertisers have pre-testing procedures in which they would have this degree of faith, and secondly because even for those who have, it is a time-taking and expensive procedure. Most campaigns are run on a rule-of-thumb basis, the rules generally being that live action commercials do not last as long as cartoon commercials; live action commercials which have some element of humour or surprise for their main effect do not last as long as more routine commercials; and that it is unwise to expose any live action commercial for many more than 20 times before replacing it. All these rules-of-thumb will be modified by the size and frequency of the campaign and by the number of commercials in the mix.

For purposes of planning it is wise to allocate between 5 and 10 per cent of the average television budget for production.

13.4   The nature of the audience

Television is a mass medium. Nine out of ten adults in the UK can receive commercial television, and there is little room for variation in this figure by demographic characteristics. Variation is to some extent introduced by patterns of viewing. The most popular programmes over the years have been the *London Palladium Show, Wagon Train, The Army Game* and *Coronation Street*. None of these could be described as making serious intellectual demands on the viewer. For all that Lord Reith and his successors may have said, for the great majority of the public television is a medium of entertainment and relaxation. The archetypal commercial viewer is a 40-year-old housewife whose husband is a skilled manual worker. The average television set is switched on for between 3½ hours in the height of summer, to 5 hours in the depths of winter, each day of each week. Who is watching it depends largely on who is in the home. The less exposed members of the population are the more mobile, that is to say men, and the 15-24 age group.

Selectivity of different target groups within the total television audience is possible to a small extent, in terms of time of day and day of week, but hardly at all by type of programme. More importantly for the planner, the degree of selectivity which exists is very largely swamped when the cost factors are applied. For many years planners were frustrated by the thought that the apparent uniformity of profile of television audiences might merely be a reflection of the insensitivity of the measuring tool. For this reason the audience research contract between 1964 and 1967 paid far more attention to demographic subgroups than had been previously possible. A great deal of analysis of the results of these years, and also of product buying from the *All Media and Product Survey,* showed that the most sophisticated analyses of the most esoteric groups produced virtually the same results as would be obtained by thinking in terms of the basic classifications of adults, men, women, housewives and children. For this reason the current contract deals in great detail with these broad classifications, and hardly at all with the finer ones.

13.5   Patterns of exposure

Because television audiences in this country are measured by the use of panels, a great deal of manipulation of patterns of coverage and frequency has taken place. Table 13.2 shows a typical example of a schedule and the analysis of it. The planner's basic task, once the critical problem of area distribution has been overcome, has been to establish the relationship between coverage and frequency which he wishes to achieve. Whilst it is customary to indicate the general balance of peak and off-peak time which he considers should produce such a pattern, it is normally the buyer's responsibility to see that this is done. The reason for this division of responsibility is the sheer difficulty of predicting far ahead of the event what television ratings and costs are going to look like.

13.6   Normal patterns of usage

The conventional patterns of buying television time were largely set in the summer of 1956. Many advertisers who had supported the opening of commercial television in September 1955 had planned campaigns to run through the winter months only, and many advertisers and agencies were appalled by the very low audiences initially attracted and the high costs-per-thousand which resulted. Consequently Associated Rediffusion, who then had responsibility for the London contract, Mondays to Fridays, and who were piling up enormous losses, offered as an inducement to advertisers two free spots for every fully paid spot which they booked. The resultant three spots a week pattern was associated with many dramatic success stories. Whether these stories would stand up

TABLE 13.2

Area: London   Target Group 1: Housewives
Spot list and cover TVR; full coverage and frequency build-up, %; Sample - 298

Spot	Description	TVR	CUM TVR	Cover TVR	CUM	1	2	3	4	5	6	7	8	9	10	11	12	13	14	15	16	17	18	19	20-23
1	76 Mar 1 Mon 13.45	10	10	*	10	10																			
2	20.57	23	33	-	28	23	5																		
3	2 Tue 19.57	31	64	*	45	29	13	3																	
4	21.28	26	90	-	49	22	16	8	3																
5	3 Wed 20.15	37	127	1	57	20	16	13	6	2															
6	5 Fri 19.14	30	157	*	63	20	14	13	9	5	1														
7	6 Sat 22.07	29	186	*	68	21	13	13	10	7	3	1													
8	7 Sun 20.47	30	216	*	71	16	17	13	10	9	5	2	*												
9	9 Tue 22.15	24	240	-	73	14	17	13	11	9	5	2	2	*											
10	10 Wed 20.15	32	272	*	75	15	13	10	14	9	5	5	2	2	*										
11	11 Thu 23.28	13	285	-	75	14	13	11	13	9	6	5	2	2	1	-									
12	13 Sat 19.45	23	308	*	77	14	11	12	12	9	5	6	3	1	2	1	*								
13	14 Sun 20.27	33	341	1	79	14	12	9	11	11	5	5	6	1	2	2	1	-							
14	15 Mon 13.41	12	353	-	80	12	12	9	11	10	7	5	6	1	1	2	1	*	*						
15	16 Tue 13.40	8	361	-	80	12	11	10	12	10	7	6	6	2	2	2	1	1	-	-					
16	17 Wed 19.40	27	388	1	81	13	10	9	11	7	10	6	6	2	2	2	1	1	1	-	-				
17	21.26	30	418	-	82	11	10	11	9	7	8	8	5	3	3	2	1	1	1	1	-	-			
18	23.09	13	431	-	82	11	10	11	8	7	7	8	5	6	3	2	1	1	1	1	-	-	-		
19	19 Fri 23.04	22	453	1	83	10	11	9	9	7	7	7	7	4	4	2	1	1	1	*				*	
20	21 Sun 20.50	26	479	*	83	8	10	10	8	7	7	8	7	5	4	3	2	1	1	1	1	*			
21	23 Tue 13.42	10	489	-	83	8	9	10	8	6	8	8	7	6	4	3	1	1	1	1	1	-			
22	24 Wed 21.12	37	526	1	84	7	10	8	8	8	8	7	6	6	5	4	2	2	1	1	1	1	*		
23	25 Thu 20.15	27	553	*	84	7	10	8	7	8	8	8	7	7	6	3	2	2	1	1	1	1	1	*	
					CUM	84	78	78	67	58	51	43	38	30	25	19	13	10	7	6	3	3	1		

Special analysis of JICTAR data by AGB

to the rigour of today's analysis is neither here nor there. It had been clearly established amongst advertisers and agencies that three spots a week on television
was a recipe for success.

Of course, three spots a week in 1956 bears little or no relation to three spots
today. The total size of the commercial television audience has multiplied about
twenty-fold whilst the average peak rating has dropped from around 70 to
around 35. The competitive effectiveness of the advertising does not bear a
simple relationship to these two factors. In the early days a high frequency of
impact was being attained on the audience in a novel and compelling way. If
your brand was being advertised on television and the opposition's was not,
there was a very fair chance that a small but vocal minority would switch
brands in sufficient quantities to make the retailer aware of what was happening,
and gain his support. The cumulative effect was, therefore, considerable. Today,
not only is the level of impact considerably lower, but it is very likely that most
competitive brands will be using the medium. The cost of producing a parallel
impact on today's audience would be astronomical; nevertheless, it is normal to
use the television medium at a much higher frequency than the press medium.

With a network 30-second spot costing over £19,000, it is clear that this philosophy militates against the use of television by advertisers with appropriations
of less than £100,000. Indeed, for advertisers wishing to cover a twelve-month
period, few media planners are happy with budgets of less than £250,000, on a
national basis. The television contractors have long been keenly aware of this
limitation of their potential custom which has resulted from this philosophy,
and have been to great pains to establish that small sums of money spent on
television can also be effective.

13.7   Related reading

A Guide to Independent Television, IBA (Annually).

14 Outdoor

As far as the media planner is concerned, outdoor advertising is usually regarded as comprising the two main divisions of posters and transportation advertising. In this chapter we intend also to deal with signs, since they can take up a relatively large proportion of the budget and similar conditions should apply in their choice.

14.1 Posters

The basic unit of size in the poster medium is the sheet, which is a double crown, 20 inches wide and 30 inches deep. Most posters come in multiples of 4-sheet, 16-sheet and 48-sheet sizes. The 16 sheet size is the most widespread and popular, 4 sheets being relative newcomers to widespread distribution, and seen particularly in re-developed areas including new towns. Planning authorities are usually loath to include large posters in comprehensively planned areas of development, with a consequence that there is no outdoor advertising at all in a number of important areas of urban renewal. It took the poster industry much time and trouble to persuade the planners that the inclusion of specially designed 4 sheet displays would enhance, rather than detract from, the amenity of such developments. Forty-eight-sheet posters, together with even larger sites coming under the general name of bulletin boards, are found most often either in city centres, or on trunk roads. Increasingly they are flood-lit, and some are in the form of transparencies, illuminated from behind. This extension of the useful life of the poster into the hours of darkness depends on there being sufficient volume of traffic along the road after dark to justify the extra expense.

A poster campaign necessitates the physical sticking of pieces of paper on perhaps 4000 different boards throughout the country. Traditionally, these boards (or sites) were individually selected, ordered and inspected. This task imposed a considerable administrative burden on the medium, aggravated by the fact that there were many owners to be contacted, and dealt with.

The solution to this problem has been the formation of British Posters, a consortium of owners accounting for about 70 per cent of the available space, and Independent Poster Sales, accounting for much of the remainder. Each Company acts as a sales agent for the individual contractors, and each offers some package deals. However, British Posters concentrate on these, to allow the advertiser, or agency, without a specialist department to buy poster campaigns with a reasonable idea of what they are getting. Independent Poster Sales concentrate on selling on a line-by-line, i.e. site-by-site, basis, which does require expertise on the part of the buyer.

Under severe cost pressures, advertising agencies disbanded their poster inspection services some years ago, and the Advertising Agencies Poster Bureau was formed to do this work, as a co-operative venture. Since this has gone into liquidation, a number of small to medium groups have been formed to carry out this work. The economics of scale involved in one organisation, rather than several, inspecting the 200,000 or so sites in the UK has led to the formation of a Poster Audit Bureau.

14.1.1 Flexibility

The outdoor medium has traditionally been the most flexible in terms of area and the least flexible in terms of time. The contractors have in recent years been taking energetic steps to deal with the latter problem. The packages referred to above may be bought for one month, or 1½, 2, 2½ ... months as required. The basis of the inflexibility has been the T/C (Till countermanded) order. Sites bought on this basis are not available for purchase by any other advertiser at any time in the future. Since some sites are thought to be more valuable than others, this has led to the practice of queueing. Thus an advertiser beginning a poster campaign will take the best sites he can obtain, and then rely on advertisers on better sites cancelling at some time in the future, when he will be given the opportunity of moving up onto the preferred site. This practice has led to the consensus that it was poor value to engage in a poster campaign lasting less than two years.

A T/C order can be cancelled at any time by giving three months' notice, provided that it does not run for less than 9 months. All other contracts are subject to a cancellation period of four months before commencement, and if they run for less than 12 months cannot be cancelled once the period within the four months before the start date has been entered.

A further inflexibility relates to copy changing. If it is wished to change copy more frequently than once a month, then a charge is made for the actual posting (in addition to the advertiser's cost of the new poster). This is not likely to be an onerous constraint in practice, since it is normal to run posters for considerably more than a month before changing designs.

The area flexibility of posters arises from the fact that each site can be purchased individually. There are occasions on which the purchase of one site strategically located may be the best way of getting a message to an individual or a small group of individuals. Its effect can be more dramatic than any direct mail shot. More generally, the boundaries of a poster campaign can be tailored to fit any marketing requirement. Packages are sold by TV areas, conurbations, and principal towns.

The cost of production in an outdoor campaign is usually higher in relation to the space cost than in any other medium. It is generally of the order of some 25 per cent. Whilst paper, printed either litho or silk-screen, is generally used for poster sites of 48-sheet size or less, bulletin boards are often painted individually on metal panels. Glow bulletins are specially prepared by painting the back of some translucent material, such as perspex. It is usual to amortise the high cost of this individual painting, by retaining the same copy over at least a twelve-month period. The effect of the display can be considerably enhanced, and the cost of production considerably increased, by the use of cut-outs, extending outside the perimeter of the board. Plate 2 shows an example of this treatment.

14.1.3   The audience

Everyone who goes out is exposed to posters. The degree of exposure is correlated to the mobility of the individual. Therefore, while the medium offers almost total coverage of the adult population, the audience has biases: up-market, towards men, and towards younger people.

Within this mass audience some variation can be achieved by careful siting of posters. Obvious examples include the use of bulletin boards on main roads and in the proximity of petrol stations, to reach an audience of motorists; and the concentration of sites in shopping areas and near supermarkets to reach a target audience of housewives. Selectivity is limited by the fact that most poster sites are located on high traffic routes in urban areas where the traffic is very mixed. It is also difficult to bias the poster audience significantly up-market since care is normally taken to exclude poster advertising from high class residential areas.

14.1.4   Site classification

The problem of value for money with poster sites is one which concerns the buyer, rather than the planner, but of which the planner must be aware. It is customary to plan in terms of average campaigns and to issue some guidance as to the type of audience required, and to leave the balance between run-of-the-mill sites and special sites to the man on the ground.

Clearly there is a wide gulf between passing a location at which a poster is displayed and looking at that poster. The gulf will be smaller if the poster is on a head-on solus position, with a long view, close to the consumer's line of vision, than if it is flat on, 50 ft up, and one of sixteen competitors. This fact is reflected in the different prices asked for different sites by the contractors, and skill in selecting sites comes from the ability to compare the price and the value. Unfortunately this is totally subjective, and therefore there is a lack of uniformity of rates between sites owned by different contractors and sited in different areas.

In order to achieve a reasonable degree of uniformity, the contractors are currently engaged in a classification process, backed by extensive research. Previous schemes have met with limited success.

Posters afford the maximum possible repetition. It is calculated that for an average campaign, the average repetition figure will be about 20 per week. Another aspect of the same basic phenomenon is the fact that the posters are there all the time. If we have a message to deliver to a housewife while she is shopping, for example, we will not know when she will go shopping but we will know that our message will be there to be received whenever it may be.

This ability to place a message in proximity to the shopping situation is important, not only in terms of time but in terms of place. There are many shopping centres in which poster sites are difficult to find, but where they are available they can form a very important last link in the communication-purchasing chain.

In terms of reproduction, the quality is entirely in the hands of the advertiser. Although 'big, bold and bloody' is not a bad slogan for poster design, some advertisers have used high quality colour photography, allied with superb litho printing, to produce very emotive posters in recent years.

Sheer size may be a virtue. Posters represent an excellent way of familiarising the housewife with a new or changed pack, and the name of a small local advertiser can be made to look big in his locality.

Geographical flexibility we have already discussed.

14.1.6   Disadvantages

In order to achieve communication, the poster has to convey its message in a very short space of time, as in most locations it is seldom accorded more than a passing glance. Thus any advertising message requiring exposition at length is normally exluded from outdoor.

Although the repetition figures produce low estimates of cost-per-thousand, in capital terms outdoor is not cheap. Examples quoted by British Posters show a national 13 week campaign of standard weight on 4- and 16-sheets costing £119,700, and a national 48-sheet campaign (heavyweight: 900 sites) for a year costing over £400,000. Added to this is the relatively high cost of production mentioned above.

In addition to the lack of flexibility of audience selection, there is no measure of what has actually been achieved. This fact hinders post-campaign evaluation.

The lack of flexibility in time has already been noted.

14.2   Transportation

Under this heading comes all poster sites on the outsides of buses, together with spaces available for advertising inside buses and trains, and sites on railway stations. There is a good deal of variation in the size, cost and effectiveness of the various spaces. Probably the most widely used and most useful of these sites is the double deck bus side. This takes the form of a narrow strip usually 5344 mm wide by 546 mm deep, and can be painted, papered, or (recently) occupied by an illuminated sign. Other commonly used exterior spaces are rears, usually about 1219 mm wide and 508 mm deep, and double fronts, each 508 mm wide and 762 mm deep, or smaller.

Inside buses, space is usually sold on front bulkheads and roof panels. These latter present the advertiser with the lowest possible capital cost outside classified advertising. It is possible, for instance, to display a roof panel poster inside a London bus for two weeks for a cost of 40p (not including the poster).

In general there are two classes of bus company operating in the UK, the district fleets and the town fleets. Reading, for example, is served by Reading Transport, which operates mainly within the confines of Reading, and Alder Valley Transport, which has routes linking Reading with neighbouring towns, and, in fact, covers a large area of the Thames and Blackwater valleys. Whether one uses one, or both, of these types of fleets depends largely on the type of coverage that is required. It may be conditioned by the fact that the colour and style of advertisement permitted on Corporation fleets sometimes conflicts with the advertiser's requirements. Some Corporation fleets refuse to take certain classes of advertisement altogether.

The planning of bus advertising depends on knowing which garages serve which routes and where these lie. Once an advertisement is posted onto a bus, its path is normally pre-destined for some time. Good coverage depends on getting the right number of buses on the right routes. However, a bus may not infrequently be transferred from one route to another and, more rarely, even from one garage to another, so that the process cannot be perfect. It is generally true to say that is is uneconomic to operate double deck buses in areas of low traffic. The general tendency is, therefore, for double deckers to operate in high traffic areas and single deckers in low traffic (usually rural) areas.

Advertisements inside London underground carriages (popularly known as 'Tube cards') are used by both local and national advertisers, and can, with correct creative treatment, be a very effective way of reaching the underground passenger.

Poster sites on stations range from double crown (single sheet) sizes up to bulletin boards. In general the remarks made previously about posters will apply to them, but there are the following exceptions.

1   Most people wait for some time on platforms and therefore posters on platform sites can reasonably carry long copy.

2   Although everyone in a town is likely to use the station from time to time, the bulk of the traffic is likely to be of a particular type, e.g. commuters from a London suburban station, businessmen from most main line stations, etc.

3   On most stations the bulk of departing traffic is in one direction. Since people waiting for a train normally wait near the edge of the platform, looking onto the track, it is therefore preferable, if the design will stand it, to place your poster on the platform opposite the busy one.

4   It is possible to buy 'general distributions' of posters up to 4-sheet size on British Rail and London Underground stations. These show considerable savings over individual displays.

5   Rear-illuminated posters may now be bought on certain British Rail and Underground stations in sizes as small as 4 sheets. As station rebuilding proceeds, more and more of these illuminated, and sometimes spectacular, sites are made available.

In general terms the audience for transportation advertising is similar to that for posters. Different positions however do tend to attract different groups of the adult population.

Double deck bus sides   The principal advantage of these over posters is that they tend to congregate in the busiest streets in city centres. It is in these streets that it is often very difficult to obtain poster displays at all and if they are available, they are usually very expensive.

Bus rear positions   These have long been popular for advertising to motorists. However frustrating it may be for a motorist to be stuck behind a bus in a traffic queue, there is no doubt that the message written on the back of a bus is pretty well inescapable.

Bus interior panels   Although buses are used by all groups in the population, outside the rush hours they tend to be used heavily by the older and poorer housewives who do not have access to a private car.

London Underground stations   These tend to cover disproportionate numbers of special groups, depending on their location. Piccadilly, for instance, is visited by most tourists and is also heavily used by theatre and film-goers. Oxford Circus, Bond Street, Marble Arch and High Street Kensington have to cope with large numbers of shoppers. Olympia will attract special groups, depending on the nature of the exhibition running at a particular time.

14.2.2   Principal advantages of transportation advertising

1   Generally the advantage of poster advertising will apply.
2   Although geographical location is less precise than with posters, all sites of a given nature are more or less equal and a first class display can be purchased immediately.
3   In general it is easier to mount short-term displays on transportation advertising.

14.2.3   Disadvantages

In general the disadvantages of poster advertising apply, but the following points have to be made.
1   The size and the nature of the viewing opportunity impose design restrictions on transport advertisements which are not invariably appreciated.
2   The mobile nature of the displays makes inspection, and therefore control, difficult. Advertisements in buses and trains spend a considerable proportion of the working week in garages and sidings.
3   When the audience is at its highest it is most difficult to see the advertisements.

4   The variety of shapes and sizes for particular spaces, and the physical restrictions imposed by some transport undertakings, tend to increase production costs.

14.3   Signs

It is unusual for a media planner's recommendation to include electric signs, but
a decision to use one, or more, will usually proportionately reduce the amount
of money he has, particularly for outdoor. Because of the cost of building, electric signs are usually on a minimum three-year contract. Rentals are usually in a
range £10,000 to £50,000 per annum, and construction and maintenance costs
can double this figure. It is, therefore, economically necessary to limit their use
to areas of the highest possible traffic density.

Size, colour and movement make electrical signs very difficult to miss. In
recent years lighting developments have made it possible to make them quite
attractive. There is a tendency for them to brighten up city centres, rather than
to sell goods other than by reminding a consumer that a product exists. Their
use tends to be confined to advertisers who have a very simple story to tell; or
who have a particular interest in the city-centre audience, or who have particularly large budgets.

14.4   Related reading

R. Nelson and A.E. Sykes, *Outdoor advertising,* Allen & Unwin (1953).

15 Cinema

Advertising time is sold in the cinema in 15, 30, 45 and 60-second lengths. Other lengths are occasionally available by negotiation. A package of films six or seven minutes long is shown immediately before the main feature in every programme. In the normal package there are about ten 30-second films, many of which are library commercials made for exhibition by local retailers. These are followed by perhaps two one-minute films usually for national advertisers. It is a condition of contract that the films are shown with the house lights down and the curtains opened.

Cinema can be one of the easiest media in which to plan, or the most difficult, depending how you approach it. As its share of media expenditure (1 per cent) indicates, it is not a particularly important medium in the United Kingdom and expansion prospects are extremely limited. The main reason for this is the continuing decline in the audience for the cinema, and the continued closing of larger cinemas (not entirely countered by the opening of new, smaller ones). An increase in the amount of advertising time permitted in each programme does not seem particularly likely and, although advertising rates have recently been increased, it looks as though further rate increases will be very difficult to apply.

The problem with planning cinema advertising is that there are still today some 1500 cinemas which take advertising, each of which may be bought separately. The simplicity comes from the fact that advertising space in almost all of these cinemas may be contracted through the three main contractors, Rank, Pearl & Dean and Presburys. Each of these contractors will, given the basic details of the campaign, produce a complete schedule showing, by television or other areas, the cinemas which have been booked, and the weeks in which the advertisements are due to be run, together with complete budget details. Thus the planner is quickly able to satisfy his objectives as to distribution of the appropriation by area and across time.

The snag with this way of operating is that the planner does not know if his plan is the best one, or indeed what it will achieve. There are two bases for discussing a cinema audience; the first are the admission figures provided on a national basis from returns made by the cinema operators to the Board of Trade. This gives a global estimate of the total size of the medium. The second relates

131

to the characteristics of this audience which are drawn almost entirely from a question asked on the National Readership Survey. As Table 15.1 shows, the cinema audience is highly skewed, compared with the adult population as a whole, towards the young and to a lesser extent towards unskilled workers.

The difficulty in using these data sources stems from the fact that hardly any cinema campaign covers more than half the cinemas in the country and very few cover more than half the weeks in a year. Cinema audiences vary markedly from one cinema to another, even where both have the same capacity, and in the same cinema variations from one week to the next can be of the order of ten to one, depending on the quality of the film which is being shown.

Most of these problems could be solved if the cinema owners would divulge the audience figures for each cinema, by each week. Although the data would be complex, a learning process would inevitably take place and planners would be able to forecast audiences with the same consistency (and the same inconsistency) as they do with television programmes. However, this state of affairs does not apply; instead the cinema contractors (who do know the figures) base their rates on them, but adjust them by a series of weightings which tend to make those cinemas most in demand the most uneconomic in terms of cost-per-thousand. This would be a perfectly proper application of economic theory were it not for the fact that the demand arises from ignorance, rather than knowledge.

For inter-media comparisons cost-per-thousand is a basic yardstick. For 1974, the average adult figure was about £4.65.

15.1 The main strengths of the cinema medium

Cinema shares with television the attributes of vision, plus sound, plus movement and adds to them the general availability of colour and the impact of the wide screen. Furthermore the cinema commercial is presented to the audience at a time when they have (with the exception of those in the back row) no distractions. The mood of the audience is also an asset in that they are engaged in the business of being entertained and relaxed. Provided that the message is not anti-pathetic, the cinema is the creative man's dream.

The fact that cinemas are bought individually means that it is a very flexible regional tool. It is possible, for instance, to attach a dealer's name and address to the end of a one or two-minute commercial so that when the consumer's intention to purchase has been established he knows where to make the purchase. Cinema provides, too, an easy way of weighting up (or down) a particular area of the country in relation to the national pattern. Advantage may also be taken of the fact that the area flexibility is not merely a question of buying one television area or another, but can, for instance, permit the mounting of a summer campaign in seaside resorts. This would seem the ideal use of the medium for selling, for instance, raincoats.

The final advantage of the medium is its relatively low capital cost. The biggest cinema campaigns are in the £100,000 to £150,000 range. Remembering the concentration of the audience into the younger age groups, it is clear that it is possible to project a brand to this group in an extremely dominant way for a cost which would not buy a very large campaign in other media.

TABLE 15.1

	Adult cinema audience, %	All adults, %
Age		
15-24	54	19
25-34	20	17
35+	26	64
Socio-economic class		
AB	16	14
C1	24	23
C2	33	32
DE	27	31
Men	55	48
Women	45	52

Source: JICNARS

15.2 Disadvantages of the medium

Clearly the cinema's strength with respect to the younger age groups is its weakness with respect to others. Although it is very flexible in terms of area, it is relatively inflexible in terms of time. The combination of availability problems and the time it takes to make a colour commercial means that it is seldom possible to mount a campaign with less than 3 months' notice, where still the cancellation clause is 17 weeks.

The high cost-per-thousand of cinema space has already been commented on, but a comparison should perhaps be made for the audience section for which cinema has the greatest strength. Considering only the 16-24 age group, for commercials of one minute or longer we would expect peak television time, on average, to produce a cost-per-thousand about 16-per cent higher than cinema. Owing to the difference in rate structures, the difference at the 30-second rate reduces to approximately 4 per cent.

An additional cost burden is that of production. A one-minute colour film can easily cost £8000 to make and prints can cost as much as £8 each. A good deal of ingenuity is shown by the contractors in moving prints from one cinema to another, but for any large scale campaign it is likely that at least one print will be needed for every cinema used. Where cinemas are used for consecutive weeks, two prints per cinema will be required.

134   Finally, owing to the pattern of cinema attendance, it is impossible to deliver high frequency of impact except to the small sub-group who make visits once a week, or more; while the total adult coverage attainable is, at 47 per cent, too low for many advertisers.

16 Radio

16.1 The present situation

Although commercial radio transmissions were received in the UK (from various Continental sources) as long ago as the 'thirties and an official station was opened in the Isle of Man in the 'sixties, legal reception to other UK-based stations started only in the autumn of 1973. The medium had a very uncertain start: this was the only country in the world in which commercial radio came after commercial TV. However, it is now established as a small, but flourishing, sector of the media spectrum.

Geographical coverage is unevenly distributed (Table 16.1). Eighteen areas are covered by nineteen contractors (two in London), but a number of important marketing areas are not covered and, at the time of writing, seem unlikely to be covered. The stations came on the air over a period of time, the last, in Wolverhampton, commencing transmission in April 1976.

The official name for the service is Independent Local Radio, and it does tend to justify the adjectives, in spite of quite large shareholdings by other media, including national media. There is a world-wide pattern of folksy, me-to-you chat which has been developed by local radio announcers/commentators; although the style is common, the link with the listener depends on frequent references to purely local phenomena.

Heavy use of radio by local advertisers, mostly retailers, may be related to this fact. Certainly, few national advertisers have tried to emulate the local atmosphere. It would be quite costly, in production terms, and could be disastrous, if imperfectly executed. The nuances of life in Bradford are seldom crystal clear in Mayfair. It is also irritating for national advertisers that they cannot use local radio in all parts of the country, although, of course, national coverage is still available from Radio Luxembourg.

16.2 Audience size

Measure of audience size take three forms: the stations' potential, the 'weekly reach' and the achievements of specified schedules. The first two vary widely, as

TABLE 16.1

Station	Potential audience, '000 adults	Weekly reach %
London		
(London Broadcasting Co.)	8300	21
(Capital Radio)	8300	37
Manchester		
(Piccadilly Radio)	2500	38
Glasgow		
(Radio Clyde)	1900	61
Birmingham		
(BRMB)	1800	39
Liverpool		
(Radio City)	1800	36
Tyne/Wear		
(Metro Radio)	1600	41
Wolverhampton		
(Beacon Radio)	1500	NA
Belfast		
(Downtown Radio)	975*	70
Edinburgh		
(Radio Forth)	940	40
Sheffield/Rotherham		
(Radio Hallam)	690	45
Teeside		
(Radio Tees)	680	41
Nottingham		
(Radio Trent)	610	42
Bradford		
(Pennine Radio)	480	29
Portsmouth		
(Radio Victory)	440	46
Swansea		
(Swansea Sound)	370	63
Reading		
(Thames Valley Broadcasting)	270*	53
Plymouth		
(Plymouth Sound)	260	67
Ipswich		
(Radio Orwell)	200	79

*Provisional figures

Table 16.1 shows. These variations have given rise to arguments about the coverage which may reasonably be claimed for the medium. Adding the potentials gives a figure a little over 60 per cent of the adult population. However, most media planners would consider that a listener not reached by a total audience package could not reasonably be counted. On this basis potential coverage is at least halved.

Most stations offer a 49-spot 'total audience package'. Analyses of these show a very steady correlation with weekly reach, the package achieving about 88 per cent of the total weekly audience.

16.3 Audience profiles

Users of local radio must beware of the considerable differences between the audience profiles of the various stations, and the way in which these vary from the station potential. This is illustrated in Table 16.2, which shows the profile of the 49-spot total audience package, together with the area profile, for four major stations. It will be seen that the appeal of the three provincial stations varies, but they are more like each other than any of them is like Capital. If we generalise by saying that the local radio audience tends to be female, middle-aged, and down-market, we see that Capital is more male than female, and markedly young rather than middle-aged. The Manchester station comes closest to it in this comparison, but its youth bias, in particular, is nowhere near as pronounced.

16.4 Principal advantages of radio

Low capital cost is often advanced as an advantage of radio, and, indeed, it is possible to buy a 30-second spot on Thames Valley Broadcasting for £7.50. However, a total audience package on all stations, which is more likely to be the way a national advertiser will enter the medium, costs over £5000.

Cost-per-thousand impacts is low, even for those audience segments least enthusiastic for the medium. Conversely, the low impact of commercial radio is reckoned largely to offset its low cost, and a rule-of-thumb of one-fifth of the cost per thousand for the same audience on TV has become regarded as a reasonable relationship.

This may be grossly unfair in particular cases. Music on radio is mostly listened to as background, but this is seldom true of special broadcasts. Equally, while many commercials may be easy to listen to without hearing, some are very intrusive.

Radio's strength in the early morning is often an advantage, particularly if one wishes to address the housewife before she goes shopping. A radio spot in the morning, acting as a reminder for a television spot seen the previous evening, could be a valuable use of the second medium.

Most radio advertising is for local firms, particularly retailers. This makes sense not only because of the pertinence of the catchment area, but because it is possible to go on the air, quickly and cheaply, with a news story about merchandise on offer. There are already several case histories showing how effective this can be. Of course, there is every reason why the national advertiser with a local story to tell should use the medium in the same way.

TABLE 16.2 Percentage profiles

	Demographic group	49-spot package	Area population
BRMB (Birmingham)	Men	42	49
	Women	58	51
	Housewives	49	43
	15-24	16	20
	25-34	22	16
	35-54	38	34
	55+	24	30
	ABC1	20	32
	C2DE	80	68
Capital (London)	Men	53	48
	Women	47	52
	Housewives	34	46
	15-24	38	19
	25-34	26	17
	35-54	24	32
	55+	12	32
	ABC1	38	45
	C2DE	62	55
Clyde (Glasgow)	Men	43	47
	Women	57	53
	Housewives	45	41
	15-24	22	21
	25-34	17	17
	35-54	38	32
	55+	23	30
	ABC1	20	31
	C2DE	80	69
Piccadilly (Manchester)	Men	46	48
	Women	54	52
	Housewives	45	46
	15-24	26	19
	25-34	25	17
	35-54	34	32
	55+	15	32
	ABC1	22	33
	C2DE	78	67

The relatively low cover available puts the medium in the same class as cinema, but without the latter's dominance of a particular audience group. For a national advertiser it is, therefore, almost inevitably going to enter consideration only as a support medium.

The patchiness of geographical coverage will also inhibit the national advertiser, except where he wishes to make a special local effort. Indeed, using radio where he can may unbalance his national effort in ways which are difficult to predict, and to monitor.

Creative considerations are difficult to advance as a disadvantage, in the face of a well directed promotional campaign to the effect that radio offers the creative man total freedom. It is true that brilliant writing, backed up with appropriate sound effects, can work wonders with the imagination. It is also true that something useful can be said about the product on radio, whatever we may feel can not. Nevertheless, if the creative will to get the most out of the potential is not strong, there will be many situations where a colour page in *Woman*, say, will have great, and obvious, prior claims.

16.6   Related reading

D. Beckett, A. Mitchell, G. Paine and W.A. Twyman, 'A radio rodeo', *Admap* (August 1976).

17 Direct mail

A very considerable sum of money is spent each year on Direct Mail advertising. Quite how much it is difficult to assess and it does to some extent depend on how you do the sum. An estimate of £75-100 million would probably meet with general agreement. Recommendation of direct mail by the media planner often presents organisational problems because departments other than the media department are usually concerned in its planning.

Direct Mail has been defined as any advertising matter sent by post, but these days the description usually includes delivery by specially employed forces of messengers and is not confined to the services of the Post Office. There are three elements in direct mail which may be purchased from three bodies, or from one: they are the list, the mailing shot and the delivery.

A number of organisations exist to supply a complete service, although often they use the Post Office for delivery purposes. Some media owners offer a direct mail service in support of their own medium, although it is normal to sub-contract the work to an independent specialist.

17.1 The list

The point of direct mail is that the advertising should be received by the whole of the target market and by nobody outside the target market. The accuracy with which this can be done depends on the quality of the address list which is used. All companies have address lists within their own organisations, for instance, lists of account customers. However, one of the chief assets of a direct mail organisation is its ability to maintain a wide variety of high-quality lists which it sells to prospective users. Another important source of lists has grown up in recent years: this is known as list broking. A perambulator manufacturer, for example, will build up a list of his new customers from a return of guarantee cards. All the mothers on this list will be very good prospects for the manufacturers of baby foods, and the perambulator manufacturer may sell his lists to such an advertiser, or, alternatively, to a direct mail organisation who will do the same thing.

A direct mail shot may comprise anything which can legally be sent through the post, or delivered to the recipient in some other way. This makes it extremely difficult to give any estimates of cost; but one can discuss the minimum amount for a shot which is delivered through the post, since the largest element will be the postage – at present 7p. It is possible by using minimum standards of paper, envelopes, etc., to confine the remaining costs on the shot to 1½p, and so produce a cost per shot of 8½p, or a cost-per-thousand of £85. Door-to-door delivery, on a shared basis, can cost as little as ½p per shot, and in this way the cost-per-thousand can be as low as £20 per thousand. This latter method will, however, not ensure personally addressed delivery to selected respondents and that, to many people, is what direct mail is really about.

There is literally no upward limit to cost.

17.3   The advantages of direct mail

The comparison is often made between mass media and shotguns and direct mail and rifles. Certainly the advertising theorist must welcome the possibility of addressing a specially tailored message to every single member of his target audience, and making sure that nobody else sees it.

Direct mail normally slips from this precise definition because of the sheer difficulty of producing correct lists. A number of companies now classify areas in the country as being particularly rich in two-car households, or mothers of young children, or houses without central heating, or what you will. They will then deliver to each household in areas having high potential of this kind, with the result that the total audience is far richer in members of the target market than it might be otherwise.

Probably the principal advantage of direct mail is its total flexibility. Any kind of advertising message can be delivered to the prospect (even including cheap film projectors containing the message on a loop). Its timing can be carried out with pinpoint accuracy, and any area can be used, from one address upwards.

A further aspect of direct mail which may or may not be an advantage is that it is possible to check immediately on its effectiveness. It is customary for mailing shots to require some sort of response from the recipient. Coupled with the controllability of the medium this can lead to some quite elegant experiments in optimising response. On the other hand the medium tends to get judged on this criterion, and if it does not produce an obviously profitable response, it is discontinued. This is not a criterion applied to any other medium (except in the case of mail order advertisers) and allowance should be made for the sheer advertising effect that the direct mail shot has.

17.4   Disadvantages

Quite clearly the principal disadvantage is the cost-per-thousand. It is possible to deliver a message to a small minority of the readership of a national newspaper much more economically than the same message could be delivered to their homes, even if you knew where they were. Another major disadvantage which really has got direct mail quite a bad name in some areas, is the antagonism which is aroused in the recipient of a shot which he, or she, thinks is inappropriate. In a way this is a compliment to the medium. Just as people never complained about detergent advertising before television began, so they safely ignore very many advertising messages which they see, but which they do not consider to be addressed to them. This is not possible with direct mail.

The question of cancellation of direct mail is a complex one. On the one hand it is possible to stop the shot going out until the time of posting; on the other hand a substantial part of the cost will normally have been incurred by this point, and will subsequently have to be met. Of course, if it is postponement rather than an outright cancellation, no problem arises.

18   Retail advertising

To devote a chapter to retail advertising in the first edition of this book would have been considered a quirk, but not to do so in the second edition would seem likewise; so great has been the growth in the importance of the retailer vis-a-vis the brand advertiser in the intervening years.

Recently retail advertising has taken over the No.1 MEAL spot from food, and on current trends will become steadily more important. This parallels the shift in the market place, affecting particularly the money spent on promoting branded goods. Much of this money is now given to the retailer to persuade him to stock the goods; some of this the retailer may redeploy in advertising to get the goods off the shelf.

We are not concerned here with the relative efficiencies of the two approaches in selling branded merchandise, but the ways in which the retailer should approach the media planning task to best build his own business.

In some ways his job is much more difficult than that of the brand marketer; he has to maximise effort spread over (usually) a multiplicity of lines. In other ways it is much easier: four of the slipperiest variables for a manufacturer, namely distribution, display, price and competition, are completely within his control.

As far as this chapter is concerned, by 'retail' we really mean 'an organisation with many independent, or semi-independent, branches'. Thus, we are not talking about the self-employed shoe repairer with a shop near the market, but we could be talking about British Rail, British School of Motoring, or British Home Stores.

Because media plans for retailers can be thoroughly tested, we shall discuss the testing procedures, and then some possible plans.

18.1   Determinants of branch volume

Before we can consider the effects of advertising on branch turnover, we have to consider the other factors. There are clearly many which play a part, of which the company reputation, type and range of goods stocked, and pricing policy, will be (more or less) common.

What will vary by branch will be the catchment area (how many customers of the right type are within reasonable range of this branch?) the size of store (or number of booking clerks, or instructors), the competition, the location of the store (how many people walk past on the average (or peak) shopping day?) and the quality of the manager. Other factors may be important on occasion, such as the age of the branch. For the particular client, it is essential that his stores are categorized by turnover, in these terms. Only by matching stores on the critical criteria can we be sure that we are testing advertising effects, and not inter-actions.

For example, if we take two stores of equal turnover, one in a high catchment area and one in a low, and measure the effect of normal advertising weight in the first versus double weight in the second, we may well find there is little difference between the results. This may be due to the fact that the second shop was close to its maximum potential and that extra advertising was therefore wasted. It does not (inevitably) mean that double weight advertising for the first shop would not have been profitable.

In order to get satisfactory tests, we must draw a sample which genuinely represents the universe of shops, i.e. the whole group, not only geographically, but also in the terms mentioned above.

18.2   Type of effects to measure

Work published to date suggests that there are a number of specific effects which we should expect to meet. These all relate to the sale of specific merchandise through specific outlets, be these Awayday tickets through BR stations, refresher courses through BSM branches, or boys' socks through British Home Stores.

Retail advertising is usually of this type, rather than the building of store image. The reason for this is that, in order to buy the merchandise, people must visit the store, and we may rely on the principle of cognitive dissonance to look after image enhancement. That is to say, if people buy at a store, they will convince themselves that it must be a good store, otherwise, what are they doing shopping there?

Of course, the premise is not necessarily true, and for completeness should certainly be checked. If ads are run which are not concerned with selling specific products, then, in addition to total store turnover, we must also collect the 'indirect' data. This is the exception to the situation described below in Section 18.3.

With respect to a particular piece of merchandise in a particular shop, we know that its rate of sale depends on:

Its relative price
Display
Promotion
Advertising
Competitive activity

given a constant demand for the product group as a whole.

We also know that the effects of these variables are lagged over time. If we advertise this week, we shall expect some sales effect this week, but also some next, and possibly some later. We know that the length of the lag varies: price and promotion, for example, are likely to be faster acting than advertising. And

are often followed by decreases next, because we have changed the timing of the
purchase, not the number of purchases made.

We know that most response curves are S-shaped, showing little return at low
levels of advertising, then a period of considerable response, then a flattening off.
We know that the dimensions of the curve will vary with the potential of the
store.

The areas in which we can, and should, seek guidance include:

1   Which media should we use?
2   In what size space/length of time?
3   With what frequency?
4   On which days?
5   With how many products?
6   Of which type?
7   How described (illustration/copy/both)?
8   How priced?

18.3   How to make the measurements

Since the end-product with which we are concerned is profit, we must measure
something which can give us a direct steer on this. Thus we will normally exclude store awareness, image, and/or traffic, and concentrate on the sales.

Background data is necessary in order to establish the nature of the pattern
which we are trying to change. For example, suppose we advertise baked beans
in week 5, in a sample of stores, and the results look like this:

	Average sales, *weeks 1 - 4*	*Sales* *Week 5*
Sample stores	38	50
Control stores	39	37

This seems very encouraging at first sight, but conceals several totally different possibilities within the data as they stand. Consider the following:

Case 1

	Week 1	*Week 2*	*Week 3*	*Week 4*	*Week 5*
Sample stores	38	37	39	38	50
Control stores	39	40	38	39	37

Here there is little weekly variation, either within the sample or the control. The
control figure for the fifth week is slightly below expectations, and confirms
that there is no significant upward movement in the market. The sample figure
shows a highly significant upward variation in week 5, which, if no other explanation is found, may reasonably be attributed to the advertising test.

	Week 1	Week 2	Week 3	Week 4	Week 5
Sample stores	16	50	52	34	50
Control stores	46	28	25	57	37

In this case, both sample and control show very wide variability from week to week, and neither of the figures for week 5 are outside the range of random variation. Therefore, we can draw no conclusions from these data. (Although we may try to establish the reason for the large variations.)

Case 3

	Week 1	Week 2	Week 3	Week 4	Week 5
Sample stores	20	30	42	60	50
Control stores	60	46	30	20	37

Here we have well defined trends (albeit very short term) in both sample and control, although in opposite directions. The control figure for week 5 suggests that the market may have experienced an upturn, whilst week 5 in the sample is a very disappointing result. If we had only these figures to go on, we would assume that the advertising test was a failure.

In general, it is unlikely that our real data are going to follow any of these patterns, so that we shall need to develop a predictive model. Great care will be needed in handling advertising weight in such a model, particularly in relation to local newspapers. With most media the absolute number of opportunities-to-see, and the catchment area, are self-limiting. That is to say, one insertion in the *Daily Express,* for example, will give one opportunity to (a percentage of) adults in the catchment area, however this is defined. But consider two stores of equal turnover, one in Liverpool and one in Luton. If advertising is assigned in proportion to sales, about five times as many opportunities to see may be bought in the latter as the former.

If it is intended to deliver opportunities to see disproportionately, then local media will have to be bought, and their cost considered in the profit equation. (See below.)

This model will enable us to say that, if we had not conducted this test, sales would have been, say, 38 ± 5. In this case 50 is clearly exceptionally good, and we can be reasonably confident that our change in marketing activity has resulted in a sales increase best estimated as 12 units on 38, or 32 per cent.

This information is not sufficient, however, to tell us whether or not the action was profitable. We have significantly increased sales of one brand of baked beans. This could come about through attracting that brand's buyers from another store, which would be fine. While in our store, they might buy other products as well, which would be finer. But they might be our regular customers just switching brand, so that our total baked bean sales do not go up. Or our regular spaghetti customers switching to baked beans, so that the total food sales do not go up.

We only profit if our total turnover is increased as a result of the promotional activity, and consequently this is a vital measurement.

Serious constraints will be placed by the management of the client company on the range and timing of experiments proposed by the media planner. Indeed they may consider, once the measurement tool is established, that other marketing factors, such as store layout and display policy, must take priority over advertising tests. If these are going to make a greater contribution to profit, the media planner should possess himself in patience.

What must be understood is that there is a severe limit to the number of tests that can be carried out at the same time, whilst producing independent results, and that we should look out for interaction effects.

Tests to be carried out simultaneously must either be on factors which may confidently be expected to be independent, or a correct experimental design, which will enable the effects to be detected, must be used. For example, the baked bean test described above could be carried out at the same time as an area test of television weight, provided that the television area is taken out of the baked bean assessment, and the baked bean promotion does not attract a significant number of new shoppers.

Experimental design, which will be used with statistical tools such as the analysis of variance, needs expert guidance, although there is nothing inherently difficult about it.

The most critical point of any test programme is ensuring that all concerned, in the client and agency organisation, know the nature and purpose of what is going on, so that they take no action which could adversely affect understanding of the test. Non-adherence to pricing policy, failure of delivery of display material, running out of stock of the promoted product, or a store manager's holiday, have all been known to make a significant difference to results. We should also be wary of the over-generosity of media owners, who can, with the best intentions in the world, foul up a carefully designed experiment (see Chapter 8).

18.5   Basic principles

So far we have discussed the ways in which a media plan for a multi-branch organisation can be refined to provide a good profit return on the advertising investment. However, if we do not run (unrefined) campaigns whilst the testing is proceeding, the client company may go into liquidation before we have finished. Some rules of thumb are needed, and are given below.

There are three broad types of multi-branch organisation, in media terms, which will probably require different types of treatment.

18.5.1   *Nationally distributed branches, uniform stocking policy*

Here we are dealing with a Fine Fare, a Curry's or a Nationwide Building Society, where the organisation is selling the same goods (by and large) throughout its outlets, which although varying one from the other, do not do so by region.

In this case, national media will almost inevitably be the correct answer, and it is highly likely that national press media, particularly dailies, will predominate.

They have four great advantages over competitive media:

1   The ability to picture a large number of products, with selling points and prices.
2   The opportunity to place the ad close in time to the expected day of purchase.
3   Short copy dates, allowing the organisation quickly to pass on to the public deals made with suppliers.
4   Economy.

Not all these points are equally relevant to all organisations of this type. With a building society, for example, where items offered for sale, i.e. investment plans, change little over time, other media, particularly television, compare more favourably. With some, the national press has another use. If there is reason to believe that the location of branches is not well known, a list of addresses may be carried in newspapers (although this takes a lot of space, and is correspondingly expensive).

18.5.2   Nationally distributed branches, local stocking policy

The best example would be British Rail, but fashion stores could qualify, and so could some department store groups. In these areas there will almost certainly be some national advertising, this being the most economical way to promote rail as a means of travel, or to establish the store name and style, and so on. But local advertising will be essential to sell this ticket from this station, or these jeans from that shop. Evening and weekly newspapers will play a large part in such campaigns, although all media capable of localisation, TV (to some extent), radio, outdoor and cinema deserve consideration.

18.5.3   Regionally distributed branches

There are important multi-branch organisations which are not national, for example, Sainsbury's, Asda, and the Area Electricity Boards. Clearly, national media are wasteful for such organisations, but are unlikely to do positive harm, as may be the case with the branded manufacturer advertising outside his area of distribution. Simply, if we see an attractive ad for Sainsbury's, and there is no Sainsbury's in our area, it is likely to have the effect of making us wish there were; of shopping at Sainsbury's if we travel to the right area; and of attracting our custom if ever a branch is opened within range. So, while we would be unlikely to buy media specifically to cover areas in which we are not represented, the wastage versus economy equation needs calculating with care. It may well be cheaper to cover the whole country with national newspapers than half of it with regionals.

18.6   Other considerations

1   *Regional copy splits* in the national newspapers, and the possibility of buying regional editions, should always be borne in mind. They may allow for the

featuring of merchandise sold only in some branches, or for national 'weight' to
be given to an area campaign. Buying them requires negotiation, and some penal-
ties, in terms of cost, and flexibility, may be incurred. Nevertheless, the benefits
may be considerable. For example, where a list of addresses is necessary, it may
be halved, or better, by featuring only those within the distribution boundaries
of the edition concerned.

2   *Weighting media coverage* by store turnover may be proposed. This is an
aspect of the general area allocation problem, dealt with in Chapter 7. How to
do it should be resolved by the testing programme, but before those results are
available some generalities can be made. Firstly, media costs in relation to turnover need careful examination. If we have one store in Liverpool and one in
Luton, and the turnover is approximately the same in each, the same weight of
media money will buy about five times as many pages in Luton as in Liverpool,
and it is unlikely that this will be justified.
   The question should be asked 'Which store is the more typical?' If the Luton
store is already doing exceptionally well, it is probable that disproportionate
further support will not be rewarded. On the other hand, if the Liverpool store
is badly situated, or too small, then its potential may never be realised.
   For stores which are achieving average results, equality of exposure is probably a better principle than equality of money. This is another argument in
favour of the nationals, although regionals may well be used to weight up particular areas of need (as with brand campaigns).

3   Notice has already been taken of the possible need to draw to the attention
of the public the actual addresses of the stores. There are other ways of doing
this, besides listing in newspapers. Many groups will have lists in the telephone
directories, and attention may be drawn to this fact in other media. The only
problem here relates to changes, which may take years to add or delete.
   Posters may also be used for branch locations; indeed, a national poster campaign can easily be 'slipped' with the address of the local branch. Cinema commercials, too, may be 'tailored' with an address caption, with or without voice
over, just as they are for independent retailers.
   Finally, leaflets may be distributed door-to-door in the area served by the
branch. It is unlikely that this would be done solely for the notification of an
address but could well be carried out in co-ordination with some special offer
scheme. This is quite often done by petrol companies for the opening of new
stations.

4   A major need for local publicity arises when a new store is opened. It is
necessary to get the new establishment contributing as quickly as possible, for
it will be bound to have accrued considerable costs during building, converting,
equipping and so on. Generally several of the options discussed above will be
used simultaneously, often together with a PR effort, such as having a person-
ality to perform the opening ceremony, or a composite feature supported by
builders and suppliers, in the local paper.

5   Just as a brand budget can be efficiently extended by dealer support, so do
many retailers expect contributions of cash or space from their suppliers to add

weight to their campaign. This may take the form of a joint listing ('Available at branches of Woolworths, Boots and other fine stores'), use of the brand's space to tie on a sales 'Available at ...' message, and simply, money, which the retailer will be expected to use to feature the brand in his own advertising.

6   Although there is some seasonality in all retail business, and much in some, the retailer cannot 'make for stock' as can the manufacturer, and will wish to have customers continually crossing his threshold. Accordingly, campaigns should be mounted to cover as much of the year as possible, reducing in size in low periods, rather than missing weeks altogether.

Of critical importance to most retail advertisers are the 'sales', and attracting the maximum possible number of shoppers at these periods is essential. Fortunately, the mere announcement of a sale seems to stimulate considerable activity, and hence the ads can be small/short, allowing high repetition at modest cost.

18.7   Related reading

Peter Doyle and Jan Fenwick, 'Planning and estimation in advertising', *Journal of Marketing Research* (February 1975).
Ambar G. Rao, *Retail outlet management—old problems, new solutions,* OR/MS Dialogue Inc. (1975).

19   Direct response campaigns

Within the scope of this title, we include any advertising campaign the purpose of which is to produce known contacts. Clearly, the majority of campaigns are intended to produce a direct response in the sense that it is hoped that consumers will go to retail outlets and purchase the goods advertised! In the context of this chapter it may not be necessary for them to make a purchase at all, but it is necessary for them to identify themselves to the advertiser.

To the media planner who is interested in his job, there is a great deal of satisfaction in dealing with this type of campaign. The lack of feed-back that has been available to the media man is decried at several points in this book. With direct response the feed-back is perfect; one knows precisely what the direct effect of the advertising was.

There are some major problems too. The chief of these is the organisation required in order to use the information generated. It is not difficult, but it *is* very tedious, to carry out the necessary experimentation and to tabulate and analyse the results with necessary care. Although direct response advertising is the only area in which the profitability of the advertising expenditure can be directly assessed, most advertisers seem singularly uninterested in it. The consequences of this is that almost all published work on this subject (and there is not a great deal of that) relates to *post hoc* analyses of campaigns that have contained many variables. The major exception to this generalisation relates to C.J. Taylor's paper (see References). This presents an extremely interesting, albeit highly mathematical, approach to campaign planning in the direct response field.

It is important to emphasise that the same advertisement in the same size, on the same page, in the same position, in the same publication can produce wide variations in response, not related to time and order effects. This makes the inclusion, or exclusion, of a trial medium on the basis of one insertion, highly questionable.

A subsidiary problem to the media planner is that of getting so interested in direct response campaigns that he either neglects his less quantifiable work, or tries to apply lessons to normal advertising which cannot be applied.

It is perhaps worth spelling out the essential difference between the two types of campaign. With normal consumer advertising the purpose of the campaign is either to consolidate the behaviour of existing users of the brand, and/or to persuade infrequent users to increase their frequency of use at the expense of other brands. Once this objective has been achieved, it is felt likely that the consumer will make a considerable number of purchases over a considerable period of time.

Direct response advertising is quite the contrary to this. In the majority of cases, once the consumer has responded to the advertisement he is likely to be out of the market for some time. Even if the response is at as low a level as an enquiry for a leaflet, then the advertiser has little interest in him applying for another.

(It is, of course, true that some advertising has a hybrid role, attempting not only to get people to write in for information concerning a product, but also in continuing to interest them once they have written. Our view is that such hybrids are less likely to succeed than a mixture of straightforward coupon getting advertisements and straightforward persuasive advertisements.)

This vital distinction may be less important to the media planner than to other members of the agency. It is common, for instance, for advertisers engaged in normal consumer campaigns to reject media in which the bulk of the advertisements are for direct response campaigns. Whilst it is true that the medium's ability to attract direct response (a fact which is presumed from its continued usage by coupon advertisers) may not prove its effectiveness with attitude-changing campaigns, it seems to us to require a fairly perverse mind to believe that it necessarily will be less effective for such campaigns.

19.1   Some actual cases

We are reprinting the two cases given in the first edition, since the methodology which they describe remains perfectly valid. Of the three companies who co-operated in providing the cases, only Atlas Lighting remains in being: but neither the disappearance of S.H. Benson nor that of Shell-Mex and BP could be attributed to lack of expertise in direct response. The interesting lesson to be drawn from both these cases is how agency and client, working together, improved the performance of the campaigns over time.

Shell-Mex and BP Limited

One of the objectives of the Shell-Mex and BP Limited Central Heating campaign is to obtain coupons. This objective is defined precisely in terms of the number of coupons required to be delivered for a given sum of money spent in a given period of time. As campaigns progress, weekly reviews are held of the state of coupon returns and adjustments made, wherever necessary, to forward media scheduling. The knowledge that the client and the agency have gained of methods of obtaining specific numbers of coupons in response to their advertising covers the whole creative and media area.

As an example of the learning process that has been at work as to media effectiveness in coupon response terms for this advertising, we may look at the data set out in Figure 1. This shows the cost per coupon reply for the years 1964 to 1968 indexed on 1968 as 100. Also shown, in Figure 2, is the absolute number of coupons obtained

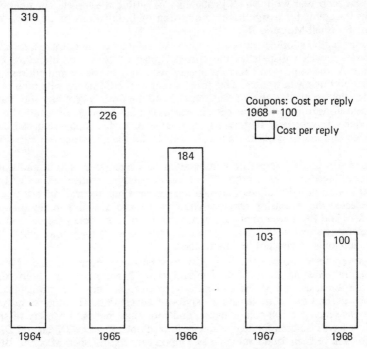

Fig. 1. Media effectiveness (1)—performance comparison 1964–1968

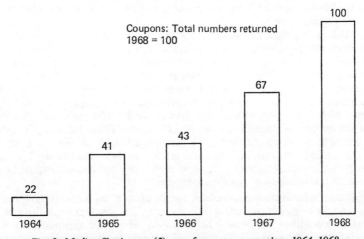

Fig. 2. Media effectiveness (2)—performance comparison 1964–1968

in each of these areas again indexed on 1968 as 100. It can clearly be seen that very considerable reductions have been and are continuing to be made in the cost per coupon reply for this advertiser.

Similarly it is shown that targets for absolute numbers of coupons obtained can be raised each year with a high probability of hitting the target. The coupons so returned account for a significant proportion of installations of oil fired central heating for Shell-Mex and BP.

The procedure adopted with each coupon is that it is sent initially to a direct mail organisation which dispatches the current range of consumer literature to the inquirer. At the same time a form is opened recording the name and address of the inquirer and its media source. This form is sent to the Company salesman responsible for that particular area of the country, and the form is kept alive until an oil-fired central-heating system has been installed or it has been clearly established that the inquiry is valueless. In this way the value of each coupon returned can be identified and linked back to the media source and the advertisement carrying the coupon.

The means used have been a combination of a creative evolution and a media evolution linked with each other. What has evolved in creative terms has been a special 'coupon carrier' style of advertising—termed the 'tactical' advertising. This has reflected the increasing range of equipment made available to the market by Shell-Mex and BP. The coupon carrier advertisement is extremely factual and direct and relatively small in size (black and white half-pages in magazines and 8 inches × 2 columns or equivalent in newspapers).

However, these are not the only advertisements appearing for Shell-Mex and BP Central Heating in a particular campaign. There have also been 'theme' advertisements, as well as the tactical advertisements. Thus, the campaigns have typically carried two complementary styles of advertising. The 'theme' advertisements have included full-colour pages, and four-page inserts. A variety of special positions have also been found efficient in, for example, *Reader's Digest* and *Drive*—gate-folds have been found valuable as coupon carriers. As Shell-Mex and BP and Bensons have learnt more about obtaining coupons in this particular field, it has been possible to be more and more precise about the proportion of the appropriation required to obtain a given target of coupons. This target itself is set by Shell-Mex and BP in terms of the installation jobs throughput required for a particular campaign that can be dealt with by Shell-Mex and BP and their appointed installers of central heating systems.

The experience gained of media values in this market gives us firm criteria for media selection (subject to over-all coverage and frequency achievement) in terms of coupon reply costs and numbers. We have been able to apply cumulative coupon response against cumulative advertisement expenditure for individual advertisements in individual media over time. The distribution of insertions in specific media shows a high and positive correlation between cumulative expenditure and coupon response with increasing returns for certain media (for example, *Drive*), and decreasing returns for others (for example, *TV Times*). Other media again appeared to be unable to get across the start line in terms of adequate coupon response. These comments on individual media do not necessarily apply in other fields. The mixture of newspapers and magazines can thus be evolved by combining predicted coupon response with coverage and frequency targets.

In this way, meaningful relationships can be established between the advertising process and the targets for the client. It is instructive to note that while there has been increasing expenditure on central heating as a whole, oil expenditure has been decreasing proportionately—oil's share of expenditure having remained static in absolute terms over the period 1964 through 1969. Although one may not know in detail how advertising works in this field, in terms of the precise mechanisms operating in the minds of the consumers, one can achieve effective results on the 'black box' approach by adjusting input to expected output and thus retain effective control over expenditure.

Atlas Lighting

Advertising for Atlas Lighting equipment in 1967 used trade and technical media. A review of this policy was undertaken by the client and S. H. Benson to assess whether it was possible to reach the decision makers in the market more effectively by using media additional to those in the trade and technical group. The thinking behind this review was that a significant group of decision makers in the area of lighting equipment would not necessarily be exposed to the specialist trade and technical media, who could be reached by national media. Those who *were* exposed to specialist media could, obviously, also be reached by the national media. To check this thinking, it was decided that research would be undertaken on the exposure of decision makers to both specialist and national advertising media.

The research was carried out among electrical contractors by Interscan, which obtained readership patterns for journals being used for Atlas in the electrical field and also exposure to daily newspapers and Sunday newspapers. This research also covered advertisement recall among lighting contractors of national advertising for Atlas Lighting and other brands of fluorescent light fittings. Research findings were that although the reach of certain of the specialist media was very high in the market, this could be matched by the net readership of an appropriate mix of the national and Sunday newspapers.

Further research was carried out as to the relative merits of advertising Atlas Lighting in the trade press as against national newspapers, on a pilot scale, among representatives of the target group. Frequency of reading and time spent reading were covered for national dailies and Sundays, and for specialist publications. Recognition of advertisements in the lighting field in each of these publications also was checked. Attitude measures as to perceived reliability of the lighting equipment advertised and the interest, informativeness and authoritativeness of the advertising was also obtained for these three media groups.

It was found that the number reading an issue and time spent per issue did not alter significantly between daily newspapers and trade publications, and that Sunday newspapers came out ahead of both of these other media groups on both these dimensions. Authoritativeness was a dimension on which trade publications scored better than national daily or Sunday media; as against interest on which dimension the reverse was true. Recognition of advertisements was found, however, to be equally high in daily newspapers and trade publications. Sunday newspapers came out ahead of daily newspapers and trade publications in this respect. This was true both of the main Sunday papers and the weekend colour magazines.

From the media point of view the conclusion reached from this work was that there was a case for adding national media to the schedule of Atlas Lighting at the expense of a proportion of trade advertising expenditure in order to reach those not covered by the latter, in the market, and that the penalty of doing this did not appear to be significantly large in terms of advertising exposure among those effectively covered by the specialist press.

In this thinking, certain elements were particularly important. Among these elements was the difficulty in the specialist press in identifying the most effective publication out of a large number reaching a particular target area. Complementing this was the problem of having to use a large number of trade and technical magazines, in each of which a very large and not particularly distinguished mass of advertising appears, in order to ensure coverage of the target groups. A third factor is that one can be over-precise in using 'pin-point' media such as specialist magazines. In pin-pointing the most relevant people, those who can also be important, even if not the *most* relevant are sacrificed.

Elements working for the national press included, firstly, their selectivity on a broad front as opposed to the extremely fragmented trade press approach with the concomitant advantage that all levels of management, purchasing and generally influential people across a variety of industries could be reached.

Secondly, there was the advantage of having Atlas Lighting appear in media of national stature which would help to reflect advantageously upon Atlas products.

Thirdly, were the implications of Atlas seen on a national scale in national media as a progressive and vital company which carried influence among people involved with the purchasing and distribution of the company's products.

Schedule analysis of available media was the next step. Marplan/Economist surveys showed that selected national newspapers could reach 85 per cent of businessmen in the market for Atlas equipment. It was therefore decided that the Atlas Lighting schedule for 1968 should comprise a balance of national media and trade press. Specialist press was felt to add emphasis to the national campaign in

Lighting equipment—Product X
Coupon Results to 21 June 1968
All data are indexed on 100=results for *Sunday Times Colour Magazine*

	Cost	Replies	Cost per reply
Sunday Times Colour Magazine	100	100	100
Daily Telegraph Colour Magazine	93	120	75
The Times	13	16	77
Guardian	11	11	105
Financial Times	15	5	324
Economist	10	2	436
Municipal Engineering	2	*	737
Municipal Journal	3	*	543
Surveyor & Municipal Engineering	2	—	—
Public Lighting	1	—	—
Shop Equipment & Shop Fitting News	4	1	278
Industrial Purchasing News	6	1	577
Modern Purchasing	6	2	360
Purchasing Journal	3	1	490
Architectural Journal	4	3	138
Electrical Times	2	4	63
Electrical Review	3	1	214
Electrical Contractor	2	1	271
Electrical Wholesaler	2	—	—
Lighting Equipment News	4	2	159
Light & Lighting	2	1	164

* Less than 1 per cent.

specific markets, and also for 'tactical' use when Atlas had something to say of more than usual news value or interest. From this emerged a main schedule for Atlas Lighting consisting of the quality daily and Sunday newspapers, a selection of general management journals, and a group of top level professional and trade magazines.

Advertising for Atlas Lighting had a built-in measure of response in that coupons were included in some of the advertisements, and enquiries invited. Analysis of the results of a mixed approach using both national and specialist journals as against a schedule confined entirely to specialist journals was therefore available, as a first measure of the effectiveness of the change of media policy.

Sales analysis obviously provided the final criterion of effectiveness but as a measure of response to advertising these coupon results have value. As shown in the table opposite, the national colour magazine media provided excellent results by quantity and cost per reply relative to the performance of specialist media in the field. Only one specialist medium was able to match cost per reply achieved by *The Times*, *Daily Telegraph* and *Sunday Times*.

One very interesting finding of general application is indicated in the table. The direct response advertiser is normally concerned not only with the cost-effectiveness of varying media, but also with the volume of business they generate. It is not uncommon to find that the 'best' medium in terms of cost-effectiveness is, like the *Electrical Times* in the table above, a special medium directly appealing to the hard core of buyers. Even though the company would dearly love to generate more replies at the same, or similar, cost without the big guns (the *Sunday Times* and *Daily Telegraph* above) they would be out of business. This is no reason for ignoring the specialist media, but it is a reason for believing that big circulation publications are likely to be very important.

19.2   The necessary learning programme

Five elements may produce very significant differences in the response generated to campaigns for a particular product or service. These are:

1   Copy, i.e. the actual advertisement used.
2   The size or length of the advertisement.
3   Its position.
4   The time lapse since the previous insertion.
5   The medium.

19.2.1   Copy

Very little experience is necessary to discover that one advertisement will pull a great deal more direct response than another—differences of two to one are common. Since this book is about media planning, we will not attempt to discuss the possible merits and demerits of different copy approaches, but will confine ourselves to discussing how the media planner gets involved in this question.

Because it is essential for certainty of results to tackle only one variable at a time, copy testing must take place in the context of A/B splits. By this term is meant the ability of some newspapers to run different pieces of copy in alternate issues of the publication. This ensures that each of the two advertisements being tested is randomly distributed across the entire circulation. It is quite different from regional splits, or demographic splits, each of which might introduce bias into the assessment of the result. It is an interesting experience to carry out such a split, using the same advertisement in both copies but with different key numbers. Although it is unlikely that *precisely* equal numbers of responses will be received, application of the correct statistical significance tests will show that any differences fall well within the permissible limits.

The quickest and easiest way of using A/B splits is to take the number of advertisements available and run each against every other one in a regional evening newspaper. For example, if four advertisements were to be tested, *a, b, c* and *d,* it would be necessary to use six newspapers, and the copy arrangement would look like this:

Newspaper	'A' side	'B' side
First newspaper	a	b
Second newspaper	a	c
Third newspaper	a	d
Fourth newspaper	b	c
Fifth newspaper	b	d
Sixth newspaper	c	d

A typical result would show that *a* was successful in the first test; *c* in the second; *d* in the third; *c* in the fourth; *d* in the fifth and *c* in the sixth. Thus *c* has beaten the other three advertisements, *d* has beaten two of them, *a* has beaten one and *b* has lost in each case. Doing the assessment this way avoids worries about the relative circulations, responsiveness and location of the newspapers. Running all the insertions on the same day ensures that there is no seasonal peculiarity involved.

19.2.2   Size

It is advisable to run the copy test in the smallest available size of the advertisement, for reasons of economy. Testing the effect of size is done only on the successful advertisement. This is considerably more difficult in organisational terms, since very few newspapers are willing to run an A/B split on different sizes of advertisement. This is quite simply because extra editorial has to be provided to fill up the remainder of the space, and this will cause editorial problems. It is often necessary to agree to the advertisement appearing on a feature page where these problems can be settled in advance.

The assessment of the results of size tests is important. Clearly, if the cost per response produced by the larger advertisement is lower than that for the smaller, there is no problem as to which to use (and this is usually the case). On the other hand, if the smaller size produces a lower response, but a more economical one, then we are in the position mentioned in the Atlas Lighting case. Suppose we are, for example, considering pages against half pages, where the space costs are two to one, and the half page pulls 50 replies, whilst the whole page produces 90. Clearly, a single insertion of the half page is more cost-effective. However, assuming the advertiser wishes to spend the whole of his appropriation, he will need two half pages in succession and, if the normal pattern of diminishing returns applies, he may not get 40 to his second insertion.

19.2.3 Position

Testing position is arguably less important than testing the other factors, for two reasons. Firstly, it is likely to have far less effect than the other factors, because the position of a particular advertisement, within a particular newspaper, on a particular day, is likely to be much less important than the content of the advertisement and the medium concerned and the day on which it is placed. Nonetheless, there are occasions on which position does seem to have a dramatic effect on response, and it is probably even more logical not to test position simply because of the unpredictability of these events. Even if we can establish that page 3 is better than page 2 in a particular context, one cannot say with any kind of certainty that the same effect will be observed on another day in the same medium, or on the same day in another medium.

Such tests too are very difficult to mount since whilst many newspaper owners do not mind varying factors on behalf of a particular advertiser, they are reluctant to vary factors affecting other advertisers, and this is inevitable in position testing. At worst, it is sometimes possible to supply two advertisements from the same advertiser (or the same agency) and switch these around.

As a final word on this subject it should be mentioned that media owners have, over the years, collected direct response advertising for particular types of goods in particular features, and there is no doubt that readers in the market for such goods come to know this.

The most worthwhile kind of position testing would, therefore, be in feature against run-of-paper on the same day.

19.2.4 Insertion interval

Testing the optimum interval between insertions is so time-consuming and complex that it may well be better to rely, in the main, on *post hoc* analyses. It is, nevertheless, well worth getting the general feel of the subject at the beginning of the learning process, and using this as a basis for campaigns over a period of years.

It is often found in direct response advertising that frequency is the enemy of economy. Each advertisement seems to work on its own, and there has to be some change of climate amongst the non-responding readers of a particular publication before an equal number of them can be induced to respond to a second advertisement. The required interval may be two weeks, or it may be eight, and the best way of finding out is to run the advertisements in different provincial media, using one-week intervals in one, two-week in the second; three-week in the third and so on. On any cycle the experiment may be stopped when uneconomical results have been produced.

The real problem comes with duplication between national media. Where two newspapers, such as, for instance, the *Daily Mirror* and *Sunday Mirror,* duplicate their readership highly, four-weekly insertions in each may produce a different result to four-weekly insertions in one alone. Where a large schedule of national media is being used, the first insertion in a newspaper, almost all of whose readers have been exposed in other media, is unlikely to produce as good results as might be expected had it appeared higher in the order. Theoretically one might be able to allow for this by calculating the duplication from the National Readership Survey. Unfortunately, the NRS duplication does not seem in any way predictive of the diminution experienced in direct response campaigns.

19.2.5 *Media*

Although it may seem strange that the actual media forming the schedule are regarded as the last in the order of testing, it must be emphasised that unless the previous factors have been established then a media test is not likely to be particularly helpful. Clearly the advertiser and his agency will either know, or be able to guess, the type of consumer most likely to respond to his advertising, and will be able to select a media list for trial on this basis. As mentioned above, because factors beyond the control, or even the discernment, of the advertiser may produce a large difference in response between two insertions, at least two trials should be given to each medium. With an initial list of ten publications, this already means 20 insertions which, with the preliminary testing, will make a considerable hole in many budgets. For the advertiser who has not yet exhausted either his patience, or his budget, further media should be tried which appear to be similar (in a subjective way) to the media which have produced the best response so far. At the same time plans will be laid for repeating insertions in all cost-effective media at the optimum time interval.

Where everything has worked perfectly, and a good estimate has been made of the rate of fall-off in return per insertion, it will be possible to draw up a table with media down the side and numbers of insertions along the top and size and cost of response in the cells. The planner will then be able to list the insertions he should have on his schedule in order, proceeding from the most cost-effective towards the least, until the budget has been spent, or the break-even point has been reached.

Everything which has been said so far has been said in relation to press media. A great deal of money is spent on direct response advertising through the medium of direct mail. Indeed, direct mail and mail order are probably the two most widely confused pieces of jargon in the business. All that relating to testing in press media, with the exception of position, is clearly applicable to direct mail, and is indeed the procedure which should be employed. It should be a great deal simpler because the requirement is not co-operative media owners, but well organised lists. If an advertiser has a list of, say, a million names of his prime prospects, then he may use randomly drawn sub-samples of, say, 10,000 names to produce test vehicles.

It is also important to remember that other media can be very effective producers of direct response, although the organisation may be rather more difficult. Radio Luxembourg have long had the reputation of producing large numbers of requests at a very low cost, for material likely to be of interest to their listeners. This is usually related to pop music, but can well be tied to consumer promotions by way of competitions and so forth. To get direct response from the television medium usually requires one of two ancilliaries. Either the commercial has to contain a reference to a coupon appearing in the *TV Times,* or some other suitable medium, or the respondent has to be invited to telephone a particular number at which he can either get action, or more likely deliver a recorded message. The first technique is used with outstanding success by holiday advertisers, and the second was used with considerable success some years ago by one of the advertisers we have been discussing—Shell-Mex and BP—for their Pink Paraffin.

The TV contractors now provide such a telephone answering service for advertisers, on a regular basis.

19.3   Related reading

E.J. Ornstein, *Mail order marketing,* Gower Press (1970).

C.J. Taylor, *Margo and Marcia,* XVIIth Annual Conference of the Institute of Management Sciences (1970).

Stephen Winship, *A review of factors affecting direct response campaigns*, Marketing Communications Research Centre, Cranfield (1975).

20 Trade and technical campaigns

20.1 Purpose

The term 'trade campaign' is normally used to denote advertising addressed to people operating the channels of distribution necessary to get the advertised goods to the ultimate consumer, the public. The purpose of the campaign is usually concerned with the encouragement of the flow of the advertised goods through the channels so that the consumer advertising, if it works, is not frustrated by lack of availability at the point of sale. Members of the target audience for such campaigns may range from Sir John Cohen to the owner of the corner general store.

The purpose of the 'technical campaign' is normally to assist in the selling of goods and services of a technical or specialist nature to professional buyers, either for their own use or for the use of their clients. Members of the target audience for technical campaigns may range from Sir Arnold Weinstock, to a mechanic in the local garage, to the principal scientific officer at Harwell, to the media buyer in the newest agency.

From these definitions the reader may wonder why the two categories are included in the same chapter. The answers are firstly administrative convenience, and secondly the similarity of the underlying problems which are quite different from the problems of consumer campaigns.

20.2 The nature of the differences

The biggest single difference facing the planner is that of the volume and quality of the information he has available. Target definitions in the trade and technical area are normally very much less precise than in consumer campaigns and media data may be completely absent.

Secondly, the advertiser's means of communication with the customer is quite different. In consumer campaigns advertising is probably the chief source of contact. In trade and technical campaigns the sales representative, either of the manufacturer or of his wholesaler, or agent, is likely to be the prime contact, and advertising will represent only a small proportion of the effort. Allied with the fact that the buyers are professional, both in the sense that they are trained and also in the sense that they are not buying for their own consumption, this means that the purpose of the advertising is quite different from that in consumer campaigns. It is most unlikely that advertising can be relied on to sell the product by itself. Its purpose is either to ensure that the products of a company are considered in competition with others, or, quite often, to ensure that the company's representative gets a sympathetic reception when he calls.

A further complexity comes from the fact that many buying decisions in this area are not taken by one man, but by a number. The processes involved in taking this decision are often complex and may not be well understood by those involved. They are likely to vary depending on the nature of the organisation and may well differ in different firms with similar organisations simply because of the different personalities involved.

20.3   Defining the target group

David Aitchison has described three levels of decision making in the trade and technical area and suggested that these may coincide with senior, middle and junior management levels. The three areas are firstly, the decision to allocate a sum of money for a general area; for instance, renewal of plant. Secondly, the decision to spend some, or all, of such an allocation on a particular piece of machinery. Thirdly, the decision as to which manufacturer that piece of machinery should come from. In the trade field these decisions could be equated with a decision to invest more in stock of convenience foods, then frozen foods, then a particular brand of frozen foods.

It is critically important that the media planner knows at which level the message will be pitched and, therefore, which group, or groups, should be covered. A considerable influence on the definition of the target is whether the product is of appeal across a number of industries and trades, or whether it is of concern solely to one industry or trade. The manufacturer of stationery, for example, has all companies to go for, whereas the manufacturer of surgical instruments will have a tightly defined market. The differences are not so sharply marked on the trade side although aspirins, for example, may be sold through grocers, chemists, tobacconists, licensed premises, department and variety stores, whereas the retail distribution of baths is considerably more restricted.

20.4   The trade and technical press

Groups of buyers, be they trade buyers or technical buyers, are often served by one or more specialised publications. These may be 'vertical' publications aiming to cover a variety of interests within a particular industry, e.g. *Campaign*, or 'horizontal', aiming to interest a particular level or type of personnel across a wide variety of industries, e.g. *The Director*. The advertising in these publications may be of as much interest to the readers as editorial matter. This fact has resulted in the growing trend towards controlled circulation. Today the best publications in some fields are distributed in this way.

At first sight it seems like the media planner's dream to have all the prime prospects for his advertising contained within the readership of a small number of relatively inexpensive publications. It is unfortunate that closer inspection turns the dream into something more like a nightmare. The key problem is the gross inequality of individuals within the prime prospect group.

With consumer advertising there are so many prospects, and the extreme range of their purchasing ability within the product field is so limited that it makes perfectly good sense to talk in terms of percentages of the total covered. With campaigns of the sort we are now considering, this is not true. For instance, when selling to the motor manufacturing industry, four companies in this country constitute the vast bulk of the market. It may be that there is one key person in each of these companies whom the advertising should reach. A campaign with 99.5 per cent coverage, but without these four men, would be of very little value.

We have already mentioned the importance and difficulty of identifying where the decision is actually taken. Eloquent testimony of the difficulty of this process is given by the fact that the identification of the decision makers in the selection of advertising media was set as one of the medal competitions by the Thomson Organisation, and attracted no entries.

Thus, clearly, the penetration of a buying group by a trade publication is of relatively little value. This point may have some bearing on the fact that very few trade and technical publications have set about the task of establishing what their readership really is. This critical lack of data makes planning in the sense used in the rest of this book extremely difficult. Experience has shown that the establishment of readership of this type of publication is in itself a difficult research task, and the cost may well not be worth the effort.

There are, however, no such excuses for the fact that many such publications do not supply audited circulation figures. It is usually the case that publishers unwilling to disclose their true circulation figures have good reason for their reticence, and planners are well advised to view such journals with considerable circumspection. Nevertheless, a glance through *Brad* will demonstrate that in a number of important trade and technical fields, it is unreasonable to expect adequate coverage without using publications which are bought in almost total darkness.

In an attempt to shed light into this area of darkness the Media Data Form has been introduced. This data sheet has the support of advertisers, agencies and publishers and aims to provide information of value in a standard form. It is completed by publishers, and includes a history of the journal, statements of editorial policy, method of distribution and various breakdowns of the circulation. Sadly, publishers who have been least informative about their journals in the past are least likely to complete the MDF; but the IPA, through agency media buyers, has been conducting a campaign to persuade them to do so.

A piece of crude, tailor-made research may well be the best solution to some of the problems. This involves enlisting the co-operation of the client's sales force. This provides a list of individuals within customer companies and prospect companies whom the salesmen believe to be important recipients of the advertising message. It is possible to get useful guidance on the relative merits of the different publications by conducting a simple and inexpensive postal survey to these addresses. Although the results of such a survey are bound to be influenced by the ability of the client sales force, and could not be put forward as industry data, they will nevertheless produce a very much better basis for media selection than the media planner sitting with a well chewed pencil and a copy of *Brad* as his only guides.

Although, as we have mentioned above, the chief purpose of many campaigns is a general one, it may be argued that a useful measure of the degree of interest which an advertisement may generate in a particular media vehicle will be proportionate to the direct response which the medium can generate. The most productive technique is undoubtedly the keyed coupon, and careful assessment of the results of such advertising, analysed not only in terms of coupon response but ultimately in terms of the value of the orders placed resulting from such coupons, will enable the relative value of the publications to be assessed. Because many technical campaigns cover a variety of different buyers with different educational levels and different skills, it may be necessary to run a series of advertisements rather than one. There is nothing wrong with this as long as each advertisement appears in each publication and the results are assessed over the whole series. No value will accrue from comparing the response from advertisement one in publication A with the response to advertisement two in publication B. This technique has been discussed in the previous chapter.

20.5   Direct mail

Most mailing houses carry lists covering a wide field of trades and of technical buyers. Comparing these lists with the client company's own account and prospect list will give an indication of their quality. If the lists are of a reasonable standard this method of advertising allows for high and unduplicated coverage of the prime prospects. Moreover, since there is normally a large volume of competitive advertising addressed to these prospects, the possibility of mailing unusual pieces may have considerable value (see Chapter 17).

A useful example of the exercise of this control is where direct mail is being used to introduce a new representative to a territory. Letters can be written from the sales manager, or from the previous representative where this is appropriate, to each of the representative's prospects, perhaps bearing a photograph of the new man. He can then arrange to post these as he goes off on his journey, so that the prospect receives the shot on the morning that he calls.

20.6   Other media

20.6.1   Print

Printed material of one sort or another often comes out of the advertising budget for a trade or technical campaign and may account for a substantial proportion of the total. It is not uncommon, these days, for the salesman to carry with him a folder, often in loose-leaf form, which contains a complete and ordered presentation of his sales story. Since few of these would normally be produced, the unit cost may be very considerable.

When any product of a technical nature is being sold, it may well be necessary to leave with each prospect expensive and detailed literature containing complete specifications of the product's performance, possibly measured against the relevant British Standard. In some fields it may also be necessary to leave swatches of the product showing surface designs and/or colours. These too can be extremely expensive but are not normally counted as part of the advertising budget.

20.6.2   Exhibitions

These represent an important way of getting at a section of the target audience for any trade or technical campaign. The fact that their audience is usually confined to the most enthusiastic section of the target is clearly not a serious disadvantage. On the other hand, the ability to entertain prospective customers in a very business-like atmosphere, when they can be shown films and other visual aids concerning the product, and orders can actually be taken, is clearly a considerable advantage. Exhibitions will only be used as a part of the trade or technical campaign where there is a serious selling job to be done in depth. They would not be recommended for the important, but relatively simple, task of communicating to the trade that a consumer campaign was to be launched.

20.6.3   Non-specialist publications

The market for some products is spread across a wide and heterogenous group of buyers. The installation of a Telex, for example, is something which is appropriate for companies in virtually all industries, and for which the purchase decision may be made by executives carrying a wide range of titles. In cases like this, resort is often made to what is loosely termed the 'business press', This term is applied to that group of newspapers and magazines which tend to be read by most business executives, as an adjunct to their more specialist press. By using the *Financial Times*, the Business News sections of *The Times*, the *Sunday Times* and the *Observer*, and the management journals, it may well be possible to reach the target market more economically than by using a long list of specialist technical publications.

20.6.4   Television

The television medium is also used on occasions for dramatic coverage of a trade or technical group. Since the potential buyers will form only a minute portion of the total television audience, the cost-per-thousand of such a campaign is enormous. Nevertheless, it may be worth it. A classic example from the United States was the campaign for the Xerox Corporation addressing messages via this mass medium to chief executives of important companies, which produced dramatic results for the sale of dry copiers. It is interesting to note that a similar campaign in this country was not judged to be successful. Certain television contractors are prepared to grant special facilities for messages addressed to retailers concerning the imminent launch of television campaigns for products which they will sell. This approach can be combined with a mailing requesting the retailer

to look at the commercial channel during a specified off-peak period, thus reducing the capital cost of the operation.

20.6.5   Outdoor

Nor should the poster medium be overlooked. By individual selection of promi-
nent sites in positions where key buyers cannot fail to see them, the message
may be delivered in an interesting and different way. Although production costs
will be very high in proportion to space costs, this may not matter for the attain-
ment of a special effect.

20.7   Related reading

D.R. Aitchison, *The advertising of industrial goods and services,* New Scientist
   Publications (1970).
Emil Hofsoos, *What management should know about industrial advertising,* Gulf
   Publishing Company (1970).
V. Markham, *Effective industrial selling,* Allen & Unwin (1970).

21 Difficult media

We must begin by stating why we feel that some minor media should present unusual difficulties to a skilled media planner.

These media share several characteristics: first of all there is little or no objective data as to the audience they reach. Secondly, they fit into no particular pattern so that inter-media comparisons, always difficult, are particularly so. Thirdly, because they are minor media, a media planner himself seldom has experience on which to base his judgements, and normally no case histories are available for his guidance. Fourthly, because they *are* minor media, any effects that they might have are usually swamped by the employment of other media directed towards the same end. Fifthly, they seldom fit into a neat organisational pattern. Who in the agency, for instance, should organise production for news-casters? The television department? The outdoor department? Sixthly, these media usually raise difficult creative problems, part of the difficulty stemming from the inexperience which the media planner shares. A matchbook cover may be an intellectual challenge to an Art Director, but is it normally one which he is pleased to be without. Finally, the media planner is at risk whenever he recommends one of these media. It is difficult for him to substantiate his choice on the criteria which he himself usually sets. It will be difficult to trace the effect of his suggestion on the campaign's success or failure, but if it does fail he knows very well that the failure may be attributed to his recommendation.

None of these reasons, jointly or severally, prevents some difficult media being of considerable size and having obvious areas of use. By their very nature, some of these media tend to be short-lived. Examination of the pages towards the end of *Brad* will give the current state of play. We shall deal here only with the three major, and permanent, classes.

21.1 Telephone directories

It may seem odd that a medium with a massive circulation, almost total reader-ship, and very healthy advertisement revenue should enter so little into the considerations of the media planner. The reason is not difficult to find. Telephone directories are almost entirely a source for people seeking information, whilst most advertising attempts to force itself upon people who are basically indifferent to it.

Nevertheless, the media planner should be aware of the possibilities. Any product which is in limited distribution (in the sense of having relatively few, named, outlets) should consider using telephone directory space to list those outlets. Large organisations may find that the freedom of layout and type size available in an ad can be used to help customers to find the right number more easily than does their routine listing. Ads can be very useful, too, as a way of listing numbers which are not in the directory as of right. The one place you do not want a hotel is in your own area; some groups have seized on this fact, and listed their addresses and telephone numbers nationally.

This is not a cheap exercise. Although a page in a Yellow Pages directory with a small circulation may be bought for £768 (S.W. Scotland, circulation 47,000), a page nationally costs over £70,000 — the directory normally being current for a year.

21.2   Sporting sites

The use of posters and banners within sports grounds, particularly football and racing stadia, has grown considerably in recent years. Pressure has come from the organisers, often glad of funds from any source, and from advertisers. Some — like cigarette manufacturers, find it increasingly difficult to spend their money in conventional media; and most are sensitive to the chance of their message being seen by a much wider audience, through TV coverage of the sporting event.

But most of the impetus has come from the entrepreneurs who saw an opportunity, and have worked hard to exploit it. A small number of these companies handle most of the available sites.

Costs vary quite widely, depending on the immediate audience (Ascot racegoers may be considered more valuable than Aldershot FC supporters) and the expected TV coverage. The type of sign used also influences the cost. Most sites are sold by the season, and range from about £2000 for a First Division football club, or a first-class racecourse, down to £150-300 for Fourth Division clubs. Since there are fewer meetings, and the TV coverage is spread over more of the course, motor racing circuits command prices in the £250-500 range.

Clearly the usefulness of this type of medium will vary markedly from product to product. Apart from those directly concerned with the sport in question, for instance, bookmakers, tyre manufacturers, or whatever, probably the best application is for something which the viewer is going to need as soon as the event is over, e.g. some form of refreshment.

21.3   Exhibitions

It may seem strange to leave the subject of exhibitions to this position in this chapter. The reason is simply that notwithstanding the importance of exhibitions in the sale of some products, they seldom come within the range of recommendations of the media planner. This is perhaps unfortunate. Exhibitions usually call for a significant investment on the part of the advertiser, and we feel that they form a subject on which the media planner should at least be invited to comment. Clearly the usefulness of exhibitions varies very much with the exhibition itself, and with the product that is being advertised. Anyone who has seen the demonstrators on the small stands at the Ideal Home Exhibition will know that a large quantity of merchandise can be shifted in this way. It is a very useful way of sampling and distributing leaflets and other printed material. The fact that the audience for the medium is self-selecting means that visitors are more likely than average to have an interest in the subject of the exhibition.

We would suggest two rules for the media planner to follow when looking at an exhibition as a way of allocating part of an advertising appropriation. Firstly, make sure that the product will get significantly better demonstration and display than it will get from normal distribution. Secondly, convince yourself that the advertiser will make his stand a really worthwhile thing. This takes a lot of effort and is very time-consuming, but a poorly staffed stand is usually, literally, a cause of more harm than good to the exhibitor.

22 Market and media research

22.1 Market research

In most agencies it is not the function of the media planner to be involved in the commissioning, or interpretation, of market research surveys; but this situation is changing, in line with the trend away from media planning to campaign planning. In any event the media planner will be much better equipped to undertake his job if he has the ability to assess whether a survey has been well executed, or not, and to distinguish those findings which are important from those which are trivial. The only way the planner is going to discover things for himself is by studying the changes shown by research to be taking place on his brands, and attempting to relate these to his own work.

22.1.1 Available information

The most important source of information to the planner should be the brand fact book (or whatever it may be called). This should record all the current facts which are known about the brand, its performance, both physically and in the mind of the consumer, the sales history of the brand, the profile of users from time to time, the state of the market as a whole, the media schedules which have been used and the advertising which has filled them. If there is not such a fact book for each of his brands, the planner should agitate until one is prepared. Extracts from this book will normally form the basis of the historical review included in each marketing plan.

Sales trends are clearly of vital importance to the manufacturer and everyone working on his account. These are most easily provided by ex-factory sales figures, but unfortunately these are often the least helpful form of data. In the majority of cases there is a substantial lack of correlation in time between sales to the wholesale and retail distributive trades, and sales to the consumer. There are two main reasons for this.

Firstly, the pressure on the consumer is exerted by consumer advertising, whereas the pressure on wholesalers and retailers is exerted mainly by the sales force. Secondly, the stock existing in the distributive trades acts as a buffer.

Thus, if the manufacturer's sales force is doing its job correctly, there will be a surge in ex-factory sales sufficiently before the break of consumer advertising to allow all retailers to be in stock by the time consumer demand is generated. Secondly, strong consumer demand following advertising may not be reflected in ex-factory sales because, for one reason or another, the trade are selling from stock.

Nevertheless, manufacturer's sales figures are of extreme importance and all clients should be exhorted to supply them in as much detail as is possible (by week, by pack size and by television area, for example). The agency has to be aware that whatever consumer demand its advertising has generated, the only source of the appropriation, and client's profit, is his actual sales. Then too, no research organisation measures the whole of a company's sales, and over the long term the only way of establishing the proportion which is measured is by comparison with the ex-factory figures.

22.1.2   Retail audits

Among the most widely used tools for measuring consumer sales, amongst other things, are the Nielsen indices. These are based on panels of retail outlets, designed to be representative of the whole, in grocers, chemists, confectioners, tobacconists and licensed outlets. Some of these reports are exclusive to a particular manufacturer, but in general this service may be purchased by anyone. The fact that most major competitors in many product fields regularly see the same Nielsen information about each other's sales, makes it difficult to justify the aura of secrecy that surrounds many of these statistics. The reports generally show:

1   Consumer purchases: grossed up to represent national figures, for the total market and for leading brands, in terms of packages, weight and sterling.
2   Retailer's purchases: in the same terms.
3   Percentage of outlets stocking, both by numbers and sterling.
4   Percentage currently out of stock.
5   Average levels of stock, in terms of number of months supply.
6   Extent of exhibition of point of sale material.

All these figures can normally be broken down both by region and by shop type. The media planner should, wherever possible, attend Nielsen presentations on his brand. The research is conducted in bi-monthly periods and presentations are usually made about seven weeks after the end of the audited period. The sheer quantity of data presented often makes it difficult to extract the relevant from the irrelevant and it is well to go to the meeting with a number of questions, related to specific problems in mind.

Nielsen, and for that matter other retail auditing companies, will carry out specially commissioned shop audits in connection with test markets and other forms of test, to order. Many of these may be arranged in conjunction with media owners.

Useful though the Nielsen service is, it suffers from a number of drawbacks from the point of view of the media planner. To begin with, the consumer sales it shows do not correspond very closely with purchases made by domestic

households, which is the figure usually of chief importance to the planner.
There is a significant consumption of a number of products by commercial
establishments, and there are a number of very important retail outlets, for
example Boots, Sainsburys, Woolworths and Marks & Spencer which do not
allow Nielsen access to their premises.

22.1.3 Consumer panels

An alternative way of arriving at the information is by recruiting a panel of
households to record their purchases. This technique is employed by the
Attwood group of companies and also by AGB. The techniques they use are
different: Attwood relies on the housewife to compile a diary showing her
purchases in detail, whilst AGB sends interviewers into the home to count
packages which have been purchased since the last visit. Since they may have
been purchased and used, the technique depends on the housewife placing
such packages in a special container. From this the technique is known as the
'dustbin' technique.

This service is known as the Television Consumer Audit (TCA) as it was
originally financed by ATV, and is still run by AGB in association with a
number of the television contractors. These contractors derive great benefit
from having the data as they can talk to advertisers, and their agencies, about
future plans from a basis of knowledge (often better knowledge than is possessed
by the other side).

Both Attwood and AGB generally provide the following information:
1   Consumer purchases during a four-week period, grossed up to represent
     a national figure in terms of packages, weight and sterling, both for the
     whole market and for leading brands.
2   Percentage of households buying during the period, and the demographic
     characteristics of the buyers.
3   Source of purchase.

Many of the most useful data available from consumer panels come from
special analyses. It is, for example, possible to trace the brand purchasing
behaviour of a given household over a long period of time and by aggregating
such data to establish the degree of brand loyalty in the market. It is also
possible to examine the effects of different marketing strategies. Consumers may
be grouped into light, medium and heavy purchasing groups; in a number of
important product fields it is found that the majority of consumption is
accounted for by a small minority of homes. If these homes can be isolated in
media treatment, clearly greater efficiency will result.

Such considerations lead to the desire to establish surveys linking use of
products and exposure to media; we shall deal with such studies in the next
chapter.

22.1.4 Specially commissioned surveys

In addition to ongoing pieces of research, there will probably be a number of
ad hoc surveys which are being carried out specifically to answer problems on a

particular market. These may range all the way from a few basic demographics of a brand's users, to large-scale segmentation studies aimed at isolating the prime prospects for a brand, and indicating how they must best be approached in advertising terms.

The more thoroughly the planner acquaints himself with such research, the better he will do his job.

22.1.5   *Evaluating surveys*

Since we have recommended that he should have some idea of how to evaluate such research, a few basic rules are called for.

Firstly, the question of sample size. This is not usually of such significance as is suggested, but it is an easy quantity to pontificate about. In general terms, the only point of increasing sample size is to enable more precise estimates to be made. In relation to the margins of error associated with most business judgements, to have 19 chances out of 20 of being within 5 per cent of the truth is fine. A sample of about 400 is quite adequate for this purpose. However, the problem comes when examination of specific groups has to be made. If we wish to examine the demographics of a brand which is not purchased by more than 10 per cent of the population, then our sample has to be multiplied by ten in order to arrive at the same degree of accuracy.

With today's emphasis on computer processing of research results, it is necessary to pay great heed to the unweighted sample figure printed at the top of each column. With complicated analyses of one question against another, it is quite easy to find that given a basic sample size of 3000, percentages are being calculated on a filtered base of two. Information of this type is seldom helpful.

Usually of far more importance, and less often looked into, is the representativeness of the sample. The whole process of calculating confidence intervals depends entirely on the sample being truly representative of the population from which it is drawn. The simplest way of doing this is to have a random sample, or, as it is more helpfully called, an equi-probability sample. This term means that every individual in the population being sampled has an equal chance of appearing in the sample. It is an ideal which is very difficult and very expensive to attain in practice. For this reason another technique is frequently employed, the most common being quota sampling.

This means that the interviewer is told how many of each category of respondent she has to interview, and contacts enough individuals to complete this assignment. The four basic faults often associated with quota sampling are those of region, time, place and interviewer selection. It is essential that if the sample is supposed to be nationally representative, enough sampling points, or places in which interviews are held, are included. There are substantial regional variations in many patterns of consumption and habit in this country, and it may well be important that each variation is included at its true value. Look askance at surveys in which fewer than thirty sampling points have been used.

Problems of time and place tend to be inter-related. If the interviewing is in the home and conducted during the daytime, it is clear that most working housewives will be missed. On the other hand, in-home interviews conducted Monday through Saturday on the subject of beer drinking, might well miss the most important consumers. The question to be asked in this connection is: is the short-fall of a particular group likely to correlate with what is being measured?

Interviewer selection contains two problems. The most conscientious interviewer is likely, at the end of a hard day or at the end of a difficult quota, to select respondents who look sympathetic, or who do not appear to be in a desperate hurry to do something else. Much worse is the interviewer's friend who is a 'quota filler'. Once an interviewer has found a willing respondent who comes in an unusual quota, it is extremely tempting to go back to the same person when a different survey calls for a similar quota. This is a problem which good supervision should solve.

Thirdly, and very importantly, we come to the question of the questionnaire itself. The most impeccably selected sample will produce bad results from a bad questionnaire. Sometimes, too, this is difficult to detect, which is the basic reason pilot surveys are conducted. What appears perfectly reasonable in the research office, sometimes strikes the consumer as being very peculiar. The most obvious pitfalls are leading questions: 'Is there anything you particularly dislike about this brand?' not balanced by a similar positive question. Beware of woolly questions: 'Which is your usual brand?' How meaningful the answers are to particular questions may be indicated by comparing answers to similar questions put in different ways at different points in the questionnaire.

Finally, we would stress the philosophical viewpoint put forward by Professor Ed Burske of the Harvard Business School. In research in this country we tend to be rather purist, which is all to the good. However, there is a tendency, if a fault is discovered in a particular survey, to discard the whole thing lock, stock and barrel. Professor Burske urges us to examine the survey in detail to see whether it does in fact tell us anything we did not know before, which is useful, and in which we can have reasonable confidence, despite whatever the defect may be. Research data are scarce and precious and this advice will often prevent us from throwing the baby away with the bath water.

22.1.6 Other data sources

If a planner is really stuck for information about a particular market there are a number of sources to which he can turn for help. Odhams (now part of the International Publishing Corporation) for many years conducted high-quality surveys into different markets, in association with various of their periodicals. These surveys are still being continued under the aegis of IPC and are available at a low cost. It is worth going through the questionnaires on these surveys because not all the results are published in the tables. The best generally available source of demographic data on the whisky market, for example, was once a question asked on (what was published as) a survey into beer and stout.

IPC have in fact recently published a substantial document called the *IPC Marketing Manual*. This is a collection of information about a number of markets in the UK and is helpful mostly as a source of reference to other publications rather than for the material itself.

A different kind of marketing manual used to be published by the British Bureau of Television Advertising. This showed in very considerable detail, for all the administrative areas within television regions, a large number of basic facts concerning population, housing rateable values, retail outlets, and so on.

The Economist Intelligence Unit in its *Retail Business,* and Mintel, in the *Mintel Report,* publish much information about various markets which is updated every few years. More frequently the *Financial Times* publishes articles concerning recent trends in markets.

Finally, trade publications can be a useful source of information. The editors of many of these are well informed about their subjects and often know what surveys have been carried out by whom. Sometimes, indeed, the journal will have commissioned a survey of the market itself for editorial purposes.

22.2 Media research

It has been calculated that the sum spent on collecting and processing media research data in the UK is currently approaching £2 million per year. It is possible that as a result of this expenditure no more time or space is bought or sold, but it is hoped that it is bought to better purpose. One of the ways in which the media planner in this country is exceptionally fortunate is that he has an agreed set of industry figures on which to base his major media decisions. Although there are many problems with research produced by committees, a great deal of work has been done, over the last few years in particular, by advertisers, agents and media owners to ensure that the data are of the highest quality possible.

22.2.1 *JICTAR – Joint Industry Committee for Television Advertising Research*

This committee is responsible for production of research into the audiences for television, and has commissioned AGB with the task of collecting and processing the data.

Sample   The sample comprises a panel of homes of net reporting size 2650 divided as follows: London 350, Midlands, Lancashire, Yorkshire 300 each, Central Scotland, Wales & West, South, Tyne Tees and East 200 each, South West, Ulster, Border and Grampian 100 each. Some 7500 individuals live in these panel homes, and it is from their viewing records that the data on individual viewing are produced.

The sample is drawn from a much larger sample, interviewed three times a year by AGB on their home audit. The purpose of this audit is basically to determine the sales of consumer durables. In the course of these interviews, information concerning the type and nature of the television set in the home, if there is one, together with the channels which can be received on it, are recorded. These base data not only provide a framework for drawing the meter sample, but also provide information on the television audience in total. This information is published in the form of the 'establishment survey'.

Method   AGB has developed, for the purposes of this contract, a sophisticated electronic meter which records the switching behaviour of the set in a form which is quickly convertible to computer in-put material (punched paper tape). They have also developed a diary completed by each member of the household for themselves, and by the housewife additionally for guests, indicating the time, or times, at which they were watching television. These diaries are read directly by a computer peripheral which also produces punched paper tape. The two streams of data are merged in the computer, and the size and nature of the audience for each minute of transmission are deduced. Additional information is fed in concerning the programmes which were transmitted and also the commercials, along with their time of transmission.

Reports: THE TV RATINGS REPORT   This is received by contributors first thing every Monday morning and relates to the viewing period which finished at the close of transmission on the Sunday eight days previous. It contains data relating to the eight major areas (Trident and Stags each being treated as an area) presented in various forms. The pages are grouped station by station, with the days running Monday to Sunday for each station. For each day a page shows information as in Figure 22.1. This contains a graphical representation of the levels of viewing in terms of the percentage of sets switched on to both ITV and BBC. Programme information for each channel is included alongside the graph, and the indentations on the line alongside it indicate the time and duration of commercial breaks. On the left-hand side of the page total set ratings, together with those for BBC and ITV separately, the number of sets switched to ITV and the share, are all shown averaged for each quarter of an hour. Figure 22.2 shows a second page in which the commercial ratings in terms of sets switched on are listed, together with the time of transmission, duration and cost-per-thousand calculated at the 30-second rate. Finally, a page intended as the major planning tool is shown in Figure 22.3. For each break during the day, the time, the programme, this week's set rating, the previous three weeks' set ratings individually, and the four-week average, are all shown, together with the four-week cost-per-thousand sets and the current week cost-per-thousand sets. The rating and cost-per-thousand is also shown both for the four-week average and the current week, in terms of housewives, adults, men, women and children. At the foot of each segment averages are shown for all the breaks in that segment, for each of the audience categories.

WEEKLY SCHEDULE OF COMMERCIALS   This report is received by subscribers first thing every Wednesday morning, two days behind the *TV Ratings Report*, but referring to the same period. Commercials are presented in product groups and within these, brands. Within brands, the commercials are shown by area in order of appearance. For each commercial is shown the day and date of transmission, time and duration, the rate card cost (this is accumulated to show a total for each brand), the rating, numbers viewing and cost-per-thousand at 30-second rates in terms of sets, housewives and adults (see Figure 22.4).

In addition to the commercial information, abbreviated TV ratings are shown for smallest areas. All these figures are for sets; no figures are shown for individuals.

ANALYSIS OF ITV VIEWING   This report appears three times a year and

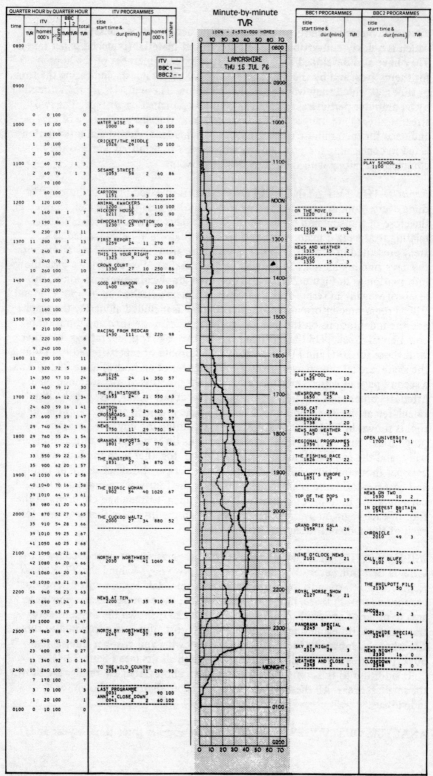

Figure 22.1

Chronological List of Commercials

LANCASHIRE   THURSDAY

****

SECS   7   15   30
RATE   £70   £125   £180

Commercial	Time	Duration	TVR	Homes viewing 000's	Cost per 000 (P)
TRILL BIRD SEED	1255	15	10	250	73
SETLERS TABLETS	1255	15	10	250	73
DOMESTOS SUPER	1255	30	10	250	73
MUNCHIES CAT FOOD	1327	15	9	230	79
UNOX CANNED MEAT	1327	30	9	230	79
WALLS MINI MILK I/C	1328	30	9	230	79
TV TIMES	1328	30	9	230	79
MARS MINSTREL	1341	30	10	250	73
NIMBLE BREAD	1342	30	10	250	73
PERSIL AUTOMATIC	1342	45	10	250	73
LUX TOILET SOAP	1343	30	10	250	73
WALLS MINI MILK I/C	1343	15	10	250	73
DRIVE	1357	30	10	250	73
HEINZ BAKED BEANS	1357	30	10	250	73
BLUE BAND MARG	1358	30	10	250	73
PLAYTEX GENERAL	1358	30	10	250	73
TV TIMES	1359	30	10	250	71
LIFEBUOY T SOAP	1426	30	9	220	81
KIT E KAT	1426	30	9	220	81
NDC MILK	1426	30	9	220	81
HOMEPRIDE WONDERLOAF	1427	30	8	210	85
TWEED PERFUME	1428	15	7	190	96
JOHN WEST CNND FRUIT	1428	15	7	190	96
HALLS PETITE RANGE	1444	30	7	180	100
FOSTER BROTHERS	1445	15	7	180	100
WILKINSON BNDED RZOR	1445	30	7	180	100
KP CRISPS	1445	30	7	180	100
TOBY LIGHT 5 STAR BR	1446	15	7	180	100
CROWN + 2 EMULSION	1446	30	7	180	100
HAVOLINE OIL	1447	60	7	180	100
MARS MINSTREL	1512	30	8	200	88
ENERGN ONE CLRIE DNK	1513	15	8	200	92
MUNCHIES CAT FOOD	1513	15	8	200	92
DOMESTOS SUPER	1513	15	8	200	92
ENGLISH CHEESE	1514	30	8	200	88
THINK ELECTRIC	1514	45	8	200	88
DENIM AFTERSHAVE	1515	30	8	200	88
WHITBREAD TROPHY	1515	30	8	200	88
HALLS PETITE RANGE	1545	30	9	220	81
HARPIC	1546	30	9	220	81
ELSEVE BALSAM H/COND	1546	30	9	220	81
STARDUST HOLIDAYS	1547	30	9	220	81
COCA COLA	1547	30	9	220	81
WILKINSON BNDED RZOR	1548	30	9	230	79
GUINNESS	1549	30	9	240	76

****

SECS   7   15   30
RATE   £135   £240   £340

Commercial	Time	Duration	TVR	Homes viewing 000's	Cost per 000 (P)
DENYS FISHER JENNY	1621	30	13	340	99
GLDN WNDR ROCK&RLLRS	1621	30	13	340	99
PERSIL AUTOMATIC	1622	45	13	330	104
COCA COLA	1622	30	13	330	104
LIFEBUOY T SOAP	1623	30	13	340	99
TREBOR REFRESHERS	1649	30	16	420	81
GLDN WNDR ROCK&RLLRS	1649	30	16	420	81
SKI YOGHURT	1650	30	17	440	77
HARPIC	1650	30	17	440	77
HEDEX TABLETS	1651	30	18	470	72
MR SHEEN H/HOLD CLNR	1651	30	18	470	72
KELLOGGS TWO SHAKES	1652	30	19	490	69

****

SECS   7   15   30
RATE   £240   £420   £600

Commercial	Time	Duration	TVR	Homes viewing 000's	Cost per 000 (P)
TAYLORS SHOP	1716	15	23	600	100
ELSEVE BALSAM H/COND	1717	30	23	590	102
BLACKPOOL ZOO	1717	15	23	590	102
ASBESTOS INFO CNCIL	1738	30	26	680	88
PLAYTFX BODY LANG	1739	30	26	680	88
M.M.B. CHEESE PROMO	1739	30	26	680	88
ANDREX	1740	30	27	690	87
PALMOLIVE SOFT&GNTLE	1746	30	28	730	82
OMEGA WATCHES	1747	30	28	720	83
HEDEX TABLETS	1747	30	28	720	83
BOOTS PHOTOGRAPHIC	1748	30	28	720	83
KELLOGGS BRAN FLAKES	1748	30	28	720	83
DOMESTOS SUPER	1749	30	28	710	84

****

SECS   7   15   30
RATE   £480   £840   £1200

Commercial	Time	Duration	TVR	Homes viewing 000's	Cost per 000 (P)
ENERGN ONE CLRIE DNK	1828	15	32	810	148
KENDAL MILNE	1829	15	32	810	148
BENSONS BED CENTRES	1829	30	32	810	148
KNOTT MILL CARPETS	1829	30	32	810	148
TV TIMES	1830	30	31	800	150
GRTR LNCASTRIA CO OP	1844	30	34	880	136
EMBRA INVESTMENTS	1844	30	34	880	136
BLACKPOOL ZOO	1845	15	35	890	134
CARLING TAKE HME PCK	1845	15	35	890	134
WILLIAMS SHOP	1845	30	35	890	134
ASBESTOS INFO CNCIL	1857	30	36	920	130
LENOR FABRIC SOFTENR	1858	30	37	940	127
GUINNESS	1858	30	37	940	127
CREST TOOTHPASTE	1859	45	37	960	125

Commercial	Time	Duration	TVR	Homes viewing 000's	Cost per 000 (P)
NDC MILK	1900	30	38	970	123
ARIEL WASHING POWDER	1900	30	38	970	123
FRESH & DRY	1901	7	39	990	
IAN ANTHONY	1901	7	39	990	
HAVOLINE OIL	1919	60	41	1060	114
WILKINSON BNDED RZOR	1920	30	41	1060	113
GOODYEAR TYRES	1920	30	41	1060	113
MARS BAR LINES	1921	15	41	1060	113
NDC CREAM	1921	15	41	1060	113
US DEODORANT	1934	15	39	1010	118
TOBY LIGHT 5 STAR BR	1934	15	39	1010	118
NIMBLE BREAD	1935	30	39	1010	119
P O TELECOMMUNICATNS	1935	45	39	1010	119
WRANGLER JEANS	1936	30	39	1010	119
ALKA SELTZER	1936	15	39	1010	119
BIRDS INSTANT COFFEE	1956	30	37	960	125
JOHN WEST SKIPPERS	1957	30	37	960	125
BOOTS PHOTOGRAPHIC	1957	30	37	960	125
CARLING TAKE HME PCK	1958	15	36	930	129
FRESH & DRY	1958	7	36	930	
IAN ANTHONY	1958	7	36	930	
ANDREX	2011	30	36	860	140
BRITISH LEYLAND	2012	60	34	870	138
ENGLISH CHEESE	2013	30	33	860	140
M.M.B. CHEESE PROMO	2026	15	36	930	129
GUINNESS	2026	45	36	930	129
KELLOGGS BRAN FLAKES	2027	30	37	950	126
MARS BAR LINES	2028	30	37	950	126
CREME SILK CONDITNR	2055	30	41	1060	113
W H SMITH LP/CSSTTES	2056	30	42	1070	112
HEINZ BAKED BEANS	2056	30	42	1070	112
KNOTT MILL CARPETS	2057	30	41	1060	114
COMPUTA CAR	2057	30	41	1060	114
WHITBREAD TROPHY	2058	30	41	1050	115
STARDUST HOLIDAYS	2123	30	42	1090	110
UNIGATE FIVE PINTS	2123	30	42	1090	110
DENIM AFTERSHAVE	2124	30	42	1080	111
JIFF LEMON	2124	30	42	1080	111
KELLOGGS BRAN FLAKES	2125	30	42	1080	111
MACLEANS NW FLUORIDE	2125	15	42	1080	111
FRESH & DRY	2126	7	42	1080	
WHITBREAD TROPHY	2126	30	42	1080	111
TAYLORS SHOP	2126	7	42	1080	
HALLS PETITE RANGE	2156	30	39	1010	118
WILLIAMS SHOP	2156	30	39	1010	118
CAMAY TOILET SOAP	2157	30	39	1000	120
HEINEKEN LAGER	2157	60	39	1000	120
TWIST SAVOURY SNACK	2158	30	38	980	122
MACLEANS NW FLUORIDE	2159	15	37	950	126
WLWRTH ICE CUBE TRAY	2159	15	37	950	126
KITCHEN QUEEN	2208	30	36	920	130
OMEGA WATCHES	2209	30	36	920	130
KENDAL MILNE	2209	15	36	920	130
VOLKSWAGEN CORPORATE	2210	45	36	920	131
NDC CREAM	2218	15	34	880	136
CARLING TAKE HME PCK	2219	15	35	900	133
NUTTALLS MINTOES	2219	30	35	900	133
MUM ROLLETTE	2220	30	35	890	134
DULUX VINYL SILK	2220	30	35	890	134

****

SECS   7   15   30
RATE   £275   £485   £690

Commercial	Time	Duration	TVR	Homes viewing 000's	Cost per 000 (P)
HARPIC	2237	30	36	920	75
JOHN WEST SKIPPERS	2237	30	36	920	75
DULUX SILTHANE SILK	2238	15	36	930	74
WILKINSON BNDED RZOR	2238	30	36	930	74
FRESH & DRY	2239	7	36	930	
ACCRINGTN ANTIQUE FR	2239	7	37	950	
DAILY MIRROR	2239	15	37	950	73
E M I BEACH BOYS	2239	30	37	950	73
TEMANA AIRFRESH BALL	2239	30	37	950	73
SKOL LAGER	2308	30	37	950	73
MCGOWAN JEWELLERS	2308	30	37	950	73
MACLEANS NW FLUORIDE	2309	15	37	950	73
ODOUR EATERS FT DEOD	2309	30	37	950	73
SENATOR CIGARS	2310	30	37	950	73
DAILY MIRROR	2310	15	37	950	73
BIRDS INSTANT COFFEE	2334	30	27	700	98
BRITISH LEYLAND MINI	2335	30	24	620	111
KRONENBERG LAGER	2335	30	24	620	111
MUM ROLLETTE	2336	30	23	590	117
WRIGLEY SPEARMINT	2336	30	23	590	117
HALLS PETITE RANGE	2337	30	22	560	124
SCHWPPS TONIC	2337	30	22	560	124

****

SECS   7   15   30
RATE   £160   £280   £400

Commercial	Time	Duration	TVR	Homes viewing 000's	Cost per 000 (P)
MARS BAR LINES	2348	15	15	380	106
ALL FRESH PADS	2349	15	15	380	104
DULUX VINYL SILK	2349	15	15	380	104
DOUBLE AMPLEX	0027	30	5	140	288
DULUX WEATHERSHIELD	0028	30	5	120	326
SPANISH SUN SHERRY	0028	30	5	120	326
P O TELECOMMUNICATNS	0028	45	4	110	349
TOBY LIGHT 5 STAR BR	0029	15	4	110	349
JOHN WEST SKIPPERS	0029	30	4	100	407
LADY GRECIAN 2000	0030	30	4	100	407

Figure 22.2

Analysis of Commercial Slots and Segments

Programmes	Slot time	Homes TVR 3 weeks ago	2 weeks ago	1 week ago	this week	Homes TVR	Homes Cost per 000 (p.)	H/wives TVR	H/wives Cost per 000 (p.)	Adults TVR	Adults Cost per 000 (p.)	Men TVR	Men Cost per 000 (p.)	Women TVR	Women Cost per 000 (p.)	Children TVR	Children Cost per 000 (p.)
LANCASHIRE	THURSDAY					2570		2570		5430		2560		2870		1490	
VARIOUS PROGRAMMES	1226	3	5	6	–	5	152	*3	238	*3	131	*2	301	*3	234	*3	407
HERE'S GOOD HEALTH / DEMOCRAT'S CORONATION	1255	5	9	9	10	18	93	8	127	7	78	7	178	8	187	3	417
THIS IS YOUR RIGHT	1327	6	10	8	9	8	97	8	108	7	78	7	187	9	188	1	
CROWN COURT	1341	5	10	7	10	18	93	8	143	7	72	2	218	9	148	1	
CROWN COURT	1357	5	8	5	10	10	192	8	138	3	87	3	291	9	182	1	
GOOD AFTERNOON	1426	4	7	5	8	8	142	4	147	3	93	2	295	3	153	1	
CRICKET / RACING/NEWMARKET	1434	–	6	–	–	5	144	*3	273	*3	118	*2	271	*3	210	*0	
SHOW JUMPING / RACING FROM REDCAR	1444	3	–	–	7	7	140	*3	203	*3	118	*2	283	*2	205	*1	
VARIOUS PROGRAMMES	1512	–	7	6	8	7	100	4	172	5	72	5	159	4	182	1	
SHOW JUMPING	1529	4	–	–	–	4	202	*2	322	*2	161	*2	377	*2	281	*1	
RACING/NEWMARKET / RACING REDCAR	1545	–	–	7	9	8	98	3	138	3	76	3	191	3	138	2	
THE UNIROYAL / CRICKET	1549	4	8	–	–	6	122	4	178	3	98	2	292	4	148	1	
30 SEC RATE £180	0400 – 1600 HRS					8	108	6	159	4	89	3	222	5	118	1	
VARIOUS PROGRAMMES	1621	5	7	10	13	13	100	6	216	6	102	7	199	5	211	10	221
SURVIVAL	1636	–	8	–	–	8	169	5	274	5	138	4	380	6	217	4	
SURVIVAL	1649	7	10	14	18	18	108	10	133	8	28	8	218	7	177	17	139
30 SEC RATE £540	1600 – 1715 HRS					10	83	8	158	8	115	8	184	8	204	14	164
THE FLINTSTONES	1718	16	15	22	23	23	101	15	157	13	86	12	204	14	150	19	216
CROSSROADS	1738	21	22	26	27	27	89	18	117	18	88	18	129	20	100	12	321
CROSSROADS	1746	22	23	27	28	28	83	19	117	17	85	19	132	21	100	12	335
GRANADA REPORTS	1809	21	–	–	–	21	110	16	143	16	70	16	148	16	135	7	
30 SEC RATE £500	1715 – 1825 HRS					23	88	17	121	17	73	18	181	18	176	13	226
GRANADA REPORTS	1828	22	24	26	31	31	148	24	193	23	97	22	218	24	177	20	402
VARIOUS PROGRAMMES	1844	23	23	26	35	38	100	29	132	28	118	18	208	29	167	17	382
VARIOUS PROGRAMMES	1857	26	31	33	37	37	123	28	188	24	82	32	210	29	128	32	348
SIX MILLION DOLLAR MAN / THE BIONIC WOMAN	1919	31	35	38	41	29	113	37	132	38	92	35	189	32	136	30	311
SIX MILLION DOLLAR MAN / THE BIONIC WOMAN	1934	32	34	38	39	36	118	38	187	27	92	35	187	38	121	30	235
SIX MILLION DOLLAR MAN / THE BIONIC WOMAN	1956	29	32	37	37	37	128	28	179	26	85	32	185	29	184	26	322
SPRING AND AUTUMN / THE CUCKOO WALTZ	2011	27	–	35	34	32	139	29	177	22	97	23	202	32	166	20	332
VARIOUS PROGRAMMES	2026	26	21	38	37	39	127	31	128	28	100	32	180	28	170	18	372
VARIOUS PROGRAMMES	2055	28	24	43	41	24	179	32	128	32	98	38	209	32	128	17	373
CLAYHANGER / THE SHADOW LINE	2116	27	22	–	–	24	194	22	215	18	125	13	348	21	195	9	
VARIOUS PROGRAMMES	2123	23	–	41	42	22	170	31	131	32	80	35	198	30	117	15	
VARIOUS PROGRAMMES	2156	24	26	41	38	38	127	30	133	28	87	32	195	33	128	10	
NEWS AT TEN	2208	–	–	–	36	38	130	33	142	27	82	38	212	31	136	7	
NEWS AT TEN	2218	26	30	42	35	33	132	32	142	28	87	31	208	38	127	7	
30 SEC RATE £1500	1825 – 2225 HRS					37	122	30	177	28	80	35	188	38	184	13	363
NEWS AT TEN	2237	25	30	40	36	36	73	29	78	27	47	22	124	32	75	7	
VARIOUS PROGRAMMES	2251	25	30	35	–	30	89	25	106	23	54	22	122	25	97	6	
VARIOUS PROGRAMMES	2308	22	25	–	37	37	72	24	118	21	41	19	100	33	93	3	
THE GREAT RACE	2315	–	–	29	–	29	92	24	113	26	49	26	102	25	95	8	
VARIOUS PROGRAMMES	2334	19	19	–	24	24	177	17	132	18	85	19	184	22	178	2	
30 SEC RATE £550	2225 – 2335 HRS					38	84	24	112	21	51	29	138	28	102	5	
THE GREAT RACE	2345	–	–	19	–	19	80	15	105	17	57	18	85	16	88	–	
VARIOUS PROGRAMMES	2348	12	13	–	15	13	163	18	128	12	66	11	149	13	182	3	
THE CHALLENGING SEA / MY SHERLOCK HOLMES	0012	6	–	9	–	7	212	5	346	6	123	7	214	5	291	0	
THE CHALLENGING SEA / LONDON NOBODY KNOWS	0019	4	–	8	–	7	222	5	296	6	130	7	234	5	296	0	
MY SHERLOCK HOLMES / TO THE WILD COUNTRY	0027	–	–	5	5	5	332	*2	473	*2	188	*2	327	*3	214	*1	
30 SEC RATE £60	2335 – HRS					10	182	7	215	8	112	9	173	7	281	1	

* AUDIENCES SHOWN FOR HOMES TV RATINGS OF 5 OR LESS

Figure 22.3

Weekly Schedule of Commercials

Day and date time and duration (seconds)	Rate Card Cost £'s	Homes TVR	Homes viewing 000's	Homes Cost per 000 (p.)	H/wives TVR	H/wives viewing 000's	H/wives Cost per 000 (p.)	Adults TVR	Adults viewing 000's	Adults cost per 000 (p.)
THREE IN ONE OIL										
EAST OF ENGLAND										
SAT JUL17 1900 15	308	27	320	137	22	260	169	19	500	88
SUN JUL18 1545 15	154	15	180	123	12	145	153	10	250	87
SUN JUL18 2240 15	154	13	155	143	11	125	175	9	230	96
	616									
	156560									
• NEWSPAPERS •										
DAILY MAIL										
LONDON										
FRI JUL16 2159 30	3000	29	1260	237	22	960	313	20	1820	165
MIDLANDS										
FRI JUL16 2123 30	1400	34	1040	135	30	920	152	25	1590	88
LANCASHIRE										
FRI JUL16 2122 30	1200	38	970	124	33	860	140	27	1490	81
TRIDENT										
FRI JUL16 2156 30	1500	29	870	173	25	740	203	21	1330	113
TRIDENT - YORKS										
FRI JUL16 2156 30 T		27	550		24	480		21	880	
TRIDENT - N.E.										
FRI JUL16 2122 30 T		34	315		28	255		23	450	
SCOTLAND										
FRI JUL16 2123 30	660	33	515	129	31	475	139	24	815	81
WALES AND WEST										
FRI JUL16 2124 30	585	33	475	124	28	390	150	22	675	86
SOUTH										
FRI JUL16 2124 30	780	26	415	188	22	355	220	21	700	112
EAST OF ENGLAND										
FRI JUL16 2124 30	700	33	395	177	31	365	192	23	590	119
SOUTH WEST										
FRI JUL16 2122 30	278	24	127	219						
ULSTER										
FRI JUL16 2124 30	145	32	128	114						
BORDER										
FRI JUL16 2124 30	115	30	58	198						
	10363									
DAILY MIRROR										
LONDON										
MON JUL12 1957 15	2590	25	1100	335	19	820	451	16	1480	250
MON JUL12 2028 15	2590	27	1200	308	19	840	439	17	1570	235
TUE JUL13 1549 15	300	10	420	102	7	300	142	5	480	90
TUE JUL13 2231 15	2100	17	760	397	14	600	502	13	1180	255
WED JUL14 2125 15	2590	30	1330	279	25	1090	339	23	2080	178
WED JUL14 2251 15	2100	23	1020	295	19	850	354	19	1710	175
THU JUL15 1919 15	2590	33	1440	257	23	1020	364	22	1990	186
FRI JUL16 2322 15	770	14	610	181	10	450	242	10	890	124
SUN JUL18 2132 15	2100	22	970	310	19	820	367	17	1550	193
MIDLANDS										
MON JUL12 1941 15	1015	28	870	161	23	710	196	20	1280	109
MON JUL12 2013 15	1015	32	980	142	28	860	164	24	1530	91
TUE JUL13 1745 15	260	23	700	52	14	420	86	12	780	46
TUE JUL13 2233 15	655	18	540	167	15	470	193	14	890	101
WED JUL14 1844 15	1015	31	950	147	27	830	168	21	1380	101
WED JUL14 2125 15	1015	33	1010	139	30	900	155	25	1620	87
THU JUL15 2237 15	510	31	930	75	25	760	93	24	1550	45
FRI JUL16 2231 15	655	33	1020	89	29	870	103	24	1580	57
SUN JUL18 2117 15	1015	24	730	192	21	650	216	18	1150	122
LANCASHIRE										
MON JUL12 1925 15	840	29	740	161	26	660	182	22	1190	101
MON JUL12 1940 15	840	35	890	134	32	820	146	26	1430	84
TUE JUL13 1746 15	420	24	620	96	17	440	137	16	860	70
TUE JUL13 2231 15	485	21	550	126	19	490	141	16	880	78
WED JUL14 2040 15	840	31	800	150	27	690	174	23	1230	97
WED JUL14 2159 15	840	37	960	125	33	850	141	29	1600	75
THU JUL15 2239 15	485	37	950	73	35	890	77	27	1490	46
THU JUL15 2310 15	485	37	950	73	34	880	78	30	1600	43
FRI JUL16 2253 15	485	35	890	77	30	770	90	24	1320	52
SUN JUL18 2045 15	840	34	880	136	29	740	162	28	1500	80
TRIDENT										
MON JUL12 1939 15	1080	31	920	163	26	770	194	22	1340	112
MON JUL12 2013 15	1080	34	1010	148	26	780	192	24	1470	102
TUE JUL13 1749 15	440	23	680	89	15	440	140	15	920	66
TUE JUL13 2231 15	520	19	560	128	15	460	156	15	930	78
WED JUL14 1941 15	1080	29	860	174	24	700	214	21	1280	117
WED JUL14 2159 15	1080	29	860	175	27	800	188	22	1390	108
WED JUL14 2232 15	520	24	730	99	23	670	107	19	1220	59
THU JUL15 1745 15	440	19	580	105	13	380	160	12	740	82
THU JUL15 2237 15	520	32	950	75	26	770	93	25	1580	45
FRI JUL16 1928 15	1080	31	930	161	25	750	199	22	1390	108
FRI JUL16 2253 15	520	29	870	83	26	780	92	23	1470	49
SUN JUL18 2044 15	1080	21	620	240	17	500	302	16	970	155
TRIDENT - YORKS										
MON JUL12 1939 15 T		33	680		28	570		23	990	
MON JUL12 2013 15 T		34	690		26	540		24	1030	
TUE JUL13 1749 15 T		25	510		16	330		16	680	
TUE JUL13 2231 15 T		18	360		13	270		13	570	
WED JUL14 1941 15 T		31	630		26	530		23	970	
WED JUL14 2159 15 T		26	530		24	490		21	870	
WED JUL14 2232 15 T		21	430		20	410		18	750	
THU JUL15 1745 15 T		21	430		14	290		13	550	
THU JUL15 2237 15 T		26	520		21	430		21	890	
FRI JUL16 1928 15 T		33	670		27	540		23	990	
FRI JUL16 2253 15 T		26	540		24	480		22	940	
SUN JUL18 2044 15 T		20	400		16	330		15	630	
TRIDENT - N.E.										
MON JUL12 1942 15 T		27	245		22	200		18	355	
MON JUL12 2015 15 T		35	325		26	245		23	440	
TUE JUL13 1749 15 T		19	175		12	110		13	245	
TUE JUL13 2231 15 T		22	205		20	185		18	355	
WED JUL14 1943 15 T		25	235		19	175		16	315	
WED JUL14 2159 15 T		35	325		33	305		26	520	
WED JUL14 2232 15 T		32	295		28	260		24	465	
THU JUL15 1749 15 T		16	150		10	95		10	190	
THU JUL15 2237 15 T		47	430		38	345		35	690	
FRI JUL16 1928 15 T		29	265		23	210		21	405	
FRI JUL16 2253 15 T		36	335		32	300		27	525	
SUN JUL18 2044 15 T		24	225		18	165		17	340	
WALES AND WEST										
MON JUL12 1941 15	410	33	475	124	28	395	149	22	670	87
MON JUL12 2030 15	410	30	430	136	23	330	176	21	625	93
TUE JUL13 1734 15	308	30	430	102	21	290	150	18	555	79
TUE JUL13 2234 15	184	18	255	103	13	185	140	13	390	67
WED JUL14 1927 15	410	24	345	169	19	275	213	17	510	115
WED JUL14 1959 15	410	22	320	184	19	265	220	16	470	124
WED JUL14 2159 15	410	29	410	143	26	375	157	22	680	86
THU JUL15 2027 15	410	34	490	120	27	380	154	24	735	80
THU JUL15 2239 15	184	31	445	59	26	375	70	25	745	35
FRI JUL16 2320 15	116	18	255	65	13	180	93	12	350	47
SUN JUL18 2024 15	410	26	365	159	20	285	207	20	605	97
SUN JUL18 2123 15	410	25	360	162	21	300	196	18	550	106
SOUTH										
MON JUL12 1941 15	545	27	425	184	24	385	201	19	645	121
MON JUL12 2059 15	545	27	425	184	25	395	198	22	720	108
TUE JUL13 1650 15	175	15	230	108	8	125	197	6	190	130
TUE JUL13 2234 15	320	11	175	261	9	150	311	9	295	156
TUE JUL13 2332 15	70	10	150	66	8	120	82	8	255	40
WED JUL14 1943 15	545	25	390	199	22	355	220	19	635	123
WED JUL14 2159 15	545	26	415	188	21	340	231	21	695	113
THU JUL15 1654 15	175	11	175	142	5	85	298	4	130	191
FRI JUL16 1736 15	545	27	425	184	23	370	211	19	640	122
SUN JUL18 2051 15	545	21	330	238	20	325	239	17	585	134
SUN JUL18 2145 15	545	22	345	227	21	330	237	18	600	130
EAST OF ENGLAND										
MON JUL12 1927 15	490	30	350	199	26	315	224	22	570	123
MON JUL12 1958 15	490	32	380	183	30	350	199	24	630	112
MON JUL12 2159 15	490	21	245	284	17	200	350	13	335	210
TUE JUL13 1749 15	154	22	260	85	15	185	120	15	375	59
TUE JUL13 2158 15	490	10	125	568	9	105	664	9	220	318
TUE JUL13 2256 15	70	14	165	60	10	120	82	9	240	42
TUE JUL13 2330 15	70	10	115	85	6	70	143	6	160	63
WED JUL14 1857 15	490	39	465	151	33	395	177	27	695	101
WED JUL14 2159 15	490	26	315	223	22	265	263	18	465	151
WED JUL14 2345 15	70	6	70	147	3	40	251	3	85	116
THU JUL15 1749 15	154	22	260	85	13	160	139	11	280	79
FRI JUL16 2214 15	189	26	315	86	26	310	88	18	465	58
FRI JUL16 2344 15	70	6	75	135	5	65	156	5	115	87
SUN JUL18 2118 15	490	21	245	284	19	230	307	16	405	172
SOUTH WEST										
MON JUL12 1942 15	195	36	193	144						
MON JUL12 2015 15	195	36	193	144						
TUE JUL13 2234 15	95	16	86	157						
WED JUL14 1846 15	195	43	233	119						
WED JUL14 2127 15	195	31	167	166						
FRI JUL16 2231 15	95	22	117	116						
FRI JUL16 2321 15	56	13	71	113						
SUN JUL18 2026 15	168	24	127	189						
SUN JUL18 2115 15	168	22	117	206						
BORDER										
MON JUL12 1941 15	83	33	64	181						
MON JUL12 2015 15	83	35	67	171						
TUE JUL13 2216 15	36	15	29	172						
TUE JUL13 2310 15	18	23	44	57						
WED JUL14 1857 15	83	38	73	158						
WED JUL14 1958 15	83	28	53	218						
THU JUL15 1749 15	32	31	60	75						
THU JUL15 2210 15	36	30	58	86						
FRI JUL16 1748 15	32	29	55	82						
FRI JUL16 2214 15	36	28	53	95						
SUN JUL18 2029 15	72	18	35	289						
SUN JUL18 2116 15	72	15	29	344						
	55747									
DAILY RECORD										
SCOTLAND										
SUN JUL18 1748 15	231	10	160	207	11	170	197	8	270	123
SUN JUL18 1941 15	462	17	270	245	14	225	295	13	450	146
SUN JUL18 2108 15	462	22	345	192	18	280	237	15	515	129
SUN JUL18 2204 15	462	16	245	269	12	190	348	10	355	185
	1617									
SUNDAY MIRROR										
LONDON										
SAT JUL17 1936 15	1820	22	950	272	17	740	354	15	1370	190
SAT JUL17 2149 15	1820	18	770	338	16	690	380	14	1260	207
MIDLANDS										
SAT JUL17 1440 15	180	9	280	91	5	140	177	6	360	70
SAT JUL17 1841 15	725	26	800	124	22	660	152	19	1220	82
SAT JUL17 2343 15	285	4	130	307	* 3	100	383	* 3	170	226
LANCASHIRE										
SAT JUL17 1729 15	320	23	580	79	16	420	111	14	770	59
SAT JUL17 1842 15	595	26	680	125	22	560	152	20	1060	80
TRIDENT										
SAT JUL17 1320 15	195	13	390	69	7	200	138	8	490	55
SAT JUL17 1421 15	195	14	400	67	8	230	117	9	550	49
SAT JUL17 1934 15	650	28	830	109	24	710	126	20	1220	74
TRIDENT - YORKS										
SAT JUL17 1320 15 T		11	230		6	120		7	300	
SAT JUL17 1421 15 T		14	280		8	150		9	370	
SAT JUL17 1934 15 T		27	540		23	460		19	820	

* AUDIENCES SHOWN FOR HOMES TV RATINGS OF 5 OR LESS

Figure 22.4

LANCASHIRE THURSDAYS

Analysis of ITV Viewing ALL INDIVIDUALS

4 WEEKS ENDING 27TH JUNE 1976

Start of 15 minute period	Total TVR	ITV SET AUDIENCE: TVR	ITV SET AUDIENCE: Homes viewing '000s	ITV SET AUDIENCE: Viewers per set	AGE GROUPS: Total 6910 '000s	%	4-9 770 '000s	%	10-15 720 '000s	%	16-24 930 '000s	%	25-34 990 '000s	%
1200	7	4	110	1.6	170	*2	50	*6	20	*3	10	*1	30	*3
1215	9	6	160	1.6	250	4	70	9	30	4	20	2	50	5
1230	9	6	150	1.7	250	4	40	5	30	4	20	2	50	5
1245	11	7	190	1.5	280	4	30	4	30	4	20	2	50	5
1300	13	9	230	1.5	340	5	20	3	30	4	20	2	40	4
1315	13	9	220	1.5	330	5	20	3	20	3	20	2	40	4
1330	11	8	210	1.5	310	4	20	3	20	3	30	3	30	3
1345	11	8	210	1.4	300	4	20	3	20	3	30	3	30	3
1400	11	7	170	1.4	240	3	20	3	20	3	20	2	30	3
1415	11	6	160	1.3	210	3	20	3	20	3	20	2	20	2
1430	11	6	160	1.3	210	3	20	3	10	1	20	2	30	3
1445	12	6	170	1.3	220	3	20	3	10	1	20	2	30	3
1500	13	7	180	1.4	260	4	10	1	10	1	10	1	40	4
1515	14	7	190	1.4	260	4	20	3	10	1	20	2	40	4
1530	15	8	200	1.3	260	4	10	1	20	3	20	2	40	4
1545	17	8	220	1.3	290	4	20	3	20	3	30	3	40	4
1600	17	9	230	1.4	330	5	30	4	30	4	20	2	50	5
1615	20	10	260	1.5	380	5	40	5	40	6	30	3	60	6
1630	22	11	280	1.5	420	6	40	5	50	7	40	4	50	5
1645	27	12	320	1.5	490	7	60	8	70	10	50	5	60	6
1700	31	14	370	1.7	620	9	80	10	90	13	80	9	70	7
1715	39	21	550	1.6	900	13	90	12	110	15	110	12	90	9
1730	44	25	640	1.7	1110	16	80	10	130	18	190	20	110	11
1745	48	24	620	1.7	1070	15	60	8	110	15	150	16	120	12
1800	50	24	620	1.8	1090	16	50	6	80	11	160	17	140	14
1815	51	25	640	1.8	1130	16	60	8	100	14	180	19	140	14
1830	50	27	680	1.9	1300	19	110	14	130	18	210	23	170	17
1845	51	29	760	1.9	1470	21	150	19	150	21	240	26	200	20
1900	55	33	840	2.1	1740	25	200	26	170	24	260	28	240	24
1915	57	35	900	2.0	1840	27	230	30	190	26	250	27	250	25
1930	58	36	940	2.0	1920	28	230	30	190	26	250	27	280	28
1945	58	35	890	2.1	1830	26	230	30	180	25	230	25	260	26
2000	59	29	760	1.8	1380	20	90	12	130	18	170	18	180	18
2015	59	28	730	1.8	1330	19	80	10	120	17	170	18	170	17
2030	58	28	730	1.7	1270	18	50	6	80	11	140	15	230	23
2045	58	30	760	1.7	1320	19	40	5	70	10	140	15	240	24
2100	60	31	790	1.8	1400	20	40	5	110	15	160	17	260	26
2115	60	29	750	1.8	1340	19	30	4	100	14	150	16	250	25
2130	56	26	660	1.7	1140	16	10	1	70	10	140	15	180	18
2145	55	25	640	1.7	1100	16	10	1	60	8	120	13	180	18
2200	55	27	690	1.7	1180	17	10	1	50	7	110	12	200	20
2215	52	29	750	1.7	1280	19	10	1	60	8	110	12	250	25
2230	46	26	680	1.7	1120	16			50	7	120	13	230	23
2245	42	27	680	1.7	1120	16			40	6	150	16	230	23
2300	36	23	590	1.7	1000	14	10	1	40	6	160	17	200	20
2315	32	21	550	1.7	930	13	10	1	40	6	150	16	180	18
2330	27	19	490	1.7	820	12			40	6	140	15	160	16
2345	21	15	400	1.7	680	10			40	6	120	13	110	11
0000	11	8	210	1.8	380	5			20	3	90	10	60	6
0015	5	5	130	1.9	250	*4		*	20	*3	70	*8	20	*2
0030	1	1	20	1.5	30	*		*		*	10	*1		*
0045	0	0	10	0.0		*		*		*		*		*
0100														
0115														
0130														
0145														

Start of 15 minute period	AGE GROUPS: 35-44 920 '000s	%	45-54 930 '000s	%	55 and over 1650 '000s	%	IPA SOCIAL CLASS: ABC1 1900 '000s	%	C2 2530 '000s	%	DE 2480 '000s	%	COST PER 000 30 sec rate (p): Homes	H'wives	Adults
1200	10	*1	10	*1	40	*2	30	*2	70	*3	80	*3	227	357	250
1215	10	1	10	1	50	3	60	3	110	4	80	3	156	250	179
1230	10	1	30	3	70	4	40	2	100	4	100	4	167	227	139
1245	20	2	20	2	110	7	50	3	90	4	140	6	132	179	114
1300	10	1	40	4	180	11	70	4	80	3	200	8	109	147	86
1315	10	1	40	4	180	11	70	4	80	3	190	8	114	147	86
1330	10	1	50	5	150	9	80	4	60	2	170	7	119	167	93
1345	10	1	50	5	140	8	70	4	60	2	160	6	119	167	96
1400	10	1	40	4	110	7	50	3	60	2	130	5	147	208	125
1415			30	3	100	6	50	3	50	2	110	4	156	227	139
1430			20	2	110	7	40	2	50	2	120	5	138	200	116
1445			20	2	120	7	40	2	60	2	130	5	129	183	110
1500	10	1	20	2	150	9	40	2	60	2	150	6	122	157	96
1515	10	1	10	1	150	9	40	2	70	3	150	6	116	157	96
1530	10	1	20	2	140	8	50	3	70	3	140	6	110	157	92
1545	10	1	20	2	150	9	60	3	70	3	160	6	100	157	92
1600	20	2	20	2	150	9	70	4	90	4	170	7	165	271	146
1615	20	2	20	2	160	10	80	4	120	5	170	7	146	238	127
1630	30	3	50	5	160	10	90	5	120	5	210	8	136	200	112
1645	40	4	50	5	160	10	100	5	180	7	210	8	119	190	106
1700	50	5	60	6	190	12	90	5	280	11	250	10	103	158	84
1715	60	7	120	13	310	19	170	9	370	15	360	15	113	155	89
1730	80	9	180	19	350	21	220	12	480	19	420	17	97	122	68
1745	70	8	180	19	370	22	220	12	430	17	420	17	100	129	69
1800	60	7	190	20	390	24	210	11	440	17	440	18	100	124	65
1815	60	7	190	20	400	24	210	11	460	18	470	19	97	122	64
1830	100	11	220	24	360	22	230	12	580	23	490	20	194	254	125
1845	130	14	230	25	380	23	280	15	670	26	530	21	174	232	113
1900	180	20	250	27	440	27	370	19	770	30	610	25	157	200	96
1915	210	23	260	28	450	27	410	22	820	32	620	25	147	191	92
1930	230	25	270	29	470	28	430	23	860	34	620	25	140	181	88
1945	200	22	260	28	460	28	410	22	770	30	650	26	148	189	92
2000	140	15	220	24	450	27	280	15	540	21	560	23	174	213	113
2015	120	13	200	22	460	28	270	14	500	20	560	23	181	220	117
2030	90	10	200	22	480	29	240	13	490	19	540	22	181	206	116
2045	90	10	220	24	520	32	240	13	520	21	550	22	174	197	110
2100	130	14	210	23	490	30	300	16	550	22	560	23	167	186	105
2115	120	13	210	23	470	28	280	15	520	21	540	22	176	197	110
2130	110	12	180	19	440	27	200	11	420	17	510	21	200	228	126
2145	110	12	180	19	440	27	200	11	400	16	490	20	206	236	129
2200	130	14	190	20	480	29	240	13	400	16	540	22	191	213	119
2215	150	16	210	23	500	30	270	14	440	17	570	23	176	194	109
2230	150	16	180	19	390	24	220	12	410	16	480	19	106	118	67
2245	150	16	180	19	370	22	230	12	420	17	470	19	106	118	67
2300	170	18	170	18	250	15	220	12	380	15	400	16	122	150	75
2315	160	17	170	18	220	13	220	12	360	14	350	14	131	167	82
2330	130	14	140	15	200	12	170	9	300	12	340	14	86	114	54
2345	110	12	130	14	160	10	140	7	250	10	290	12	105	140	66
0000	70	8	70	8	80	5	70	4	150	6	160	6	200	300	117
0015	50	*5	60	*6	40	*2	60	*3	80	*3	110	*4	323	525	183
0030		*	10	*1	0	*0	10	*1	10	*0	20	*1	100	200	400
0045		*	0	*0	0	*0	0	*0	0	*0	0	*0	200		
0100															
0115															
0130															
0145															

* AUDIENCES SHOWN FOR HOMES TV RATINGS OF 5 OR LESS

Figure 22.5

LANCASHIRE THURSDAYS

4 WEEKS ENDING 27TH JUNE 1976

Start of 15 minute period	ITV PROGRAMMES	MEN Total 2560	MEN under 45 1430	MEN 45 and over 1130	WOMEN Total 2860	WOMEN under 45 1410	WOMEN 45 and over 1450	HOUSEWIVES Total 2570	HOUSEWIVES under 45 1110	HOUSEWIVES 45 and over 1460	HOUSEWIVES with Children 970	HOUSEWIVES without Children 1600	Start of 15 minute period
1200	RAINBOW (15)(WK3&4)												1200
1230	HERE'S GOOD HEALTH (WK2364)												1230
1245	FIRST REPORT (23)(WK1364)												1245
1300	THIS WEEK (23)(WK2)												1300
1315	CROWN COURT (27)												1315
1330													1330
1345													1345
1400	ROOMS (27)(WK2&3)												1400
1430	VARIOUS PROGRAMMES (WK164)												1430
1445													1445
1500	MOODY AND PEGG (55)(WK263)												1500
1515													1515
1530													1530
1545													1545
1600	QUICK ON THE DRAW (25)(WK263)												1600
1615	SURVIVAL (24)												1615
1630													1630
1645													1645
1700	THE FLINTSTONES (22)												1700
1715	CROSSROADS (22)												1715
1730	NEWS (11)												1730
1745													1745
1800	GRANADA REPORTS (26)												1800
1815	COMMAND PERFORMANCE (27)												1815
1830													1830
1845	SIX MILLN DOLLAR MAN (52)												1845
1900													1900
1915													1915
1930													1930
1945													1945
2000	SPRING AND AUTUMN (26)												2000
2015	CLAYHANGER (55)												2015
2030													2030
2045													2045
2100	THIS WEEK (26)(WK1364)												2100
2115													2115
2130													2130
2145													2145
2200	NEWS AT TEN (29)												2200
2215	MAUDE (27)												2215
2230													2230
2245	THE ZOO GANG (49)												2245
2300													2300
2315													2315
2330													2330
2345													2345
0000	THE CHALLENGING SEA (26)												0000
0015													0015
0030													0030
0045													0045
0100													0100
0115													0115
0130													0130
0145													0145

* AUDIENCES SHOWN FOR HOMES TV RATINGS OF 5 OR LESS

Figure 22.6

covers at each appearance a four-week period. The four-week periods correspond to February, June and October, unless varied by agreement. Figures 22.5 and 22.6 illustrate a typical spread from this report showing the division of the audience by quarter-hour segments across a number of demographic breaks. There is a similar spread for each area on each day; rather more sub-groups are shown for London and fewer for smaller areas.

On a number of the examples, asterisks occupy the positions of figures in a number of places. The reason for this is that JICTAR has decided that viewing figures associated with ratings of less than five are subject to such large sampling fluctuations, they may be misleading.

FACILITIES FOR FURTHER ANALYSIS   AGB provide, with the authority of JICTAR, a number of further analyses of the data on a standardised basis. They can also carry out schedule analysis in terms of coverage and frequency, or, by agreement, anything else which the advertiser may require. This service is available to companies with computer terminals through CRC.

They are further able to provide to users with their own, or with Bureau, computing facilities, various types of data suitable for further analysis. These data need careful handling because AGB naturally record the viewing of the gross panel, whilst they produce reports only for a net panel. There may well, therefore, be discrepancies between privately processed data and the published reports.

22.2.2   JICNARS – Joint Industry Committee for National Readership Surveys

This committee was set up in the image of JICTAR to take over the supervision of what were known for many years as the IPA surveys. The survey has been conducted, without a break, since 1955, and subject to more methodological study and experiment than any other survey in the world. The research has been conducted by either BMRB or Research Services in recent years, but the contract is awarded on a short-term basis and put out to tender. The survey changes frequently, in detail; we will describe its current state and must warn readers to look out for changes.

Sample   Some 30,000 individuals aged 15 and over are interviewed each year as a strict probability sample of the total adult population, based on the electoral register. Interviewing does not take place in Northern Ireland, nor in Scotland north of the Caledonian Canal. The method of sampling implies omitting the readership of the peerage, criminals and the insane. Interviewing takes place continuously throughout the year.

Method   Interviewers are equipped with booklets containing reproductions of the 'mastheads' (that is to say the form in which the title of the publication appears) of some 90 British publications. On each 'masthead' is a scale prefaced by the statement (for dailies) 'in an average week these days, I see this number of issues, 6, 5, 4, 3, 2, 1, less than 1, none'. For Sundays and weeklies the period is a month and for monthlies the period is six months. The qualifying statement varies slightly with each category.

The first thing that happens in the interview is that the interviewer takes the respondent through the booklet, seeking a response on this scale to each publication. The respondent is then taken back through the list, and for each publication where any reading is claimed, the time of last reading (other than today) is established.

After this the respondent is asked a number of questions about exposure to other media, various purchasing and ownership questions, and finally exhaustive classification data about the respondent and also the household to which he belongs.

Reports   The main reports are produced every six months on data covering the previous twelve-month period. They show the readership of each publication covered in terms of percentage and estimated actual numbers for the categories adults, men, women and housewives, each sub-divided by age, class, survey regions and ITV regions. Examples are given in Figures 22.7 – 22.9. The data are then represented as profiles of adults, men, women and housewives. All these data are presented in terms of the 'average readership' of each publication. To qualify for this a respondent must have read a daily yesterday, a Sunday or weekly within the last seven days and a monthly within the last month.

The next section shows exposure to television and cinema, sub-divided by rate of exposure and analysed in all the previous categories.

Then comes the long section showing readership of all the publications broken down amongst the special groups. These vary from time to time, but are currently:

    Members of car-owning households – by social grade.
    Members of two-car households.
Petrol buyers:
    with heavy mileage
    with heavy expenditure on accessories
    with new car 1975/74/73
Men petrol buyers – by social grade.
Housewives:
    working full or part time – by social grade
    with children 0-15 – by social grade
    with infants 0-4 – by social grade
    with 0,1,2,3,4 + full time earners
    by number of years housewifely duties
        carried out
    in owner-occupied households – by social grade
Male heads of household:
    by social grade
    moved in last 2 years
Single women.
Married women.
Young people:
    men aged 15-20
    women aged 15-20
Holiday takers.

TABLE 9

ALL ADULTS

	TOTAL	\ AGE \ 15-24	25-36	35-44	45-54	55-64	65+	\ SOCIAL GRADE \ A	B	C1	C2	D	E
UNWEIGHTED SAMPLE	29681	4980	5358	4753	5081	4185	5344	757	3128	6709	9806	6571	2710
EST. POPULATION 15+(000'S)	41500	7645	7310	6246	6824	5947	7528	1061	4379	9380	13696	9207	3777
	000 %	000 %	000 %	000 %	000 %	000 %	000 %	000 %	000 %	000 %	000 %	000 %	000 %

GENERAL WEEKLY PERIODICALS

	TOTAL	15-24	25-36	35-44	45-54	55-64	65+	A	B	C1	C2	D	E
A T.V.TIMES	10497 25	2313 30	1991 27	1539 25	1498 25	1449 24	1537 20	264 25	1124 26	2521 27	3578 26	2224 24	787 21
RADIO TIMES	9947 24	2061 27	1779 24	1524 24	1651 24	1373 23	1558 21	441 42	1565 36	2723 29	2902 21	1680 18	637 17
WEEKLY NEWS	4320 10	751 10	700 10	628 10	783 11	684 12	774 10	15 1	165 4	711 8	1666 12	1295 14	468 12
WEEKEND	4208 10	1098 14	960 13	597 10	687 10	469 8	397 5	36 3	191 4	853 9	1783 13	1111 12	236 6
A REVEILLE	2712 7	499 7	473 6	443 7	559 8	393 7	345 5	9 1	107 2	461 5	1138 8	805 9	192 5
A TITBITS	2661 6	701 9	504 7	361 6	491 7	316 5	267 4	11 1	147 3	506 5	1104 8	714 8	157 4
A NEW MUSICAL EXPRESS	1403 3	985 13	198 3	95 2	78 1	30 1	18 *	21 2	132 3	348 4	556 4	315 3	32 1
MELODY MAKER	1378 3	956 13	195 3	90 1	92 1	29 *	17 *	42 4	158 4	399 4	509 4	253 3	17 *
MOTOR	1133 3	327 4	238 3	226 4	199 3	109 2	33 *	43 4	199 5	334 4	388 3	156 2	14 *
A AUTOCAR	1087 3	386 5	236 3	179 3	158 2	91 2	36 1	35 3	179 4	325 3	370 3	157 2	22 1
PUNCH	1016 2	362 5	212 3	145 2	134 2	94 2	69 1	80 8	254 6	345 4	237 2	83 1	17 *
COUNTRY LIFE	1013 2	138 2	200 3	132 2	194 3	183 3	166 2	112 11	244 6	271 3	228 2	99 1	59 2
SOUNDS	713 2	570 7	68 1	33 1	33 *	8 *	1 *	6 1	78 2	195 2	274 2	153 2	18 *
SHOOT	709 2	278 4	120 2	160 3	84 1	46 1	21 *	5 *	85 2	143 2	289 2	171 2	23 *
TIME	529 1	150 2	121 2	95 2	84 1	58 1	21 *	54 5	149 3	174 2	110 1	36 *	7 *
THE ECONOMIST	511 1	157 2	138 2	70 1	71 1	60 1	15 *	72 7	194 4	156 2	61 1	29 *	1 *
NEW SCIENTIST	467 1	172 2	107 1	78 1	61 1	39 1	10 *	30 3	160 4	172 2	69 1	28 *	9 *
THE FIELD	422 1	57 1	66 1	59 1	86 1	85 1	69 1	43 4	104 2	107 1	83 1	65 1	20 1
NEW STATESMAN	270 1	50 1	70 1	53 1	46 1	33 1	19 *	20 2	85 2	99 1	46 *	11 *	2 1
INVESTORS CHRONICLE	176 *	25 *	36 *	36 *	39 1	28 1	15 *	46 4	63 1	47 1	13 *	8 *	1 *
1 ANY GENERAL WEEKLY	21677 52	4912 64	4002 55	3183 51	3533 52	2905 49	3142 42	682 64	2587 59	5157 55	7252 53	4495 49	1504 40

WOMEN'S WEEKLY PERIODICALS

	TOTAL	15-24	25-36	35-44	45-54	55-64	65+	A	B	C1	C2	D	E
A WOMAN'S OWN	7584 18	1608 21	1421 19	1117 18	1237 18	1045 18	1157 15	159 15	803 18	1931 21	2546 19	1563 17	503 15
A WOMAN	7190 17	1486 19	1413 19	1012 16	1206 18	995 17	1078 14	167 16	774 18	1904 20	2398 18	1412 15	534 16
A WOMAN'S WEEKLY	5293 13	708 9	767 10	794 13	973 14	896 15	1155 15	95 9	489 11	1328 14	1779 13	1055 11	547 14
A WOMAN'S REALM	4371 11	713 9	749 10	663 11	782 11	651 11	814 11	83 8	410 9	1130 12	1494 11	872 9	361 10
MY WEEKLY	3337 8	465 6	503 7	398 6	614 9	579 10	779 10	26 2	208 5	665 7	1181 9	799 9	458 12
PEOPLE'S FRIEND	2743 7	281 4	303 4	305 5	503 7	505 8	847 11	24 2	148 3	529 6	854 6	688 7	500 13
JACKIE	1590 4	807 12	125 2	290 5	204 3	42 1	13 *	25 2	130 3	308 3	646 5	423 5	57 2
LOVING	824 2	520 7	83 1	93 1	79 1	31 1	18 *	4 *	36 1	146 2	373 3	237 3	28 1
LOVE AFFAIR	591 1	353 5	79 1	71 1	53 1	19 1	15 *	7 1	20 *	86 1	268 2	192 2	18 *
A NI	515 1	324 4	52 1	52 1	55 1	16 1	15 *	20 2	57 1	157 2	183 1	83 1	83 1
A MIRABELLE	466 1	272 4	39 1	74 1	46 1	10 1	18 *	7 1	23 1	75 1	185 1	160 2	15 1
A FABULOUS 208	465 1	315 4	34 1	54 1	47 1	10 1	16 *	3 *	38 1	80 1	182 1	146 2	16 1
1 ANY WOMEN'S WEEKLY	16124 39	3351 44	2650 36	2279 36	2626 38	2292 39	2926 39	318 30	1520 35	3918 42	5471 40	3394 37	1504 40

MEN

| | TOTAL | | WEIGHT OF VIEWING ITV | | | | | | | | | | | | TERMINAL EDUCATION AGE | | | | | |
			HEAVY		MEDIUM HEAVY		MEDIUM		LIGHT MEDIUM		LIGHT		NEVER VIEW ITV		15 OR UNDER		16-18		19 OR OVER	
	000	%	000	%	000	%	000	%	000	%	000	%	000	%	000	%	000	%	000	%
UNWEIGHTED SAMPLE	13016		2313		2897.		2970		2229		1796		811		8767		3179		1009	
EST. POPULATION 15+(000'S)	19827	000	3502	000	4364	000	4537	000	3429	000	2779	000	1215	000	13159	000	4964	000	1609	000

GENERAL WEEKLY PERIODICALS

	000	%	000	%	000	%	000	%	000	%	000	%	000	%	000	%	000	%	000	%
A T.V.TIMES	4744	24	920	26	1123	26	1136	25	810	24	610	22	144	12	3017	23	1353	27	364	23
A RADIO TIMES	4603	23	552	16	920	21	1101	24	901	26	867	31	262	22	2536	19	1449	29	599	37
A WEEKEND	2054	10	433	12	505	12	485	11	257	10	210	8	81	*	1425	11	541	11	86	*
A WEEKLY NEWS	1869	9	469	13	542	12	440	10	197	7	119	4	43	4	1460	11	359	7	47	3
A TITBITS	1429	7	421	9	344	8	369	8	201	7	149	5	65	5	1026	8	350	7	49	3
A REVEILLE	1328	7	349	10	333	8	308	7	182	5	104	4	52	4	1036	8	254	5	37	2
A MELODY MAKER	916	3	105	3	168	4	221	5	176	5	186	7	60	5	306	2	478	10	128	8
A NEW MUSICAL EXPRESS	897	4	113	3	193	4	239	5	158	5	151	5	42	3	313	2	512	10	70	4
A MOTOR	866	4	124	4	187	4	187	4	189	6	162	6	36	3	430	3	328	7	104	6
A AUTOCAR	866	4	116	3	147	3	195	4	172	5	164	6	52	4	422	3	336	7	87	5
PUNCH	656	3	40	1	86	2	132	3	150	4	187	7	61	5	174	1	308	6	167	10
SHOOT	474	2	103	3	122	3	108	2	69	2	60	2	18	1	271	2	189	4	18	1
SOUNDS	474	2	57	2	92	2	139	3	95	3	71	2	18	1	137	1	300	6	36	2
COUNTRY LIFE	446	2	57	2	61	1	97	2	91	3	105	4	36	3	203	2	175	4	68	4
THE ECONOMIST	377	2	13	*	24	1	67	2	93	3	143	5	37	3	63	*	169	3	142	9
TIME	352	2	25	1	38	1	86	2	77	3	94	3	31	3	102	1	127	3	123	8
NEW SCIENTIST	344	2	10	*	32	1	58	1	73	3	131	5	41	3	50	*	150	3	140	9
THE FIELD	229	1	14	*	42	1	50	1	39	1	67	2	17	1	100	1	82	2	34	2
NEW STATESMAN	192	1	8	*	15	*	35	1	38	1	76	3	28	2	38	*	82	2	70	4
INVESTORS CHRONICLE	139	1	8	*	7	*	24	1	35	1	45	2	13	1	35	*	66	1	38	2
1 ANY GENERAL WEEKLY	10697	54	1924	54	2272	52	2502	55	1878	55	1652	59	569	47	6407	49	3161	64	1092	68

WOMEN'S WEEKLY PERIODICALS

	000	%	000	%	000	%	000	%	000	%	000	%	000	%	000	%	000	%	000	%
A WOMAN'S OWN	1508	8	311	9	333	8	354	8	267	8	170	6	73	6	1000	8	401	8	98	6
A WOMAN	1251	6	274	8	265	6	308	7	227	7	128	5	49	4	803	6	342	7	100	6
A WOMAN'S WEEKLY	919	5	186	5	216	5	210	5	162	5	111	4	34	3	657	5	205	4	59	4
A WOMAN'S REALM	725	4	162	5	182	4	137	3	122	4	95	3	27	2	505	4	175	4	44	3
MY WEEKLY	519	3	135	4	110	3	125	3	70	2	55	2	15	1	385	3	115	2	20	1
PEOPLE'S FRIEND	508	3	94	3	145	3	121	3	74	2	51	2	24	2	386	3	104	2	18	1
JACKIE	368	2	70	2	79	2	113	3	55	2	58	2	5	*	185	1	165	3	17	1
LOVING	90	*	25	1	16	*	28	1	9	*	8	*	5	*	50	*	35	1	5	*
A FABULOUS 208	88	*	13	*	15	*	31	1	11	*	10	*	6	*	43	*	59	1	6	*
A MIRABELLE	87	*	16	*	12	*	20	1	14	*	19	1	6	*	46	*	57	1	5	*
A LOVE AFFAIR	75	*	24	1	15	*	11	*	10	*	11	*	4	*	41	*	34	1	7	*
A NIL	67	*	13	*	7	*	7	*	20	1	15	*	6	*	30	*	31	1	1	*
1 ANY WOMEN'S WEEKLY	3499	18	684	20	792	18	842	19	615	18	413	15	153	13	2354	18	913	18	224	14

HOUSEWIVES

	TOTAL	LONDON & SOUTH EAST	SOUTH WEST & WALES	SURVEY REGION MIDLANDS	NORTH WEST	NORTH EAST & NORTH	SCOTLAND	GREATER LONDON
UNWEIGHTED SAMPLE	14364	4783	2060	2318	1696	2238	1269	1809
EST. POPULATION 15+(000'S)	18450	6481	2401	2953	2234	2710	1670	2544
	000 %	000 %	000 %	000 %	000 %	000 %	000 %	000 %
WOMEN'S MONTHLY PERIODICALS								
FAMILY CIRCLE	2906 16	1289 20	369 15	425 14	206 9	391 14	226 14	472 19
A WOMAN & HOME	2527 14	959 15	377 16	375 13	237 11	339 13	241 14	292 11
GOOD HOUSEKEEPING	1885 10	825 13	236 10	260 9	171 8	234 9	159 10	313 12
VOGUE	1530 8	706 11	196 8	197 7	136 6	182 7	114 7	321 13
A IDEAL HOME	1387 8	520 8	176 7	204 7	164 7	193 7	129 8	172 7
LIVING	1354 7	608 9	156 6	215 7	108 5	155 6	112 7	226 9
TRUE ROMANCES	1325 7	415 6	155 6	208 7	146 7	218 8	182 11	167 7
SHE	1272 7	577 9	166 7	185 6	135 6	144 5	65 4	223 9
TRUE STORY	1271 7	402 6	172 7	236 8	136 6	177 7	147 9	139 5
HOMES & GARDENS	1142 6	537 8	157 7	138 5	97 4	145 5	67 4	164 6
COSMOPOLITAN	860 5	394 6	94 4	124 4	94 4	105 4	49 3	183 7
HOUSE & GARDEN	844 5	389 6	109 5	119 4	66 3	102 4	59 4	155 6
5 TRUE MAGAZINE	831 5	271 4	124 5	140 5	72 3	119 4	105 6	90 4
HOME & FREEZER DIGEST	717 4	322 5	91 4	124 4	38 2	89 3	54 3	116 5
PINS & NEEDLES	657 4	234 4	80 3	107 4	55 2	102 4	80 5	71 3
A WOMAN'S JOURNAL	652 4	293 5	93 4	85 3	55 3	62 2	63 4	96 4
A SEWING & KNITTING	577 3	222 3	76 3	88 3	52 2	84 3	56 3	61 3
ANNABEL	553 3	157 3	82 3	76 3	66 3	73 3	100 6	65 3
MONEY & VANITY FAIR	443 2	207 3	48 2	68 2	44 2	43 2	32 2	90 4
HARPERS & QUEEN	413 2	235 4	44 2	45 2	29 1	33 1	27 2	105 4
ROMANCE	380 2	128 2	45 2	63 2	40 2	47 2	58 3	46 2
WOMAN'S STORY	365 2	119 2	56 2	62 2	36 2	37 2	57 3	35 1
'19J'	348 2	149 2	42 2	51 2	33 1	47 2	27 1	63 2
A MOTHER	321 2	145 2	44 2	45 2	34 2	29 1	24 1	51 2
HERS	278 2	98 2	45 2	55 2	17 1	28 1	35 2	33 1
OVER 21	269 1	168 3	28 1	29 1	18 1	20 1	6 *	93 4
MY STORY	235 1	74 1	31 1	29 1	24 1	35 1	42 3	24 1
LOOK NOW	147 1	71 1	13 1	20 1	19 1	17 1	8 *	44 2
6 ARGUS WOMEN'S 3	2042 11	654 10	251 10	353 12	226 10	304 11	253 15	245 10
1 ANY WOMEN'S MONTHLY	8661 47	3355 52	1177 49	1340 45	882 39	1130 42	778 47	1223 48

FOR INTERPRETATION OF SYMBOLS SEE PAGE 17
FOR DEFINITION OF TERMS USED SEE APPENDIX E

JULY 1974 – JUNE 1975

TABLE 66

Owners of:
> central heating
> telephone
> consumer durables
> colour television

Adults moved in last 2 years.

A separate report is issued with the main report, showing the claimed frequency of readership, and the same figures adjusted to correspond with the claimed last readership. This is done to remove inconsistencies. For example, some readers who claim to read six copies of a daily newspaper in an average week, will not claim to have read one 'yesterday'. On the other hand, some respondents who claim to read no issues in an average week, will have read one 'yesterday'.

22.2.3   JICPAS – Joint Industry Council for Poster Advertising Surveys

Unlike JICTAR and JICNARS, it is not the function of JICPAS to produce regular surveys. What it has done has been to produce various pieces of research, carried out over the years, to establish the relationship between patterns of travel and potential exposure to the outdoor medium. This relationship is clearly not likely to vary until there are substantial changes in the pattern of our urban life.

The result of all this work has been to suggest that given the size of the town and the number of sites which are to be used, coverage and frequency can be calculated. The formulae for calculating coverage and repetition for a given number of sites are given in Chapter 24.

How should the media planner use these figures? It is clear that they are different in kind from the figures produced by the previous two surveys. The problem is that they relate to sites distributed at random over the possible locations and most campaigns do not have their sites so distributed. Moreover, most of the mystique built up by those closely engaged in outdoor advertising has depended on the fact that all towns are different in their physical make-up, and in the location of poster sites. Only local knowledge, it is maintained, can determine how many sites are needed to cover a particular town, whatever its population may be. Clearly it would be nice to have an objective appraisal of this claim.

In the meantime it is certain that the JICPAS approach is preferable to the old method of allocating posters on a basis of one per so many thousand of population. The formulae show that there is a kind of economy of scale operating: a town which is five times as large as another does not require five times the number of sites to obtain the same coverage and frequency. This has the virtue of being reconcilable with common sense.

Other useful findings concern the build-up of coverage in time (see Figure 22.10) and the realisation that reduction in sheetage affects frequency far more than coverage.

The surveys, and therefore these calculations, deal only with the adult popula-

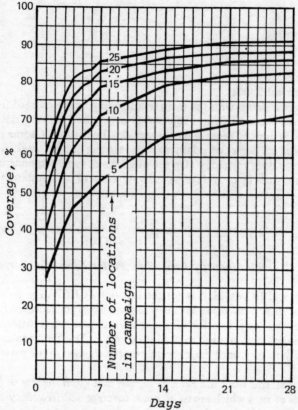

Figure 22.10 Build-up of coverage with time

tion as a whole. Information about sub-groups of the population may be obtained from the Target Group Index, in the form of weights which may be applied to the basic figures.

These show some big variations. Amongst men, for example, those heavily exposed to posters are six times more likely to come from the 25-34 age group than the 65+ age group; and more than twice as likely to be C1s than Ds. Amongst women, the 20-24 group are the most heavily exposed, while those living in the Anglia area are twice as likely to be heavily exposed than those in Westward.

22.2.4 JICRAR – Joint Industry Committee for Radio Audience Research

Although before the commencement of local radio, it was said that the stations would not be able to afford to supply research information, nor the agencies to look at it, we now have the full panoply of an industry service. Although JICTAR is the model, there are some important differences. The stations bear the entire cost of the research, and can therefore choose when to carry out any

survey, and hold the copyright. They are also the only source of special
analyses.

However, the specification for the research was agreed by the industry committee, who appointed a sole contractor (RSGB) to carry out any surveys required, on the basis of a competitive tender. Technical control of the surveys, although resting with the stations, is exercised through JICRAR.

Sample   For stations with a VHF potential in excess of one million, a net sample of 1000 has been agreed. For smaller stations, this figure is reduced to 800. If an area wider than the VHF area is sampled (as is sometimes the case) the sample has to be increased proportionately.

The method of selection allows for one adult to be interviewed in each household, on an equiprobability basis, with another adult below electoral age in the correct proportion of households (about 3 per cent).

Method   At a recruitment interview, demographic characteristics and broad listening habits of the respondents are collected, and a one-week diary is placed, where possible. This diary is a personal pocket diary designed to cover all radio listening, in and out of the home, for 24 hours a day. For each quarter hour, or half hour between midnight and 6 a.m., the respondents are required to record whether or not they are listening to radio, and, if so, to which station.

At the end of the week the diaries are collected by the interviewer. Since some respondents refuse the invitation, and some do not complete the week, the figures are weighted back to the correct demographic representation of the area. The survey is not accepted at a lower success rate than 65 per cent (60 per cent in London).

Reports   One report is issued for each survey, and, although there is a common format, the information will vary somewhat according to the requirements of the commissioning station owner. Children may be added, for example, as may be coverage outside the VHF area. Special analyses may also be reported on.

All surveys contain information about the structure of the universe, and the extent of listening (cumulative weekly penetration and average hours per listener) for all stations transmitting in the area. For the ILR station, average audiences are given for rate card segments, and half-hours, for Monday-Friday, Saturday and Sunday.

Standard demographic breaks used are Men, Women and Housewives; four age groups; two class groups; and housewives with children. In and out of home listening is also reported. The figures reported may be absolute numbers (of thousands) or percentages, and on the smaller stations it may not be obvious which is which. The presentation of audiences by absolute numbers, in demographic breaks, means that additional work is necessary to get the figures into a familiar format.

Radio Luxembourg   Some information on this station is available from the ILR reports, and more could be obtained by special analysis. An overview of the station's performance is available from the NRS, although this deals only with weight of listening, and not listening to any particular segments or combinations thereof.

Audience studies commissioned by individual media appear at a tremendous rate. They cover the entire gamut of possibilities in standard of execution and usefulness. Media planners are wont to cry that the studies would have been much more useful had they been consulted first. This overlooks the fact that the surveys are usually commissioned in order to enable the seller to sell, rather than the buyer to buy, and that the two aims do not necessarily coincide.

It may be asked with so much industry data available, why are special studies necessary? There is, of course, the very large area of non-consumer readership left untouched by industry research (see Chapter 20). There are also groups of considerable importance both to media and advertisers which the industry surveys do not cover sufficiently comprehensively, for example, A-class businessmen. Two attempts to cover this gap are extant: the NBRS, sponsored by the *Financial Times*, and the BMRC, sponsored by a consortium of 'up-market' media. These illustrate the point that where there is strong competition between rival media in a given field, there is likely to be equal competition between respective surveys. It is perhaps unfortunately true that the basic rule of media research is 'the publication commissioning the survey has the largest/most economical readership'. Conflicts of evidence of this sort may leave the media planner no better off than he was without any research. It is also true that the universe surveyed may be more appropriate to the medium than to the advertiser, and subtle changes in the framing of the question concerning readership can have quite dramatic effects on the figures produced.

Faced with these problems, the media planner will normally take recourse to the careful appraisal of the survey issued by the IPA's appraisal committee. This extremely hard-working body often throws up valuable warning signals concerning particular surveys, but unfortunately is often not in a position to say which of two conflicting pieces of data represents the best estimate of the truth. Whenever a media planner is short of readership data in a particular instance, a 'phone call to one of the obvious candidate media will usually produce something.

22.2.2 *Qualitative research*

All the media data produced by the surveys so far described have measured the largest possible number of people who have come in contact with the medium. What the media planner really wants to know is: if I place an advertisement in this medium, what quantity of my client's goods will it sell? The two measures are a long way apart.

For a very long period of time attempts have been made to bring them closer together. The best known work in this field has been the 'reading and noting' surveys pioneered in the United States by Daniel Starch, and employed in this country mostly by Social Surveys. Basically the technique has been to take a proved reader of a publication through an issue, asking him to indicate any elements on each page which he recalls seeing. Exploration is then made of all the claimed items to see how much of them the respondent remembers. The products of such research include an estimate of the percentage of readers being exposed to any item on each page, and the percentage paying various degrees of attention to each advertisement in the publication. The resulting data have been put to a wide variety of uses, including the determination of the optimum size of space, and recently in media models to convert probabilities of exposure to a medium into probabilities of exposure to a particular advertisement within that medium.

Over the years, too, doubts have been cast on the validity of the technique to measure what it was purporting to measure. Some of the doubts were concerned with the way in which the field-work was carried out, and this led to the formation of the Agencies Research Consortium. This body commissioned various research organisations to carry out field-work, and at the same time made an attempt at an independent evaluation of what the measures meant. The only evaluation which has proved practicable has been a laboratory testing method developed in Germany and applied in this country by BMRB, which has photographed respondents' eye movements whilst reading publications, and compared the results with standard 'reading and noting' surveys conducted later. As predicted by many critics, the experiment suggests that reading and noting data has practically no value for media work.

On the television side studies have been carried out, notably by J. Walter Thompson, the London Press Exchange and Research Bureau Limited on what else people are doing whilst they are watching television, and what effect this has on their ability to recall commercials. Many people have been particularly worried by the possibility that break audiences may not bear a one-to-one relationship with the audiences to the programmes surrounding them.

In an attempt to establish a technique which could be used to determine such relationships, and to provide corrective factors if these were found necessary, the IPA (with financial assistance from the ISBA) commissioned a study combining unmonitored diaries with semi-coincidental interviewing. Although the study ran into severe technical problems, the general conclusion was that the unmonitored diary was not a sufficiently accurate measuring tool for this specific purpose. Although there was confidence in the coincidental technique as a measuring tool, its cost prevents its general commercial use.

Clearly the distance between the two measures is greatest in the poster medium. Some work has been done to establish the effectiveness in terms of recall of given poster campaigns. It would be very helpful if JICPAS could extend this work on a co-operative basis so that the planner could be provided with firmer guidance as to the value of outdoor.

22.3   Related reading

Brian Allt, 'The MGN second household readership, income and consumption survey', *Admap* (March 1975).

H.A. Smith and N. Webb, 'How do women use advertisements?', Annual Conference of the Market Research Society (1974).

W.A. Twyman, *Review of consumer research sources for products and media,* Institute of Practitioners in Advertising (May 1976).

R.M. Worcester, (Editor) *Handbook of consumer market research,* McGraw-Hill (1971)

23 Product/multi-media research

Techniques for describing consumers in the target market and for describing the audiences to different media, have become increasingly sophisticated. The problem for the media planner is that whilst knowing more about the constituents with which he has to work, he has known no more about the relationships between the constituents. Thus has arisen in recent years a demand for sources of information which can enable him to view the picture as a whole, or to establish the relationships which exist between a consumer's behaviour in the market for a particular product, and his exposure to different media.

Whilst this statement of need is simple, satisfying it is not, and it is necessary to examine the need in some detail in order to answer the criticisms of those who say that difficult though the matching is, the perfection of the unmatched data provides greater overall efficiency than can single source data (as it is often called).

23.1 Increasing planning efficiency

There is a group of apparently straightforward reasons for the planner wishing to employ product/media wherever possible.

23.1.1 Operational facility

First comes its sheer ease. Target markets are almost always ideally defined in terms of brand usage. For example, we may wish to reach existing users of our brand, plus the users of the brand leader, as our prime target, or, alternatively, the users of brands X, Y and Z, under 55, living in the south. Given product/media data no further analysis is required. The media exposure habits of these groups are immediately apparent.

23.1.2 Pro's and con's of the accuracy claim

It is important to note that the efficiency of this process may be more apparent than real. Two technical problems are involved. Firstly, the definition of a user of brand X is a difficult one. Given a long enough time period most consumers in a particular market purchase most brands. In a short enough period each consumer will only purchase one brand but it may not be his, or her, regular brand. The consumer may in fact have a number of regular brands. The second technicality centres round sampling error. The way of defining target markets, in the absence of product/media data, is of course, to weight each individual in the sample according to their demographic characteristics. In this way the total sample is used, whereas by defining the market in terms of brand usage, it is likely that only 10 or 20 per cent of the sample will be used. For this reason differences in the media exposure of the two target markets arrived at by the different paths, may be due to no more than sampling error. This question is under investigation and, hopefully, by the time this book is published this question will have been answered.

On the other hand, the demographic weightings used as an indirect method of producing the target market, may in themselves lead to serious errors. They are invariably used multiplicatively, and with some product fields this process may not be justified. Let us consider the hypothetical case of a liqueur which is consumed after dinner by young to middle-aged ABs, and as a way of adding a boost to Colas by young C1s and C2s. Then, if we ignore regional variations, our market will divide like this:

	16–24	25–34	35–44	45–54	55–64	65 +
AB	0	25%	25%	0	0	0
C1	25%	0	0	0	0	0
C2	25%	0	0	0	0	0
DE	0	0	0	0	0	0

We have supposed that each age/class group drinking at all account for an equal amount of consumption. A survey of the market, analysed in the usual way, will lead to target market weightings that look like this:

AB	100	16–24	100
C1	50	25–34	50
C2	50	35–44	50
DE	0	45–54	0
		55–64	0
		65 +	0

The computer multiplies these figures to produce our weighted target market, which looks like this:

	16–24	25–34	35–44	45–54	55–64	65 +
AB	100	50	50	0	0	0
C1	50	25	25	0	0	0
C2	50	25	25	0	0	0
DE	0	0	0	0	0	0

Comparing the two tables shows that the derived prime prospect actually accounts

TABLE 23.1 *Daily Mirror*

		Readers '000s	Predicted hol.-goers '000s		Readers '000s	Predicted hol.-goers '000s
15–24	ABC1	878	273	C2DE	2194	303
25–34		696	143		2010	181
35–44		467	106		1669	134
45–64		1045	264		3149	368
65+		242	44		1166	82
Total predicted.....			830 +			1068
			i.e. 1,898,000			

Source: 1975 TGI

TABLE 23.2 *Daily Telegraph*

		Readers '000s	Predicted hol.-goers '000s		Readers '000s	Predicted hol.-goers '000s
15–24	ABC1	410	128	C2DE	240	33
25–34		469	97		178	16
35–44		431	98		162	13
45–64		992	251		317	37
65+		441	79		174	12
Total predicted.....			653 +			111
			i.e. 764,000			

Source: 1975 TGI

for no consumption whatsoever. Of course, real life cases are never so clear-cut or as difficult as this, but two examples serve to illustrate the point.

The first concerns people taking holidays abroad. The following percentages of demographic groups fall into this category:

ABC1	15–24	31.1	C2DE	15–24	13.8
	25–34	20.6		25–34	9.0
	35–44	22.7		35–44	8.00
	45–64	25.3		45–64	11.7
	65+	18.0		65+	7.0

It will be noted that these are age-within-class weights, and thus considerably less fallible than the separate age and class weights normally used. Applying these weights to the readership of the *Daily Mirror* and *Daily Telegraph,* we get

TABLE 23.3 *Woman*

		Readers '000s	Predicted slimmers '000s		Readers '000s	Predicted slimmers '000s
15-24	ABC1	626	172	C2DE	978	230
25-34		522	148		819	201
35-44		481	161		689	179
45-64		982	297		1419	358
65+		346	68		740	127
		Total	846 +			1095
			i.e. 1,941,000			

TABLE 23.4 *Daily Express*

		Readers '000s	Predicted slimmers '000s		Readers '000s	Predicted slimmers '000s
15-24	ABC1	624	172	C2DE	807	190
25-34		542	154		668	164
35-44		556	186		791	206
45-64		1291	399		1776	448
65+		598	118		1266	218
		Total	1029 +			1266
			i.e. 2,255,000			

predictions of the number of people taking holidays abroad, and reading each paper, as shown in Tables 23.1 and 23.2, respectively.

When we look at the direct figures, we find that they are 1,819,000 for the *Daily Mirror* (very close to the estimate) and 1,126,000 for the *Daily Telegraph* (47.4 per cent above the estimate). Thus the age-within-class weighting is shown to give a very distorted picture of the value of these two publications.

The second example is about women who are self-defined as interested in slimming. Here the age-within-class percentages are:

ABC	15–24	27.5	C2DE	15–24	23.5
	25–34	28.4		25–34	24.6
	35–44	33.4		35–44	26.0
	45–64	30.2		45–64	25.2
	65+	19.7		65+	17.2

These percentages applied to the readership of the *Daily Express* and *Woman*, work out as shown in Tables 23.3 and 23.4, respectively.

In fact 2,224,000 of the readers of the *Daily Express* fall within this group — again, a close match to the predicted figure. But the actual number of *Woman* readers in the group is 2,612,000, 34.6 per cent more than predicted.

With most products, and most media, such differences may not emerge. Two points should be borne in mind: firstly, if product/media data are available, they should be used, and used directly, for safety's sake. Secondly, if product/media data were not available, we should never be aware of the existence of such potential traps.

23.1.3 *Multi-media models*

In addition to simple analyses of the type presented above, product/media data, allied to multi-media models, allow mixed media schedule evaluation. A good deal of the discussion, not to say controversy, about mixed media schedules concerns coverage of the light viewer. A classic study of the launch of a new coffee product showed that the few opportunities to see delivered to light viewers were just as motivating as the many delivered to heavy viewers. For this reason, it should not be taken as axiomatic that the levelling out of exposure frequencies is necessarily a good thing. A far more powerful reason for going into mixed media schedules is the different contribution which each medium brings to the overall campaign objective — a point well made by Whitley.

It is nevertheless interesting to examine the changing pattern of frequency distribution caused by the addition of press to a television schedule. We are fortunate to be able to quote a real life example, by courtesy of Spillers French Limited, and their agency, BBDO.

The target market was defined as:

Housewives who purchase wrapped bread in the C2DE socio-economic grades in households with 4 or more members with at least one child 0–15.

The campaign period (for the assessment) was three weeks; a network TV coverage, with 236 housewife ratings, and costing £50,050, was combined with a national campaign in women's weeklies, giving 335 housewife ratings, and costing £48,664.

Computer Projects Limited (as it then was) carried out the analysis on their expanded TGI model. The important point about this model is that it re-weights TV exposure, derived from TGI, to bring results in line with those obtained from the JICTAR data. This having been done, spots were selected on a national basis to give the correct total rating level, and a fair estimate of the shape of the schedule used, which actually varied in terms of spot timing from area to area.

When the market weights were applied to the media schedules, it was found that TV ratings were increased from 236 to 266, but press ratings marginally reduced, from 335 to 332. This bias is to be anticipated from the class structure of the target market.

The analysis showed the results in Table 23.5. Clearly, the addition of the women's weeklies has had precisely the desired effect, with both coverage and frequency achieved in the various sub-groups finishing remarkably even, compared with the gross disparities of the TV only schedule. In addition, it

TABLE 23.5

	Non-viewers	Light viewers	Medium-light viewers	Medium viewers	Medium-heavy viewers	Heavy viewers
TV only coverage	0	46	68	88	98	99
TV only frequency	0	1.3	1.6	2.1	3.0	4.5
TV only GRPs	0	60	108	186	294	447
Combined coverage	68	76	92	96	98	99
Combined frequency	5.2	5.4	5.2	6.0	6.1	7.4
Combined GRPs	353	415	480	570	598	743

should be noted that coverage at the 3-level, which was considered important, was raised from 48 to 77.5 per cent. Of course, this coverage figure would have been increased had the additional money also been spent in TV, but probably not to the same extent.

Finally, it should be noted that no inter-media weight was applied, the colour pages in the women's weeklies being judged equivalent to 30 second TV spots. This equivalence is quite commonly used and there is some empirical support for it (e.g. Smith).

23.2   Source of product/media data

Any *ad hoc* survey of purchasing can have media questions added to it. Indeed, if our market is too esoteric to be covered by the syndicated services listed below, we will be forced into this method of obtaining our data. But production of media exposure data, sufficiently reliable to be used as a base for schedule construction, is not easy. Many studies, even some using NRS questions, combined with other non-media questions, have demonstrated this.

For the fortunate majority one or more of the following surveys will provide useful information.

23.2.1   Target Group Index

After a somewhat shaky start, this continuous survey, run by British Market Research Bureau, is now firmly established as the principal source of product/media data. It covers purchasing a very large number of products and services, from baked beans to motor cars to life insurance. Information is also available on such matters as the respondent's financial expectations, some psychometrics, whether trading stamps are collected, and so on. Readership information is collected in the same form as on the NRS, and is weighted to conform with current NRS figures. Exposure to other media is mostly calibrated by weight, and covers ITV viewing, cinema going, listening to Radio Luxembourg, and travel information, to give a measure of exposure to posters and London Underground sites. Yellow Pages are covered as 'used in the last 4 weeks', or not.

The annual sample size is about 25,000 adults, and data are collected by a personal interview, at which is left a self-completion questionnaire containing the majority of the questions. The volume of the data has caused problems in reporting, and also in handling the database.

23.2.2   The National Readership Survey

Although the prime concern of the NRS has naturally been with readership, questions have been asked concerning exposure to other media and also concerning 'special interest groups' since it started. These so-called 'special interest groups' were used to define certain markets for media analysis. Prime examples include cigarette smokers, drinkers of various alcoholic beverages and petrol buyers. Press schedules were analysed in terms of readership amongst these categories for years before the term 'product/media' was coined.

Market information currently collected is changed from time to time, usually as specialist reading groups are covered, e.g. motoring categories and specialised motoring press. The data do not give much detail and concern categories, rather than brands.

23.2.2   Consumer panels

Consumer panels run by Attwood, AGB and others regularly produce purchasing data of considerable accuracy capable of sophisticated analyses across a wide field of product groups. For a long time now attempts have been made to ally the media exposure of the panel members to purchasing data, so as to provide good quality product/media information. The problems arising from this type of approach fall under two main headings.

First of all the panel members are already involved in considerable research investigation in order that their purchasing habits may be correctly recorded. To carry out further extensive media research on them may be felt to overload them to the point at which they become totally atypical. It is axiomatic that making a measurement distorts what is being measured, and it is felt that this could be dangerous with too much investigation of media exposure of panel members.

The second area of problems revolves around the sample size. Although the panels consist of four to five thousand households each, there are many markets in which purchasers in a particular field, during a particular time period, may well account for no more than 10 per cent of this number. The amount of useful media analysis which can be carried out on sub-samples of this size is clearly limited.

23.3   Related reading

H.A. Smith, 'The "presenter effect" or does the medium affect the message?', *Admap* (February 1972)

E.W. Whitley, 'The media mix: some considerations', *ibid.*, (January 1975).

24 Analysis techniques

24.1 Press

It is not many years since the media research executive spent much of his time attempting to calculate the net coverage of a press schedule with the aid of the duplication tables in the NRS and one of a handful of useful formulae. (Indeed, some may still be at it.) However, today virtually all assessments are concerned with the frequency distributions of opportunities to see, on weighted markets, produced by schedules containing irregular numbers of insertions in different media, such formulae are quite irrelevant.

The media planner who, for one reason or another, cannot resort to his own, or someone else's, computer, nevertheless may have to produce an estimate of coverage and average frequency very rapidly. Fortunately, press media owners have made a great variety of data available, and most agencies will have in their possession coverage figures for a wide variety of market sub-groups by many combinations of media. By choosing an analysis concerned with a market reasonably approximating to the one he is looking into, and adjusting for the numbers of insertions concerned, the planner should be able to arrive at a tolerable estimate of the coverage his schedule will obtain. Then, by multiplying up the readership of each publication within the relevant sub-group, by the number of insertions in that medium, he is able to calculate a gross readership figure; dividing this by the coverage figure produces an average opportunities to see figure.

24.2 Television

The A. C. Nielsen Company, when they were offering a television audience research service at the beginning of commercial television in this country, were responsible for introducing many media and marketing people to the idea of frequency distribution. Nothing is easier than to produce a frequency distribution for a spot pattern covering, say, a four-week period, when panel data is available. Such analyses may now be commissioned from AGB, or produced for their own use by subscribers holding data tapes. An example is shown in Chapter 13.

It is possible to get a good approximation to the basics of such an analysis (coverage and, therefore, average frequency) by consulting one of the many tables which have been produced over the years. AGB themselves, by collating the results of many such analyses, and several of the major agencies, in the same way, have shown that the results are reliably predictable given certain key information.

It is necessary to know the gross TVRs for the schedule, and also the average rating. Some tables also require the highest rating. For planning purposes, when all these inputs will be estimates, the tables must be the best way of estimating the results. For evaluation, after the event, the computer analysis will give greater accuracy, and, if there is something odd about the pattern of spots involved, may be worth the money.

For a long time people conducted arguments on the optimum shape of the frequency distribution and what could be done to achieve this. It is now generally accepted, on the basis of work published by several different authors, that such sophistication in television analysis is seldom necessary. Provided that a reasonable percentage of peak time is included in the schedule (and with the structure of the present rate cards it is very difficult to avoid peak time) most of the audience will be exposed. Although the frequency distribution will be weighted towards heavy viewers, even if these do not constitute the target audience for the campaign, the greatest number of impacts will be delivered to the target audience by buying at the lowest possible cost-per-thousand. (Taking one of the categories, adults, men, women, housewives or children, as the closest approximation to the target.) It is important to remember that light viewers form a larger proportion of the total audience in the highest rated programmes; in the main, the 'speciality' programmes are watched by the heavy viewers.

24.3 Outdoor

The calculation of coverage and average frequency figures for poster campaigns is theoretically very simple. The formulae are:

Cover = $100 \, AS/(AS + b)$

Repetition = $AS + b$

whence

$$S = bC/A \, (100-C)$$

where S is the number of poster sites bought in a given town and A is a value] derived from a table (appearing in various publications) and dependent on the population of the town concerned; b is currently valued at 3.6 and C represents cover. For readers who wish to do their own calculations, the equation for A is

$$\log A = -0.6813 \log p + 1.3304$$

where p is the population in thousands.

There are a number of problems with these simple calculations. The first is the obvious one that the calculations must be performed for each town covered

204 and for a national schedule this involves a very large amount of repetitive work. Moreover, only the towns themselves are included in the formulae. The BPA suggest that for the hinterland population a coverage of 40 per cent with a repetition of 8 in any one week may be considered a safe average for a normal weight campaign.

The second problem is that they do not apply to conurbations, where the pattern of travel, and therefore exposure, is significantly different from that in towns. For conurbations, the planner has to do the calculations twice: once to get the total allocation, and once to decide the allocation between the parts of the conurbation.

For the former, the valid calculation is:

$$\log A = -0.6142 \log p + 0.8713$$

where b remains as 3.6. For the latter, he must calculate the number of sites per town within the conurbation in the normal way, and then reduce the number proportionately to equal the total calculated for the conurbation as a whole.

The third problem is that the figures refer only to all adults, and for subgroups weighting factors will need to be used (see Chapter 22).

Fourthly, the figures are calculated on the basis of a random distribution of sites and we do not know the relationship with the figures for a campaign.

Fifthly, the repetition figures really concern the passage of people past locations at which posters are displayed, and we have no idea of the relationship between this figure and useful exposure to the advertising.

Brian Copland of Outdoor Research International recently produced formulae for making calculations for bus campaigns similar to those for poster campaigns. These have been derived from research work carried out principally in Italy. The basic nature of the problem is very similar to that with posters, but two further factors have to be introduced. Both of these are connected with the fact that the buses are not static and depend on the frequency of the service: clearly a bus going over a particular route twice may be counted as two buses going over the same route once. The second which affects coverage arises from the fact that if the average frequency is not sufficiently high, a number of people making short journeys may be missed altogether.

As with the poster formulae, a calculation of A has first to be made and the formula for buses is

$$\log A = -a \log P + b$$

Here P is population, b is found to be about 0.6 and a seems to depend on the country in which the buses are running. Given this value for A, then the formulae are

Cover = $100\ tAV/(tFAV + 0.6)$

Repetition = $tFAV + b$

In these formulae t represents the number of weeks over which the calculation is required, A has been derived as above, V represents the number of vehicles used in the campaign and F varies with the frequency of the service and takes values ranging between 1.2 and 1.8.

The NRS includes for each respondent their claimed frequency of visiting the cinema. Thus, if one were running a cinema campaign in all cinemas, in all the weeks of the year, it would be possible to produce a sophisticated market weighted analysis of cover and frequency. Unfortunately, no cinema campaign takes this form and there are serious difficulties in producing estimates. Moreover, the probablistic nature of these estimates may prove to be significantly inaccurate in result, simply because the agency has been lucky, or unlucky, in the films exhibited during the weeks in which the advertisements appeared. The fact that these variations cancel each other out across the whole industry is, of course, of little value to the individual advertiser.

Given below are two of a series of formulae produced by David Corkindale when with BBDO, London, which enable the planner to make the best use of the NRS figures.

$$C = R (1 - F^x) + A (1 - G^x) + I (1 - H^x) \tag{1}$$

where C (%) is the coverage,

$$F = [1 - (r/4Y)] \qquad H = [1 - (i/4Y)]$$
$$G = [1 - (a/4Y)] \qquad x = M/X$$

and the total target population is P divided into

1   *Regular* — attend at least once a week, an average of r times per 4 weeks; R per cent of population P.

2   *Occasional* — attend at least once a month but less than 'regulars', an average of a times per 4 weeks; A per cent of population P.

3   *Infrequent* — attend less than once a month, an average of i times per 4 weeks; I per cent of population P.

4   *Never* — never attend.

Values of R, A and I can be read from the NRS table under the appropriate target group. The values for r, a and i can be determined from special analysis of the NRS tape, but setting $r = 4$, $a = 2$, $i = 0.5$, gives generally acceptable results.

The campaign details are: showings in one in every Y cinemas; campaign period M weeks; periodicity once every X weeks.

$$Q = 100 \, T/CP \tag{2}$$

where Q is average frequency, T is total number of exposures in the target group, C is coverage and P is population of the target group. And the planner can arrive at a value for T by dividing his total budget by his estimated cost-per-thousand.

24.5   Radio

Most national advertisers buy radio in the form of packages, and most of these packages have audience estimates produced by the JICRAR surveys (see Chapter

16). The planner faced with making an estimate for a different pattern of spots will first have to calculate his gross audience (from the detailed reports) and then make a best estimate of coverage by interpolating from the figures for the various packages. Average frequency is then found, as usual, by dividing coverage into the gross audience.

24.6 Related reading

J.A. Pounds and M.A. Newman, 'A review of the poster model', *Admap* (May 1976).

25 Media models

In Chapter 4 we discussed the use of marketing models in budget setting, and we have referred to them elsewhere in other contexts. The basic formulation of an empirical marketing model is given on page 23.

The difficulty with such models comes with the estimation of the actual numbers to be used: this difficulty hardly arises in media models. They are based on relationships like:

Value of schedule = (Market weight x Number of readers of publication
A x Number of OTS) +
(Market weight x Number of readers of publication
B x Number of OTS) +
. . .

where each sub-group has its own market weight. If we have specified a response function, we shall have to weight the frequency distribution of OTS., (opportunities to see) and not just multiply by the total, as we have above. The dots indicate that the sum has to be continued until all the publications have been covered. Readership surveys (or JICTAR data for TV) give us good estimates of the relevant numbers, and our own research will enable us to estimate market weights. Response weights are more difficult, and will be dealt with in the next chapter.

The problems with media models arise mainly from the size of the numbers involved. The NRS has 30,000 individuals in the sample; a schedule may have ten publications on it, with up to ten insertions in each. Even with modern computing facilities, actually counting the numbers involved gets very expensive. That it can be done economically is largely due to Dick Metheringham, who showed that, by taking duplications of pairs of publications, and their reader-ships, good estimates of the frequency distribution of a schedule could be made, using the formula which he developed. This has been improved since, and forms the basis of the Comshare models which are quoted in this book. Other groups have also developed efficient means of reducing the computational effort.

25.1 Evaluation models

The example given above supposes that a schedule has been specified, and that the model is being used to assess its value. Such a model is known as an evaluation model. Most will take a series of schedules, designed to reach the same target audience, and produce analyses of each, in one run.

The basis of the evaluation normally includes the cover of the schedule (at the 1 level), the gross OTS figure, the average OTS on those covered at all, and gross and net costs per thousand. A frequency distribution may also be produced, and, if a response function has been specified, a response value.

From the scatter diagram (see Figure 25.1) the planner may select groups of publications, with numbers of insertions in each which will be within his total budget. By getting a series of, say, six of these schedules evaluated in this way, he can see what range of values is open to him.

Some years ago the Media Research Group did the industry a considerable service by commissioning a number of different models to assess a number of different schedules. This showed, firstly, that different *models* (based on different mathematical approaches) produced very similar results; and secondly, that many different *schedules* produced very similar results.

25.2   Optimisation models

The earliest media models were designed simply to produce the 'best' schedules. They were very helpful in stimulating thinking in the media planning area, since, before faced with the awful logic of the computer, planners had not clarified in their own minds what they meant by 'best'. Early (US) models were set to maximise gross OTS on weighted markets, but it was immediately apparent that this did not require a computer. All available space in the lowest cpt medium was purchased, and, if there was any budget left over, this was spent in the next lowest, and so on.

In fact, much British planning was done on the basis of matching the schedule profile to the market profile, and a model was produced which did this rather well. However, it was clear that coverage and economy must be relevant, and this approach was also abandoned. In the end, since coverage, frequency, and economy were generally recognised as the vital variables, and since coverage and frequency are inversely related, it became clear that only the specification of a response function would resolve the problem. This gave us the ability to say: 'This schedule reaches 10 per cent of our weighted market 10 times, 20 per cent 9 times, . . . , etc., and we reckon that 10 exposures will sell every-one, 9 will sell 95 per cent, . . . , etc.' The computer multiplies the exposure and its effect, adds up the products, and produces a single value, called the response of the schedule.

Now we can give the computer the task of finding the schedule with the highest response, and there are a variety of different ways that it can do this. All depend on trial and error, or iteration, to use the more impressive name. At the simplest level, this means examining the effect of putting one insertion into each of the available media in turn, and choosing the one with the highest response, and then examining the effect of adding to the first an exposure in each of the media, including the original choice. Each time, we choose that additional insertion which produces the greatest gain in response, until the budget is exhausted.

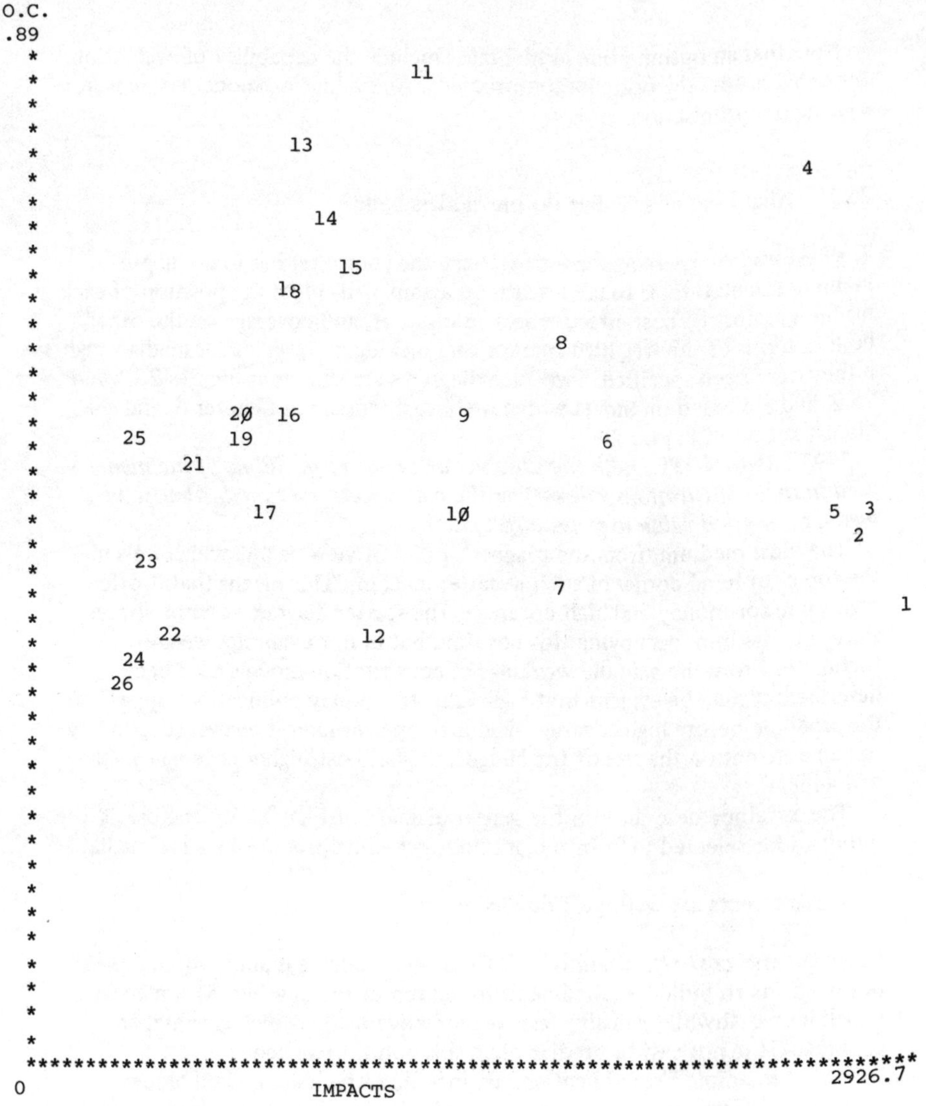

```
I.O.C.
  .89
    *                                          11
    *
    *
    *
    *                          13
    *                                                            4
    *
    *                      14
    *
    *                          15
    *                    18
    *
    *                                        8
    *
    *
    *              2Ø  16              9
    *        25    19                      6
    *          21
    *
    *              17              1Ø              5  3
    *                                                2
    *        23
    *                                      7
    *                                                            1
    *          22          12
    *        24
    *      26
    *
    *
    *
    *
    *
    *
    *
    *
    *
    *
    * .
    *
    *
    *
 ***********************************************************************************
 0                        IMPACTS                              2926.7
```

Ref.No.   Publication name

Ref.No.	Publication name	Ref.No.	Publication name
11	Good Housekeeping	21	Do It Yourself
13	My Weekly	17	Cosmopolitan
4	Reader's Digest	10	Woman's Realm
14	She	5	Woman
15	Ideal Home	3	Woman's Own
18	Homes & Gardens	2	TV Times
8	Family Circle	23	Woman's Journal
16	Living	7	Sunday Times Magazine
20	House & Garden	1	Radio Times
9	Woman & Home	12	Observer Magazine
25	Annabel	22	Practical Householder
6	Woman's Weekly	24	Punch
19	Home-Freezer Digest	26	Homemaker

Figure 25.1

Note that an optimisation model must include the capability of evaluation, since that is how the optimisation proceeds. An evaluation model *per se* is not capable of optimisation.

25.3 What kind of schedule do the models build?

The best way of assessing the results, once the computer has done its preliminary calculation, is to use a scatter diagram. This plots the position of each medium against its cost-effectiveness on one axis, and coverage on the other, both in terms of the weighted market, and making allowances for media weights, if they have been specified. Two such diagrams are shown in Figures 25.1 and 25.2, and are based on inputs which we have discussed in Chapter 6, and shall discuss again in Chapter 26.

WARNING NOTE: *Both the absolute and relative positions of the media used in these illustrations will vary as the parameters are varied. Almost all media offer good value to some target audience.*

The ideal medium, from the planner's point of view, is one which falls in the top right-hand corner of such a scatter diagram. This means that it offers high value for money and high coverage. The scatter diagrams do not always show any medium occupying this position, but in our examples we are fortunate. From the way the workings of construction models have been described, it may be evident that high value-for-money publications appear on the schedule before high coverage media. Sooner or later, however (depending to some extent on the size of the budget), higher cost/higher coverage media will appear.

The envelope described on the scatter diagram of Figure 25.1 encloses those publications selected to form the optimum schedule produced by the media model.

Three effects are worthy of discussion:

Coverage and cost-effectiveness   Without the model, a planner should select publications to build his schedule from the top of the ranking. At some stage it will be worthwhile choosing less cost-effective media which give higher coverage. It is not easy to predict when this point is reached.

In the example five publications are included which are ranked below *Homes and Gardens,* which is not included. The *Sunday Times Magazine* is included in preference to eleven publications ranked higher.

Duplication   The reason for the omission of cost-effective media is the duplication they suffer with previously selected media. The omission of *Woman,* for example, is clearly brought about by the inclusion of *Woman's Weekly* and *Woman's Own. Homes and Gardens* is considered after the inclusion of *Good Housekeeping, Ideal Home, Reader's Digest* and *She,* which probably leave it few valuable readers to contribute.

Without the model, the planner might guess that no more than two of the IPC weeklies should be included, but which two would he choose?

The effect of media weight   In this candidate list, the media weights varied

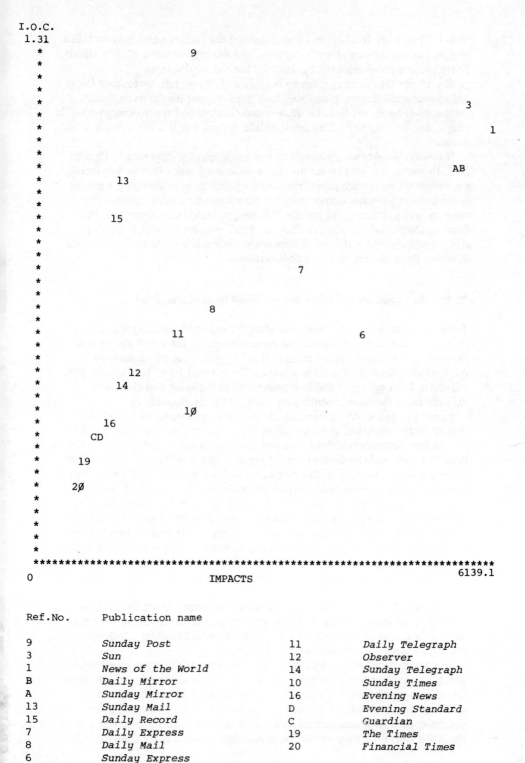

```
I.O.C.
1.31
     *                           9
     *
     *
     *
     *
     *
     *
     *                                                           3
     *
     *                                                               1
     *
     *
     *                                                       AB
     *
     *           13
     *
     *         15
     *
     *
     *
     *
     *                                               7
     *
     *
     *                               8
     *
     *                   11                               6
     *
     *             12
     *           14
     *
     *
     *                         10
     *
     *       16
     *     CD
     *
     *   19
     *
     *   20
     *
     *
     *
     *
*************************************************************************
0                        IMPACTS                              6139.1
```

Ref.No.	Publication name		
9	*Sunday Post*	11	*Daily Telegraph*
3	*Sun*	12	*Observer*
1	*News of the World*	14	*Sunday Telegraph*
B	*Daily Mirror*	10	*Sunday Times*
A	*Sunday Mirror*	16	*Evening News*
13	*Sunday Mail*	D	*Evening Standard*
15	*Daily Record*	C	*Guardian*
7	*Daily Express*	19	*The Times*
8	*Daily Mail*	20	*Financial Times*
6	*Sunday Express*		

Figure 25.2

from 0.75 to 1.00. In Chapter 10 we discussed the factors which may be taken into account in arriving at media weights, and the general trend of their effects. These become more apparent by studying the scatter diagrams.

The 15 per cent penalty given to *Woman and Home*, relative to *Ideal Home* and *Homes and Gardens,* might well have been responsible for its exclusion. On the other hand, the fact that *Homes and Gardens* had the maximum possible weight, and still did not get on the schedule, means that it is very hard to argue its case.

No media weights were assigned to the newspaper list displayed in Figure 25.2. However, it is easy to see that to *exclude* the *Sunday Post* or *Sun* from a schedule would require unrealistic down-weighting, as to *include* the groups in the bottom left-hand corner would require unrealistic up-weighting. The sensitive group is that in the middle, the *Sunday Mail, Daily Record, Daily Express, Daily Mail* and *Sunday Express.* Small changes in weights for this group could mean the difference between inclusion and exclusion, and should therefore be given very serious consideration.

25.4 How good are the schedules produced by media models?

Today's models have been developed after the expenditure of a great deal of thought by the best minds in the business throughout the world and by the expenditure of a great deal of money. It is likely that the schedules they produce as optimal do not differ significantly in result from theoretically best schedules, both optimum and best being used in the sense that they flow logically from the criteria which have been set by the planner.

In spite of this many computer-built schedules produce a great deal of anguish in the breasts of their recipients. There are two main reasons for this.

The first concerns schedules directed towards 'quality' markets. Traditionally, these have always been drawn from lists comprising 'quality' media. The planner might have selected the *Observer* and rejected the *Sunday Telegraph,* but both would always have been considered, whilst the *News of the World* would not. However, the only real reasons for excluding any candidate medium from a computer input are problems of colour, or copy-date, or some such over-riding physical attribute. What one then finds is that the cost differential between the 'quality' newspapers in general, and the populars, is so great that for any reasonably up-market product, popular newspapers offer competitive value. Thus, instead of finding either the *Observer* or the *Sunday Telegraph,* one finds the *Sun* heading the schedule.

The second reason is that for any schedule someone's favourite publication may have been omitted. If it has not appeared on the print-out, the planner is able to say, confidently, that its inclusion would produce a less cost-effective schedule — and demonstrate his point.

The weakness of the present state of the argument is that the schedules to which we are all accustomed have not been produced as logically as the model solutions, and the fact that they sold a great quantity of merchandise does not mean that they were not open to improvement. What is needed is an objective method of comparison which measures the results in real terms. Since this calls for a total marketing model, little work has yet been done in this area. However, American experience suggests that quite small changes in media schedules can produce measurable sales changes. Clearly, familiarity has a part to play. The inevitability with which some publications appear on optimised schedules will probably have some effect in persuading advertisers that they really do have some merit. It is important to note that this will not happen unless the planner does his duty and includes them on the candidate list.

The validation of some of the figures we currently use as input (particularly unresearched market weights and all response weights), so that everyone can be more confident the computer is being asked to perform a meaningful task, will also help.

Media models do represent the only way of using the data which is currently available in a logical manner, and it is worthwhile for advertisers, planners and media owners trying very hard to get them to produce the right results.

25.5   The pattern of optimisation

One fascinating thing which Comshare's optimisation programme can do is to show the way the optimum schedule develops as more money is allocated. Normally this information is not printed, since an optimisation run will evaluate hundreds of schedules, and the cost of printing, to say nothing of the paper, is wasted, unless one has a specific purpose in mind. We had two purposes in the run which we commissioned.

The order of entrance   Firstly, we wished to demonstrate the way in which the schedule was built up, and particulary how the individual media entered. It will help the reader to refer to Figure 25.2 as we comment. To begin with, the most cost-effective medium, the *Sunday Post,* was chosen. Nothing surprising there, but what is interesting (and dependent to some extent on the shape of the response function) is that the medium justified six insertions before another was worth adding. This was the second most cost-effective medium, the *Sun.* This also justified six insertions before a third medium merited a place on the schedule. Third comes the *News of the World,* again echoing its place on the cost-ranking, but this time only four insertions are justified before the next medium becomes more efficient.

The fourth medium to enter is not the *Daily Mirror,* but its sister-paper, the *Sunday Mirror.* The difference in cost efficiency is almost zero, and the *Sunday Mirror* must have had marginally less duplication than the preceding paper, or to have provided its duplication at a useful level. (Particularly the three impacts level: see the response weights.) With the *Sunday Mirror* included, the *Daily Mirror* will have to wait for its opportunity, and the *Sunday Mail* and *Daily Record* stand no chance after the *Sunday Post.*

So, after allocating three insertions to the *Sunday Mirror,* the program allocates four to the *Daily Express.* Finally, to spend the balance of the appropriation, it reaches down and left (on the scatter diagram) to pick up the *Daily Mail* for two insertions.

Growth in response   Plotting the response levels for the optimum schedules at different appropriation levels produces the somewhat erratic line shown in Figure 25.3. If only one medium was being considered, then the line would echo exactly the S-shape of the response function. If a geometric function was used, the line would be of the same shape. As it is, we have a confusion of two factors.

Although a new medium is added when the ratio of its contribution (in terms of response) to its cost is greater than any other, including the last, a second insertion in the same publication will, with this response function, prove much better. The program shows how this happens by printing the ratio at each step. Thus, when the *Sun* is first added, the ratio is 7.23; higher than that obtained by adding a seventh insertion in the *Sunday Post.* But the next insertions in the *Sun* give ratios of 19.00, 32.31, 18.81, 14.35 and 9.95. A seventh insertion gives a lower ratio than a first insertion in the *News of the World,* which is then worth 8.64. But the second insertion is worth 11.52, and so on.

The perceptive reader may wonder why, if the first insertion in the *Sun* gives a ratio of 7.23, and that in the *News of the World* 8.64, the latter is not added first. The reason is simply that the readers of the *News of the World* are less valuable until they have received some exposure from the *Sun.*

25.6   Future developments

This chapter has been concerned almost entirely with press scheduling. There is no theoretical reason, provided the data are available, for media models to be so confined; indeed many have already been applied to mixed media scheduling. The over-riding problem is that of assigning a meaningful intermedia weight. Such is the fragility of this figure in our present state of knowledge that arguments about it cannot satisfactorily be resolved. Ideally one would hope for enough schedules to be tried with different weights to enable one to build up a case-book of the relative success and failure of different judgements. In practice this is not likely to happen for many years.

An alternative solution is to impose minimum and maximum constraints on the amount of money allocated to each medium. This is done in BBDO New York's model Media-Max. Although this is a valuable tool in the United States, where the number of media vehicles involved is enormous, it is probably easier in this country to make a judgement about the proportion of the budget allocated to different media, and plan separately within each of these.

Other developments which have been, or are being, tried concern extending the scope of the models to deal with the allocation of money over time; the effects of competition; and the use of different response functions for different market sectors.

At the moment most planners use a response function which they feel seems sensible for the time period concerned. They then spread the insertions fairly evenly across the period. This method is open to the criticism that it implicitly assumes that the advertising has an immediate effect. On the assumption that the effect is spread over some period of time, insertions would tend to be bunched towards the beginning of the period. Against this it may be said that the consumer sees a campaign as something which has usually been preceded

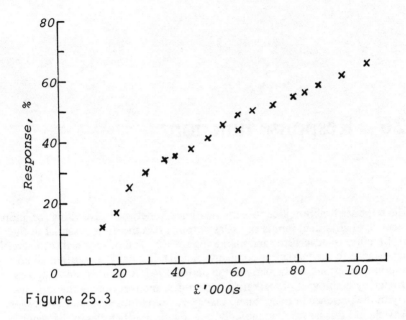

Figure 25.3

by another, and will be succeeded by a third. Since he is unaware of the company's financial years, he will perceive the advertising effort as a continuum.

The influence of competition on a campaign is not understood in any precise way, and once more probably needs the development of a total marketing model for its evaluation. It is worth pointing out that Errol Jackson has argued persuasively that in some product fields competitive claims probably have little, or no, inter-action.

If the task of a campaign is to retain current users, whilst switching users of the brand leader (and this is achievable) it may well be that the two groups have quite different response functions. There is, therefore, a strong theoretical argument for using two (or more if there are more distinct groups). Some critics would say that our knowledge of response functions is so limited that their use is never justified; but every schedule which is designed contains one, however implicitly. Provided the use of a number of different functions within one model produces sufficiently different schedules to justify the increased cost of computation, there seems every reason to pursue this path.

25.7 Related reading

Media Research Group, 'Media model comparison — an investigation into computerised press schedule construction models', *Admap* (September 1970).

26   Response functions

The response function describes the relationship between advertising (or, more generally, marketing) inputs and sales outputs. It is therefore essential to the profitability of advertising and marketing activity, and of very real commercial importance to the marketing company. A great deal has been written about response functions, particularly in the period 1965-70. Hardly anything was written by employees of marketing companies, and mentioning the term to-day in the presence of many brand managers will induce an embarrassed silence. Why should this be so? Undoubtedly, the practical difficulties in the way of estimating the response function have meant that it has been firmly established as 'theoretical', and that is not a good word in marketing. Further, the prime use of response functions being in the context of media models, not only theoretical, but agency rather than client, and agency media department at that, has been an added inhibition.

As their importance in marketing models grows, and as more media decisions are taken in client companies, we expect interest to revive. In this Chapter we shall confine ourselves to the effect on the schedules, but it may be worth referring back to Chapters 4 and 7 for a reminder of some wider implications.

26.1   The purpose of the response function in the media model

For a long time the two measures of a schedule most generally used were net coverage and cost-per-thousand. With a given appropriation the costs-per-thousand of two alternative schedules are clearly inversely proportional to their efficiency — at any given level of net coverage. For instance, if two alternative schedules each reach 90 per cent of the target market, then the one with the lower cost-per-thousand will deliver a higher average frequency. The more common case is when the schedule which has the higher cost-per-thousand also has the higher coverage: the selection in this case is much more difficult. Closer examination of the problem, together with an attempt consider the basic premises of schedule construction, led to the questioning of net coverage as a concept. If the measure of average exposure to a particular schedule was, say, 50, how valuable were the 5 per cent who only had one exposure? Underlying these problems was the general assumption that the first exposure a member of the target market had to a particular advertisement did not necessarily have the same value to the advertiser as the hundredth. There were two extreme points on this: specifying maximum coverage as a goal implies that the first exposure is totally important and all other exposures are totally unimportant. A schedule geared exclusively to produce the lowest cost-per-thousand, on the other hand, assumes that the value of all exposures is equal.

The response function is the term applied to the weights given to specified exposures to represent the value which they are felt to have. The two most commonly used are the convex curve and the S-shaped curve. Clearly, at some point in time further expenditure on advertising is not likely to have any effect (when everybody is buying as much of the product as they can possibly consume). The difference between the two curves is merely the difference in the way it is felt that this point is reached. With the convex curve each successive exposure is somewhat less valuable than the one that preceded it. This flows from the argument that the first exposure to an advertisement has the greatest effect. It is supported by many measurements which have been made comparing the recall of advertisements with the amount of exposure that they have had. The S-shaped curve implies a 'threshold effect'. That is to say, its proponents feel that until a certain level of exposure has been reached, nothing very much happens to the consumer. Beyond this point, successive exposures have a considerable effect until the levelling-out point is reached. Support for this approach comes from some psychological studies and some empirically estimated curves. Most managers behave as though they believe that this is the correct shape, i.e. they take the view that advertising appropriations may be too small to have any effect.

There is nothing, in theory, to stop a response curve going down to the right. This implies that too much advertising can actually dissuade people from purchasing the product. This form of curve is not generally used.

26.2 Specifying the function

26.2.1 The response function in the model

It should first be noted that, although much writing about response functions is in terms of the effect on the individual in the market, this is not only a difficult concept to understand, but it is not the way the models use the data. By a cumulative response weight of 85 at the fifth exposure it is easier and more practical to mean that 85 per cent of the target market will have been effectively covered by five exposures than that the average individual in the target market will be 85 per cent of the way towards being effectively covered at the fifth exposure.

26.2.2 S-shaped or convex?

The best advice we can give is that it seems reasonable to use convex curves where the advertising task is a simple one; that these curves should tend to flatten as the task gets more difficult and should become S-shaped for most persuasive campaigns.

To illustrate this we would cite the case of an advertisement offering a recipe leaflet. Repetition is unlikely to have much effect on increasing the response to such an advertisement and the chief objective of the campaign must be cover. For this purpose a steep convex curve would be appropriate. In the case of a campaign in which action is likely to stem directly from awareness, a more normal convex curve will probably be adequate. For the majority of brand competitive campaigns, we would recommend an S-shaped curve.

Some examples are given below of the effect of such decisions.

26.2.3 The period of the campaign

One of the principal factors influencing the numbers we attach to response weights is the length of the period we are considering. To produce a given advertising effect over a twelve-month period is likely to require substantially more exposures than to produce the same effect for a thirteen-week period. In fact, from the other point of view, the sheer possibility of exposing the target audience to a given number of advertisements must be greater, the longer the time period involved.

26.2.4 The effect of the budget

When we can determine the shape of the response function, we can deduce the most profitable budget level. If we are not in this position, we have to make a judgement as to whether the budget seems to be about right for the task allotted, or whether it is too much or too little. This view will colour the value we set against the number of exposures necessary to achieve the maximum, or near maximum, effectiveness.

26.2.5 A poster example

Figure 26.1 shows the research results of a poster campaign. The campaign was mounted by the Poster Industry for research purposes, and used a specially produced design, featuring the NSPCC. This was shown in four towns, using 16- and 4-sheet sites. The research, carried out by Research Services, on a sample of 1473 housewives, calibrated the respondents' exposure to the campaign, and collected various measures of awareness. They were asked if they could recall seeing any posters recently, then whether they could recall definitely seeing a poster for the NSPCC, and then whether they recognised a photograph of the poster as being what they had seen. All questions were put in the context of other poster campaigns currently in the area.

As will be seen from the graph, not only the levels of claim vary with the ease of the response, but the shapes of the graphs, too. In particular, if 'recognition' were the objective of the campaign, it would clearly be much better to

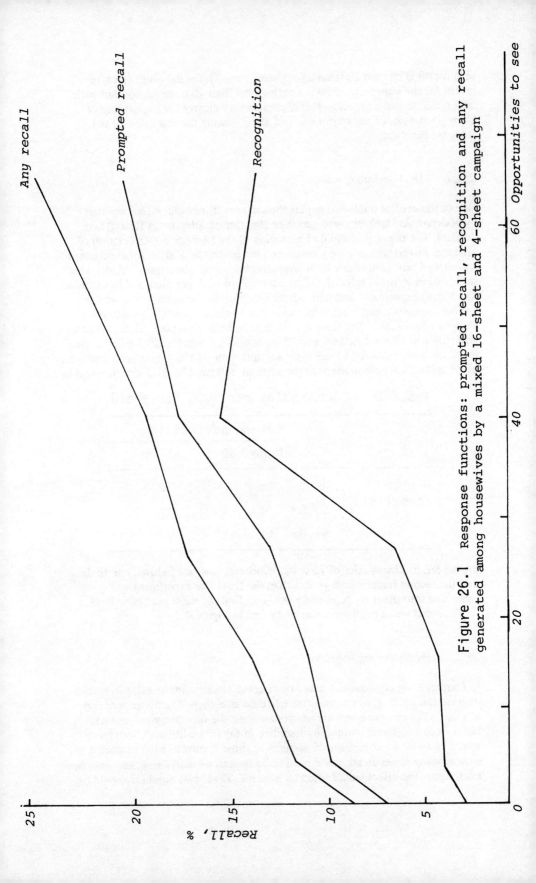

Figure 26.1 Response functions: prompted recall, recognition and any recall generated among housewives by a mixed 16-sheet and 4-sheet campaign

plan for 40 OTS than 20 (over a four-week period). On the other hand, in return for the expenditure, 20 is a better level than 40 if we are content with 'any recall' to our campaign. This illustrates very clearly the importance of being precise about our objectives, and also knowing the real shape of the response function.

26.2.6   An American campaign

One of the earliest published papers showing the 'threshold' effect was that by Malcolm A. McNiven, who was then Manager of Advertising Research at du Pont. The paper [delivered at a meeting of the (American) Association of National Advertisers in 1966] concerned the launch of Teflon. An experiment was carried out, concerning both levels and timing of advertising. Results were measured in terms of sales of Teflon-coated cookware per thousand households. The timing experiment was with advertising both in the autumn and winter periods, and with winter only; and with two levels in each. The results are shown in Table 26.1. The table may be read in both directions. Thus, whilst no advertising at all produced sales of 25 units/000 households, $0.5 million spent in the autumn, followed by the same amount spent in the winter produced sales of 29 units. $1.0 million spent in the autumn, followed by $1.0 million spent in

TABLE 26.1   Unit sales per 1000 households

		Autumn advertising		
		None	$0.5m	$1.0m
Winter advertising	None	25	26	32
	$0.5m	29	29	35
	$1.0m	49	53	70

the winter, produced sales of 70 units. Whichever line one follows, one finds that the second increment is greater than the first. The experiment was continued into other areas, at other levels, to find *the* most profitable level.

The result was a graph very similar to that in Figure 4.2.

26.2.7   Producing the numbers

In Chapter 6 we considered a schedule directed towards adults living in homes with central heating; to produce this schedule an S-shaped response function was used. The response weights which described the function were, in fact, taken from a different campaign, described in the first edition. A better way would be to take a concensus of opinion of those involved in the campaign as to how many times an ad would need to be seen to be motivating; and after how many times the effect would begin to wear off. These two numbers should be taken as the turning points of the curve.

A very useful all-purpose formula has been put forward by John Little, for his Adbudg model (see Chapter 4). This can be adapted as:

$$R = 100\,I^n / (K + I^n)$$

where R is the response, I the number of insertions and K and n are constants. The beauty of this expression is that if n lies between 0 and 1 it produces a geometric function, while if n is greater than 1 it produces an S-shaped function.

Multiplying by 100 only expresses R as a percentage. There is no reason why this should be done, as long as it is remembered that the maximum value for R is then 1.0. In our example, the reader may like to check that a reasonable approximation is given by $K = 12$ and $n = 2$.

26.3   How much difference does it make?

In the marketing model, the choice of geometric or S-shaped functions can lead to fundamentally different courses of action. Within the media model the differences are smaller. Continuing with the same example, we tried a geometric response function:

Cumulative response 1

0	0
1	35
2	53
3	67
4	77
5	85
6	91
7	95
8	97
9	99
10 and over	100

TABLE 26.2

Publication	Number of insertions	
	Geometric function	S-shaped function
Sunday Post	3	6
Sun	4	6
News of the World	3	4
Daily Mirror	3	–
Sunday Mirror	2	3
Daily Express	2	4
Sunday Express	1	–
Daily Mail	2	1
Daily Telegraph	2	–
Sunday Mail	1	–
Daily Record	1	–
Observer	1	–
Sunday Telegraph	1	–

The schedule produced by the different functions (all other factors remaining the same) is shown in Table 26.2. These are evaluated at similar levels, 92.1 and 82.3 per cent of possible response, respectively. However, from the point of view of News International, for example, or Mirror Group Newspapers, they are significantly different.

26.4   Related reading

Malcolm A. McNiven, 'Choosing the most profitable level of advertising', Association of National Advertisers Workshop (December 1966).
Ambar G. Rao and Peter B. Miller, 'Advertising/sales response functions', *Journal of Advertising Research* (April 1975).
Research Services Limited, *The ability of posters to communicate,* British Poster Advertising Association (December 1968).

27 Feedback

Once the media plan for Brand A has been accepted, it is alarmingly easy to move on to the next, not expecting to be further bothered about Brand A until this time next year, if then. For the media planner in an agency, trained to respond to client requests, and under heavy time pressure, such behaviour is understandable, if regrettable. For anyone concerned with media planning in a client company, it has to be wrong.

All marketing companies have a regular flow of information regarding their performance in the market place: factory sales, certainly; hopefully, retail and/or consumer audit data. Most will also collect information on consumer awareness of their products, attitudes to them, and so on.

If the media planner is to advance in his understanding of his job, these data must be fed to him in as meaningful a format as possible. Just to let him know how 'his' brand is faring in the market place will make him feel involved, and this involvement will almost certainly produce a better effort from him than he would otherwise produce. But, by itself, this information will not tell him much, or possibly anything, about the performance of his media plan. For this, one thing is essential, and another highly desirable.

The essential ingredient is a formalised approach to the market, so that all concerned know what they expect from the campaign. The highly desirable ingredient is experimentation.

27.1   Assessing results

Ideally, marketing management will have available a quantified marketing model of the type discussed earlier (in Chapter 4). This will involve all aspects of the advertising campaign, including media, and will enable assessments to be made over long periods (time-series analysis) and also across areas, and/or a number of brands (cross-sectional analysis). The planner must look at the analyses in relation to his plan, particularly for differences. With the best will in the world, no media plan comes out with the intended distribution of effort over areas and time, and these unintentional aberrations should give an indication of the media effect. (Not assuming all other things are equal, which they will not be: the beauty of the model is that it will allow you to quantify the other inequalities.) Of course, none of these aberrations may produce differences which lie outside the statistical confidence limits. However, this is, in itself, an important piece of information, and gives an indication of the insensitivity of the media plan; or, looked at another way, how flexible we can be without materially affecting performance.

If we do not have a quantified marketing model, then we must, again as described in Chapter 4, get as close to it as we can. The essential points are: to have an objective measuring tool, measuring something which we have reason to believe must be related to profit; and to use this so as to distinguish the contributions made by different elements in the marketing mix (including the media plan) as far as is possible. If targets are set, however subjectively, they are testable. If they are not, nothing can be achieved.

It may be necessary to issue at this point the time-honoured warning: correlation does not prove causality. For instance, if we observe that sales go down when we have a television burst, and go up when we are off the air, it does not prove that television advertising depresses sales. It could be, for example, that there is a 'lag' in the advertising effect, equal to the length of the burst; so that we reap the benefit of the advertising during the rest period, and suffer for the rest period during the next burst.

However, it must also be pointed out that there is no causality without correlation. That is to say, if we can establish no pattern connecting advertising with sales, even in the long term, it is unlikely that advertising is affecting sales. In the previous example, it would be a simple matter to run two bursts together. If sales continue to fall, then our first hypothesis looks correct; if they rise again, then the second looks more probable.

27.2 Conducting experiments

We have just suggested an alteration to the media plan which is not a response to a specific marketing objective, but which is designed to increase our knowledge of the way in which media advertising is contributing to the overall marketing objective.

The simple fact is, controlled experimentation does enable one to learn much faster, and more surely, than the types of analysis described above.

However the reader will find, when he comes to try, that setting up experiments is not easy; it is as well for him to be forewarned. There are two main types of hazard he is likely to encounter.

The first of these is a set of very sensible, practical reasons why such a test should not be put into effect:

1 Production costs will be increased, possibly considerably, by extending into a second medium and this may have a serious effect, especially on a small budget.
2 It may be (although it very rarely is) genuinely impossible to translate copy from one medium to another, and so the change in the advertisement may well be a bigger factor than the change in the medium.
3 Clearly there is little point in carrying out an experiment of this nature unless there is a good system for evaluating the results. If special research has to be done, this again may take too big a proportion of the budget.

More difficult to overcome than practical objections may be emotional ones. The process of bringing an advertising campaign to presentation stage within an agency is a long and difficult one. The necessity of producing advertisements for two different main media, implicit in a media test of this sort, may just be too much to cope with. On the other hand, if the agency succeeds in getting to presentation stage, the client may feel unjustified in risking some of his profit, since one treatment is bound to be judged superior to the other. He may also say (correctly) that his sales force in the 'under-privileged' areas will consider themselves under-supported and their selling effort may, therefore, suffer.

Tests that do not involve dramatic changes in main media may more readily gain acceptance. These may include, for example, the use of burst patterns against continuous advertising; weight tests of differing sizes and lengths, and other intra-media activities of this nature. All of them are very pertinent to the media planner's daily tasks and any genuine knowledge acquired would be of considerable value to him.

Although it is obvious, it is necessary to state that if one variable is under test in the marketing mix, it is very important that all the others are kept constant. For this reason it is important that everyone in the client company, on the marketing side, is aware of what is being attempted. Since the activities of competitors cannot be so controlled, it is extremely important to have at least two areas carrying the test treatment, preferably with wide geographical separation. A keen watch must be maintained during the course of the test to see that any unusual competitive activity is spotted and allowance made for it, where possible.

It is important to remember that the value of an experiment will be maximised if its purpose is to test some hypothesis derived from previous study. This study may well include competitive activity; we increase the amount of data available for analysis if we include brands other than our own. (Sometimes this is inevitable; where, for example, competitive promotions have a significant effect on *our* brand's sales.)

Rather than asking 'Why don't we try adding in women's magazines this year?', we should be saying 'We believe that re-allocating £X000 from TV to women's magazines would have this and this beneficial effect on the marketing plan'. Then, if people agree, it can be done, and the achievement measured.

27.3 Case histories

As the reader may have gathered from the number quoted in this book, we believe that the study of published cases is usually rewarding. However, more may be available within the reader's own company. If so, there will probably be more detail, and an opportunity of asking questions; both these points should be of value.

The best use of case histories is undoubtedly as part of a large-scale systematic study. Only in such a context can patterns be seen to emerge, and can the exceptional cases be identified as such. Such a project has been running for some years now, at the Cranfield School of Management.

Several occasional papers, and two books, have emerged already. Sadly, though, media work has received little attention so far, and there seems little demand from the sponsors that this situation should be changed.

If those engaged in media work wish to learn more about their calling, it will be by their own efforts, or not at all.

27.4   Related reading

R.A. Westwood (Editor), 'Integrated information systems', *Journal of the Market Research Society* (July 1975).

Index